T0330253

Fiscal Accountability and Population Aging

KDI/EWC SERIES ON ECONOMIC POLICY

The Korea Development Institute (KDI) was established in March 1971 and it is Korea's oldest and best-known research institute in the fields of economic and social sciences. Its mission is to contribute to Korea's economic prosperity by drafting socioeconomic development plans and providing timely policy recommendations based on rigorous analysis. Over the decades KDI has effectively responded to rapidly changing economic conditions at home and abroad by conducting forward-looking research as well as putting forth significant efforts in formulating long-term national visions.

The East-West Center promotes better relations and understanding among the people and nations of the United States, Asia and the Pacific through cooperative study, research and dialogue. It serves as a resource for information and analysis on critical issues of common concern, bringing people together to exchange views, build expertise and develop policy options. The Center is an independent, public, nonprofit organization with funding from the U.S. government, and additional support provided by private agencies, individuals, foundations, corporations, and governments in the region.

The KDI/EWC series on Economic Policy aims to provide a forum for scholarly discussion, research and policy recommendations on all areas and aspects of contemporary economics and economics policy. Each constituent volume in this series will prove invaluable reading to a wide audience of academics, policy makers and interested parties such as NGOs and consultants.

Titles in the series include:

Macroprudential Regulation of International Finance
Managing Capital Flows and Exchange Rates
Edited by Dongsoo Kang and Andrew Mason

Economic Stagnation in Japan
Exploring the Causes and Remedies of Japanization
Edited by Dongchul Cho, Takatoshi Ito and Andrew Mason

Competition Law and Economics
Developments, Policies and Enforcement Trends in the US and Korea
Edited by Jay Pil Choi, Wonhyuk Lim and Sang-Hyop Lee

Human Capital Policy
Reducing Inequality, Boosting Mobility and Productivity
Edited by David Neumark, Yong-seong Kim and Sang-Hyop Lee

Fiscal Accountability and Population Aging
New Responses to New Challenges
Robert L. Clark, YoungWook Lee and Andrew Mason

Fiscal Accountability and Population Aging

New Responses to New Challenges

Edited by

Robert L. Clark

Professor of Economics and Professor of Management, Innovation and Entrepreneurship, North Carolina State University, USA

YoungWook Lee

Fellow, Department of Public Finance and Social Policy, Korea Development Institute (KDI), South Korea

Andrew Mason

Professor Emeritus of Economics, University of Hawaii at Manoa and Adjunct Senior Fellow, East-West Center, Hawaii, USA

KDI/EWC SERIES ON ECONOMIC POLICY

A JOINT PUBLICATION OF THE KOREA DEVELOPMENT INSTITUTE, THE EAST-WEST CENTER, AND EDWARD ELGAR PUBLISHING LTD

Cheltenham, UK • Northampton, MA, USA

© Korea Development Institute and East-West Center 2021

All rights reserved. No part of this publication may be reproduced, stored in a retrieval system or transmitted in any form or by any means, electronic, mechanical or photocopying, recording, or otherwise without the prior permission of the publisher.

Published by
Edward Elgar Publishing Limited
The Lypiatts
15 Lansdown Road
Cheltenham
Glos GL50 2JA
UK

Edward Elgar Publishing, Inc.
William Pratt House
9 Dewey Court
Northampton
Massachusetts 01060
USA

A catalogue record for this book
is available from the British Library

Library of Congress Control Number: 2020952707

This book is available electronically in the **Elgar**online
Economics subject collection
http://dx.doi.org/10.4337/9781800370470

ISBN 978 1 80037 046 3 (cased)
ISBN 978 1 80037 047 0 (eBook)

Typeset by Servis Filmsetting Ltd, Stockport, Cheshire

Printed and bound by CPI Group (UK) Ltd, Croydon, CR0 4YY

Contents

Contributors

Andrew G. Biggs is a Resident Scholar of the American Enterprise Institute, USA.

Yongok Choi is a Professor in the College of Business and Economics, Choong-Ang University, South Korea.

Robert L. Clark is a Professor in the Poole College of Management, North Carolina State University, USA.

Dohyung Kim is an Assistant Professor in the Department of Economics of Myongji University, South Korea.

Kang-soo Kim is the Director and Vice President in the Department of Land and Infrastructure Policy, Korea Development Institute, South Korea.

SeongTae Kim is a Fellow in the Department of Macroeconomic Policy, Korea Development Institute, South Korea.

Taesuk Lee is a Vice President and the Director of the Department of Public Finance and Social Policy at the Korea Development Institute, South Korea.

YoungWook Lee is a Fellow in the Department of Public Finance and Social Policy, Korea Development Institute, South Korea.

Andrew Mason is a Senior Fellow of the East–West Center, USA and a Professor Emeritus in the Department of Economics of the University of Hawaii at Manoa, USA.

Marilyn Moon is an Institute Fellow of the American Institutes for Research, USA.

Weh-Sol Moon is an Associate Professor in the Department of Economics of Seoul Women's University, South Korea.

Chang Gyun Park is Senior Research Fellow in the Fund and Pension Division, Korea Capital Market Institute, South Korea.

Louise Sheiner is a Senior Fellow and Policy Director of the Hutchins Center on Fiscal and Monetary Policy, the Brookings Institution, USA.

Sylvester J. Schieber is a private consultant and the former Chair, US Social Security Advisory Board, USA.

Foreword

Jeong Pyo Choi

For most of the past three decades Korea successfully held its public debt at a low level, leaving ample fiscal space even in the aftermath of the global financial crisis. In recent years, however, a noticeable slowdown in the growth rate, combined with serial fiscal deficits, have posed concerns for long-run fiscal sustainability. Indeed, there is a growing perception that the current fiscal framework, which emerged from favorable macroeconomic environments in the past, may no longer work effectively in maintaining fiscal soundness in a more decentralized and especially a rapidly aging society.

In this sense, Korea's current fiscal framework which includes fiscal institutions and government expenditures needs to be examined and assessed from the perspective of government's fiscal accountability. Fiscal accountability is the key factor in maintaining fiscal sustainability by mandating that the government's decision be informed and justified. Fiscal accountability requires the answerability of the government about fiscal decision, the transparency of fiscal process, and enforcing mechanisms that ensure these qualities. Enhancing fiscal accountability could improve rationality and transparency in fiscal decision-making and strengthen the government's responsibility in fiscal areas.

In the context, the Korea Development Institute, in cooperation with the East–West Center, commissioned an international team of experts for a study on enhancing fiscal soundness through strengthening fiscal accountability. They discussed the weakness of the current fiscal framework and the ways to improve fiscal accountability and fiscal transparency. They reaffirmed the desirability of more fiscal oversight and accountability in both budget preparation and public spending, and discussed the fiscal issues for such various fields as budgeting, social assistance, pensions, health insurance, social overhead capital investment, and financial support to small and medium-sized enterprises. Their findings will be useful for understanding the problems involved and designing future policies.

On publishing this volume, I would like to thank Dr Robert L. Clark of North Carolina State University, Dr YoungWook Lee of the Korea

Development Institute and Dr Andrew Mason, Senior Fellow of the East–West Center and Professor Emeritus in the Department of Economics at the University of Hawaii, for organizing and editing the chapters for publication. I also wish to thank all the authors and reviewers who contributed to the volume.

Jeong Pyo Choi
President
Korea Development Institute

Abbreviations

APIFS	Agricultural Policy Insurance and Finance Service (Korea)
ASEC	Annual Social and Economic Supplement (US Census Bureau)
BOK	Bank of Korea
CBO	Congressional Budget Office (US)
CPI	consumer price index (US)
CPS	Current Population Survey (US Census Bureau)
CTC	Child Tax Credit (Korea)
DB	defined benefit (pension plan)
DC	defined contribution (pension plan)
EITC	Earned Income Tax Credit (Korea, US)
FICA	Federal Insurance Contributions Act (US)
GDP	gross domestic product
GEPS	Government Employees Pension System (Korea)
IBK	Industrial Bank of Korea
IMF	International Monetary Fund
IPPF	Investment Pool for Public Funds (Korea)
IRA	individual retirement account (US)
IRS	Internal Revenue Service
KDB	Korea Development Bank
KFoF	Korea Fund of Funds
KODIT	Korea Credit Guarantee Fund
KTFC	Korea Technology Finance Corporation
KVIC	Korea Venture Investment Corporation
MFMP	Medium-term Fiscal Management Plan
MMF	money market fund
MOSF	Ministry of Strategy and Finance (Korea)
NBLS	National Basic Livelihood Security system (Korea)
OASDI	Old Age, Survivors and Disability Insurance (US Social Security System)
OECD	Organisation for Economic Co-operation and Development
PAYGO	pay-as-you-go
PCMF	Public Capital Management Fund (Korea)
PIM	public investment management
PIMI	efficiency index of the public investment management system

R&D   research and development
RCGFs   Regional Credit Guarantee Foundations (Korea)
SBC   Small and Medium Business Corporation (Korea)
SIPP   Survey of Income and Program Participation (US)
SMEs   small and medium-sized enterprises
TFP   total factor productivity
UK   United Kingdom
US   United States

1. Introduction to *Fiscal Accountability and Population Aging*

Robert L. Clark, YoungWook Lee and Andrew Mason

Population aging and increased life expectancy at older ages are having significant economic and policy effects in all developed countries. Aging of national populations can substantially increase the cost of national retirement systems and health plans. Increased longevity places higher burdens on individuals and households to save more and work longer. Slower growth in the labor force and the preferences of older workers to delay retirement require firms to reconsider employment and compensation policies. A question of national importance is: how are governments and workers responding to the challenges posed by population aging? This volume focuses on the developing economic challenges confronting Korea and the United States in response to the aging of their populations. The following chapters examine the how public policies in these two countries are evolving in response to the demographic changes, the impact of aging on governmental expenditures, and changes in the labor force associated with aging.

During the past three decades, Korea has successfully maintained its public debt at a relatively low level which has left fiscal space for policy reforms even in the aftermath of the financial crisis. In recent years, a slowdown in the economic growth rate combined with the unexpected fiscal deficits poses concerns for the long-run fiscal sustainability in Korea. Indeed, there is a growing perception that the current fiscal framework, which emerged from favorable macroeconomic environments in the past, may no longer work effectively in maintaining fiscal soundness in a more decentralized and rapidly aging society. Several of the following chapters examine Korea's current fiscal framework, including fiscal institutions and government expenditures, and assess it from the perspective of the government's fiscal accountability. In 2016, the Department of Public Finance and Social Policy concluded that fiscal deficit in Korea has gradually widened from 1 percent of gross domestic product (GDP) in 2010 to 2.5 percent in 2015. An important policy concern is whether the continuing population aging will exacerbate the fiscal problems facing Korea.

In the United States, the federal government confronts similar problems associated with the funding of its primary retirement programs, Social Security and Medicare. Current projections indicate that as soon as 2033 not all promised Social Security benefits can be paid, while the cost of providing Medicare benefits continues to rise as a proportion of GDP. Several chapters examine whether the rising cost of retirement benefits that follows the aging of the population will limit the government's ability to fund other national priorities. State and local governments must deal with the rising cost and unfunded liabilities associated with pension and retiree health plans for these public employees. Some states face the prospects that their pension funds will be depleted in the next decade. In addition, many analysts worry that the rising annual cost of these plans will limit the ability of governments to fund public education infrastructure needs and to provide other public services.

Analyzing the public policies of Korea and the United States illustrates that two very different countries face similar challenges concerning the aging of their populations. Key factors to consider include funding pressures on retirement plans, how the aging of the labor force affects economic growth and productivity, and how governments, employers and individuals respond to these challenges. The chapters in this book provide evidence on the magnitude of the challenges in each country and possible policy changes that may occur in response to the rising cost of retirement benefits.

FISCAL POLICY AND PUBLIC DEBT IN KOREA

In Chapter 2, SungTae Kim concludes that Korea's fiscal soundness has gradually worsened in recent years and is expected to continue to do so in response to rapidly aging population. Research suggests that maintaining a debt to GDP ratio of between 50 and 70 percent would be desirable to prevent a future fiscal crisis. Based on simulations, Kim shows that to maintain this debt ratio, the annual fiscal deficit has to remain between 1 and 2 percent of GDP. He concludes that to sustain this level of debt, the tax burden in Korea must rise to 25 percent of GDP, and the level of discretionary spending must remain below 10 percent of GDP. The analysis in this chapter implies that increases in tax rates and significant restructuring of government expenditures are inevitable.

Despite well-managed fiscal soundness in Korea, concerns about fiscal sustainability are expanding as the government debt continues to increase and the population ages further. Population aging is expected to weaken growth potential and deteriorate fiscal soundness, implying that Korea's fiscal situation will decline and consequently that the country will be unlikely to sustain the desirable financial stability. The estimate of the fiscal sustainability gap based on interest rate and output growth is forecast to gradually deteriorate, showing current fiscal soundness cannot be maintained.

Simulation results are presented for fiscal adjustments needed to anchor debt-to-GDP ratio at 50 to 70 percent. If the fiscal adjustment is equally distributed between increased taxation and expenditure cuts, the tax burden ratio should rise from 18.4 percent in 2016 to about 23 percent, while discretionary expenditure should fall from 13.1 percent to about 9 percent of GDP in 2060. With the rapid population aging, a fast-growing mandatory spending share and a weakening revenue base, substantial fiscal reforms should be undertaken as soon as possible. On the expenditure side, expenditure restructuring of health, welfare, labor, education and general administration – accounting for about two-thirds of total expenditure – would be an essential part of fiscal reform. On the revenue side, revenue policy should give first priority to expanding the tax base and to reinforcing growth potential.

POLICIES TO SUSTAIN SOCIAL SECURITY IN THE UNITED STATES

The United States must confront similar financial changes to its overall federal budget and especially the sustainability of its retirement programs. Social Security is the primary national retirement program in the United States (US). For the past three decades, projections have shown that future funding problems demand new policies if this program is to be sustained for future retirees. Sylvester J. Schieber (Chapter 3) explores the underlying explanations for the underfunding of the US Social Security pension system that has persisted since the late 1980s, despite repeated calls for reform by the program's trustees and various advisory groups.

Both micro and macro estimates of the cost, shifting from older to younger generations because of the delay in financing reform, are provided in Chapter 3. The analysis shows that recent proposals, calling for balancing financing reform adjustments between benefits and revenues, would result in most of the cost being shifted to future generations of participants. Because reforms have been delayed and many current proposals call for greater welfare transfers in the program from high to low career earners, the case is made that the costs of reform should be imposed on the basis of participants' ability to pay rather than on the basis of the year in which they were born.

Recent proposals for reforming the system are consistent with the pattern policymakers have followed over the past quarter-century: most of the costs of balancing system financing will be placed on our children and grandchildren. In addition, many proposals call for improving benefits for participants with lower lifetime earnings histories including those who have already retired. The delayed adjustment in the financing and the potential for increasing the welfare transfers suggest that the costs of Social Security financing reform should be equitably shared on the basis of the ability of participants to bear the costs of reform rather than on the basis of birth date. In the United States, the financial challenges facing Social Security have been known for decades. As yet, Congress has failed to act to address the underfunding of the system; however, over the next decade new legislation must be enacted to sustain this important program.

MANAGING PUBLIC FUNDS IN KOREA

In Chapter 4, Yongok Choi discusses institutional arrangements of the government funds system in Korea. How these various funds are managed can contribute to fiscal soundness. For efficient management of government funds, Choi proposes that Korea create a fund of funds by pooling the surplus money of business-oriented funds. This enables the board of directors of each fund to focus on the fulfillment of its own project, which is their primary responsibility. Also, efficiency gains in fund management can be expected arising from the economies of scale and reduction in liquidity risks, which will lead to lower costs of short-term financing.

Choi analyzes the problems of the government fund system in terms of fiscal accountability and then proposes policies to improve the management of these funds. He outlines the problems associated with the current government funds systems and identifies three primary areas of concern. First, accountability goals are not properly established. Second, accounting is undertaken on each fund separately, so there is no overall assessment of the total strength of the funds. Third, Choi notes that there are several cases where surplus funds are used as pocket money by government departments. As Choi's chapter shows, these problems can be alleviated and the efficiency of national finances can be improved through the consolidated management of surplus money from budget-type funds.

IMPACT OF POPULATION ON THE FEDERAL BUDGET IN THE UNITED STATES

Chapter 5 by Louise Sheiner documents that the United States is in the midst of a demographic transition and assesses the impact of population changes on the federal budget. Ten years ago, the share of the population that was 65 or older was only 12.5 percent. Today, it is 15 percent, and in 20 years, the population share of this group is projected to reach 21 percent. These demographic changes have produced considerable concern about the US fiscal future. These demographic trends are important, since a large component of the budget of the federal government is allocated to old-age entitlement programs. In particular, the cost of Social Security, which provides public pensions, and Medicare, which provides health insurance to the aged, will rise as a share of GDP as the baby boom generation enters into retirement.

Demographic change is relatively easy to forecast, and economists have been studying and debating the budgetary pressures associated with aging for a long time now. But, in addition to the expected consequences of demographic change, it is possible that some other changes that we have been experiencing in the economy may also be linked to population aging. Specifically, low interest rates and lower productivity growth may directly affect fiscal challenges facing the government.

Population aging will put significant pressure on the federal budget in coming years, and policy changes are inevitable. With a permanently older population, and with health spending continuing to rise faster than GDP, it seems likely that overall government spending will have to be higher. But, given the size of the challenge, some combination of spending cuts and tax increases will likely be required. It is difficult to find policies to lighten the future burden. Increases in labor force participation can help, but without concomitant cuts in benefits they are not likely to make a large dent. How the United States addresses these population-driven fiscal challenges will determine the future economic well-being of retirees and the tax burdens of working Americans.

COST OF TAX EXPENDITURES AND THEIR IMPACT ON WORK INCENTIVES

YoungWook Lee examines the effect of tax expenditures for specific programs on the national budget of Korea in Chapter 6. Unlike the usual government spending programs, tax expenditures are often "hidden," both because they are counted as revenue losses, not outlays, and because tax administrative data are barely accessible in Korea. In consequence, government programs involving tax expenditures are often left unmonitored and are administered in isolation from other social programs. This chapter shows that when considered jointly with the Basic Livelihood Security System, a major public assistance program in Korea, the Earned Income

Tax Credit (EITC) creates an extensive income range where after-tax total household income actually falls with higher wage earnings. To improve fiscal accountability of tax expenditure programs, Lee suggests that a board of social policy be installed to ensure a harmonized design of these programs, and that the government provide greater information, so that tax expenditures are disclosed for wider public scrutiny.

Lee believes that concern about tax expenditure may weaken fiscal accountability without systematic and comprehensive reviews of tax and direct expenditure programs. The chapter examines this concern by studying Korea's case of the Earned Income Tax Credit, a tax expenditure program to support the working poor. In Korea, the EITC, as a welfare program, has been continually expanding since its introduction in 2008, but has not been checked within the welfare system. This analysis focuses on the interconnections between the EITC and other transfer programs through direct expenditure from a perspective of an integrated welfare system.

These results suggest that while tax and direct expenditure programs are independently managed by different ministries and are not reviewed comprehensively, the current interconnections between tax and direct expenditure programs are not in line with their common policy goal to encourage recipients' employment and self-reliance. The comprehensive reviews covering both tax and direct expenditure programs are also absent in other fields as well as welfare. To improve fiscal accountability of tax expenditure, the overall effectiveness of tax and direct expenditures needs to be jointly evaluated, and it should be possible to link micro-level data on tax and direct expenditure programs with the same policy objectives.

UNDERFUNDING OF US STATE AND LOCAL RETIREMENT PLANS

Chapter 7, written by Andrew Biggs, begins by describing the movement away from traditional defined benefit (DB) pensions toward greater reliance on defined contribution (DC) plans. However, in the United States, one sector where DB plans remain dominant is the public sector. Nearly all employees at all levels of government are offered a traditional pension, and the majority of employees receive most or all of their retirement benefits from a DB plan. However, the cost and risk of DB pensions has become a pressing issue for US cities and states, where pension funding has suffered, despite rising contributions and increased risk-taking through plan investments. Rising costs have placed pressures on government budgets, squeezing out resources available for other budget priorities such as education and healthcare. Biggs describes the structures, investment practices and funding health of US state and local pensions, while examining some of the policy issues pensions present to lawmakers, and certain reforms that have been considered.

In most states, pension funding ratios have fallen and unfunded liabilities have increased despite a near-tripling of government contributions since 2001. Moreover, public sector pensions have taken on increasing levels of investment risk as a means to counteract the decline in yields on safe investments. While for many years public pensions invested relatively conservatively, today nearly three-quarters of pension investments are in stocks or other risky assets. While this strategy has mitigated increases in required contributions that otherwise would have been substantially greater, rising risk-taking by public plans entails greater volatility of investment returns and required contributions in future years.

In states around the country, policymakers have considered reforms that would reduce the costs and risks of public employee pensions. Some proposed reforms are incremental and would retain the basic defined benefit structure while changing the way in which pension plans are funded or contributions paid. Biggs examines various reforms of state and local pensions in the United States and how these reforms would strengthen the funding states of at-risk plans.

IMPACT OF 2015 REFORMS ON COST OF PENSIONS IN KOREA

Chapter 8 by Dohyung Kim, Taesuk Lee and Yongok Choi explores the historical origin of fiscal rules and examines the effects of such policies on fiscal outcomes in the European Union and Organisation for Economic Co-operation and Development (OECD) countries in order to contribute to the debate on reforming fiscal frameworks in Korea. The authors highlight that the fiscal rules introduced in the European countries during the 1990s are designed to maintain the currency union without fiscal integration by preventing an excessive budget deficit of local governments (namely, the European Union member states) and hence, may not be pertinent to Korea's institutional environment. Rather, the authors suggest that the statutory "pay-as-you-go" system adopted in the United States may help to enhance the fiscal accountability of policymakers and constrain a potential rise in mandatory government spending due to the aging population in Korea.

Using an actuarial model of the Government Employees Pension System (GEPS), the authors quantify the fiscal impacts of the 2015 GEPS reform in Korea, which gradually raised the contribution rate as well as the pensionable age, while reducing the accrual rate for benefits. Projections indicate that the 2015 reform will substantially decrease the deficits (by 40.5 percent) over the next 70 years, but the overall fiscal burden due to the GEPS, which includes subsidies for closing the deficits, retirement allowances and government's matching contributions, will remain substantial over the same projection period. The analysis in Chapter 8, focusing on the marginal impact of individual measures in the reform package, reveals that about a third of the reduced pre-reform deficits (hence government subsidies) are simply replaced by the increased government matching contributions after the reform, leaving the annual fiscal burden sizeable even after the reform, which amounts to about 0.85 percent of the gross domestic product over the next 70 years.

POLICIES TO SUSTAIN THE US MEDICARE SYSTEM

In Chapter 9, Marilyn Moon describes the debate in the United States concerning the future of Medicare and shows how the discussion focuses on the question of whether we as a society can "afford" to continue funding this program at current levels. The chapter examines objective measures to assess the burdens of financing Medicare on both taxpayers and beneficiaries and suggests how to apply these measures to the debate regarding affordability. Although much of the discussion about reducing Medicare is to ease burdens on younger taxpayers, it is important to recognize that beneficiaries also contribute to the costs of the program; and to an extent not often appreciated. A second popular measure of Medicare's burdens has centered on comparing what various cohorts of Americans will have paid into the Medicare program over their working lives with what they can expect to draw out of the program. This is a useful measure only under the assumption that we expect each generation to pay for itself; a consideration explicitly rejected at Medicare's passage.

The discussion of affordability needs to recognize the context surrounding Medicare. As social insurance, Medicare differs from private insurance in important ways, principally by assuming that access is determined not on the basis of ability to pay but on the basis of membership in a particular defined group. Social insurance explicitly assumes that some groups, usually those with low incomes or with special needs such as health conditions, receive subsidies that give them access to benefits. In addition, Medicare was explicitly created as a "pay-as-you-go" system in which younger individuals pay taxes (both payroll and income taxes) that fund the current needs of beneficiaries, primarily those aged 65 and over. Finally, the debate about Medicare's future is also part of a larger debate about the size and scope of the federal budget.

Moon asks whether the burdens of future Medicare benefits place too high a burden when examined on a current accounts basis. Her findings indicated that burdens on both future taxpayers and beneficiaries will rise. But, the claim that reforms are necessary because Medicare is simply unaffordable is overstated. The magnitude of those burdens on taxpayers is less than often argued, and the impression that beneficiaries themselves are not paying much toward the costs of their own care is incorrect. A more balanced discussion is needed to determine how future burdens should be shared.

GOVERNMENT FINANCIAL SUPPORT FOR SMALL AND MEDIUM-SIZED ENTERPRISES

In Chapter 10, Chang Gyun Park explores the reasons for lack of effectiveness and efficiency in government financial support to small and medium-sized enterprises (SMEs) and suggest solutions to enhance the accountability of policymakers. He notes that the policy scheme providing financial support to SMEs in Korea has an extremely complicated structure, where no single government agency has the full responsibility to report integrated information. Also, unclear policy objectives make performance evaluation almost impossible based on which funds can be allocated. To enhance accountability in governmental financial support to SMEs, he proposes to create a public holding company with the responsibility to distribute funds based on performance evaluations, which ultimately depend on clearly specified policy objectives.

As the era of rapid growth led by large-scale conglomerates started to show the signs of gradually coming to a halt in late 2000s, interest in SMEs was increasing as an alternative engine for growth and employment in Korea. On the other hand, a lot of SMEs confront difficulties in securing the credit that is essential to growth, due to various frictions in the financial market such as information asymmetry and institutional misalignment. Many countries have taken measures to help bridge the financing gap that SMEs experience in the financial market. However, many critics argue that financial support by the government resulted in major inefficiency in allocation of credit resources. It is not difficult to identify SMEs that benefited from credit guarantee programs for a very long period of time. Responding to the criticism, policymakers have constantly adjusted the policy framework to eliminate the faulty incentive structure embedded in government programs, and to improve policy performance. Yet, several

important problems still remain unsolved. For instance, the size of government programs to help SMEs is too large compared with that of other
countries, without clear evidence of the effectiveness and efficiency of the
programs.

SME financial policy in Korea has a long history. The first serious
attempt by the government to provide financial resources to SMEs dates
back to the early 1960s. Many commentators seem to agree that the policy
has been playing a significant role in promoting the development of the
SME sector. It is also true that a serious criticism has been raised pointing
out problems such as repeated provision of scarce financial resources to
small groups of SMEs, and provision of financial support to SMEs in
better shape in terms of financial stability. In addition, some analysts argue
that the size of financial support to SMEs has been increased without due
regard to demand conditions, to replace the market allocation mechanism
rather than to complement it.

PUBLIC INVESTMENT MANAGEMENT AND ECONOMIC GROWTH

In Chapter 11, Kang-soo Kim and Weh-Sol Moon examine the relationship between the public investment management system (PIM) and economic growth. They find that the strength of PIM was a significant factor
for past economic growth. Furthermore, this study shows that efficient
PIM was essential for the establishment of high-quality infrastructure,
which has a positive effect on productivity. The discussion notes that good
PIM can enhance fiscal soundness by managing risks and uncertainties
in public investment, because successful PIM involves identification,
analysis, mitigation and management of budget deficits as a result in
public investment. Returns of the public investment will depend on the
effectiveness of management of the public investment. The authors report
that their examination of the relationship between the PIM system and
economic growth shows that the strength of PIM was a significant factor
for economic growth.

The analysis finds that there is a need for further improvement of the
appraisal (*ex ante* evaluation) of public investments. In the preliminary
feasibility study, which is a representative *ex ante* evaluation in Korea,
the proportion of qualitative analysis consisting of policy analysis and
regional balanced development analysis is gradually increasing in the
evaluation of the comprehensive feasibility on the infrastructure. The
authors believe that there is also a need for reliable and subjective appraisal
evaluation methods that can eliminate inefficient projects that are signifi-

cantly less cost-effective. Finally, they argue that it is also necessary to seek a governance reform that can positively exclude the political influence on the appraisal of the public investment.

THE ROLE OF POPULATION AGING IN GOVERNMENT BUDGETS AND ECONOMIC GROWTH

The research studies presented in this volume provide important new evidence on the impact of population on government budgets, the financing of specific retirement programs and economic growth in both Korea and the United States. The direct impact of an aging population on the cost of providing pensions and healthcare is clear: a larger proportion of the population that is over age 65 means that more individuals are receiving retirement benefits and there are fewer workers to finance higher annual costs.

This higher burden to finance retirement benefits may result in fewer resources available for other national priorities such as education and infrastructure. Difficult choices must be made. The following chapters consider various options concerning smaller benefits per retiree or higher tax rates on workers. In part, this trade-off will determine how the cost of population aging is shared across generations. These policy issues are facing Korea, the United States, and virtually all developed countries.

It is also important to consider policy in a broader context that includes other public policies, welfare programs and general tax policies. In addition, methods of stimulating economic growth to increase national resources, management of government trust funds and policies that influence labor force participation of the young and old play important roles in sharing the costs of an aging population. The analyses and research in this volume should be useful to policy analysts as they struggle to develop appropriate responses to these difficult challenges.

PART 1

Fiscal sustainability and accountability

2. An evaluation of fiscal sustainability in Korea

SeongTae Kim

INTRODUCTION

The Korean economy was confronted by serious external and internal challenges amid slowing growth after the global financial crisis of 2008. Externally, major economies were gradually strengthening their protectionism, as weak growth continued and antipathy toward globalization expanded. In particular, the United States took tougher protection trade measures, such as imposing tariffs, eliminating trade imbalances and adjusting exchange rates with China, Mexico and Japan, which had run large trade surpluses. Internally, a negative impact stemming from population aging emerged along with weak domestic demand. In recent years, the Korean economy has experienced a real annual growth rate of less than 3 percent, with sluggish private consumption, mainly due to the increase in life expectancy and the rapid shift to an aging population. Domestic investment, consequently, has slowed, and the growth potential has been gradually weakening.

In response to internal and external challenges, some policymakers and experts are emphasizing that a more active role of fiscal policy is inevitable. As the United States gradually tightens its monetary policy stance by raising its policy rate, most countries do not have room for conducting an accommodative monetary policy, given the historically low interest rates. Furthermore, high household debt, equal to more than 90 percent of gross domestic product (GDP), is another restriction for monetary policy easing in Korea. In contrast, the Korean economy has maintained a sound fiscal position with a debt-to-GDP ratio of less than 40 percent in recent decades. For this reason, Ghosh et al. (2013) classify Korea as one of the countries with sufficient fiscal space, and international organizations such as the International Monetary Fund (IMF) recommend a more active role for fiscal policy under the limits of monetary policy.

However, fiscal soundness of a country needs to be taken into account with a dynamic point of view. Although Korea's debt-to-GDP ratio remains at a secure level of around 40 percent of GDP, the ratio has been on an increasing trend since the end of the 1990s, partly due to expansionary polices during the Asian financial crisis in 1997 and the global financial crisis in 2008. Fiscal expenditures related to population aging, which have accelerated since the beginning of the 2000s, also contributed to the increase in government debt. Social welfare expenditure accounts for more than one-third of total government expenditure and is expected to increase rapidly. This trend raises concerns that the Korean economy – which has a population structure similar to Japan's, but with a 20-year lag – may follow the experience of Japan. It is worth noting that the debt-to-GDP ratio in Japan remained at a level of around 60 percent in the early 1990s, but has rapidly increased in the subsequent decades due to expansionary fiscal measures and a heavier burden of social welfare expenditure. The population aging in Japan led to a gradual decline of potential growth and consequently a weakened tax base, while its fiscal policy focused on the short-term economic fluctuation (Cho and Kwon 2014; Kim 2014). Similarly, there have been recent negative signs of economic erosion in Korea, including a shortage of tax revenue amid slow growth.

In this regard, this chapter evaluates Korea's fiscal sustainability and discusses policy directions to secure it. Fiscal sustainability in general refers to the ability of a government to sustain its expenditure without infinite bursts of new government debt or a sharp increase of financing costs. It has been evaluated along multiple dimensions: fiscal solvency risk and balance sheet problems, including debt maturity and the foreign share of government debt (which are related to rollover or liquidity risk), and contingent liability risk in the public sector. This chapter focuses on fiscal solvency risk in Korea by investigating debt dynamics, because population aging is forecast to directly affect both fiscal expenditure and revenue. Specifically, three questions are addressed: (1) What factors will determine fiscal sustainability in Korea? (2) Can the fiscal sustainability be maintained? (3) How much fiscal adjustment will be needed to maintain a target for government debt?

The following section reviews recent changes in Korea's fiscal condition, focusing on the effects of population aging for a medium- to long-term point of view. The third section discusses safe levels of government debt and investigates the debt dynamic necessary to sustain a target level of government debt. The concluding section summarizes the results and policy issues.

ASSESSMENT OF FISCAL CONDITION

Fiscal Soundness in Korea

Korea's fiscal soundness with its low debt-to-GDP ratio in recent decades is attributable to two main factors: strong fiscal discipline and a prematured social welfare system. First, Korea has maintained fiscal discipline, including the principle of annual revenue appropriation,[1] since the early 1980s, although no fiscal rule has been introduced. Checks and balances have been maintained between the administration and the legislature. For example, the National Assembly cannot modify the amount of the expenditure in the annual budget, submitted by the administration, without the consent of the government, and the new bills that could entail fiscal burdens are strictly restricted by Article 57 of the Constitution. On the other hand, the administration must obtain approval of the annual budget from the National Assembly if it makes contracts that require fiscal resources. or issues government bonds to finance a fiscal deficit (Article 58 of the Constitution). The National Finance Act (Article 89) also constrains discretionary fiscal expansion by specifying the conditions of the supplementary budget. Supplementary budgets are allowed: (1) if a war or major natural disaster occurs; (2) if significant changes occur or are likely to occur in internal and external conditions, such as a recession, mass unemployment, changes in inter-Korean relations or economic cooperation; or (3) if an expenditure arises (or increases) that has to be paid in accordance with the Act.

Second, public pensions and health insurance have not reached the mature levels that are observed in most developed countries. Thus, the negative impact of population aging has not yet caused significant erosion. According to Organisation for Economic Co-operation and Development (OECD) social expenditure statistics, Korea's welfare expenditure in 2014 was 10.4 percent of GDP, which was far below the averages of the OECD (21.6 percent) and G7 countries (24.0 percent). Most of these differences are explained by Korea's national pension, which was introduced in 1988; very late in comparison with advanced countries that introduced pensions in the late nineteenth and early twentieth centuries. Welfare expenditure in Korea is forecast to increase rapidly, driven by pension and medical expenditures, as population aging progresses.

Fiscal soundness, however, has been gradually deteriorating since the global financial crisis of 2008. Fiscal deficits remained at about 2–3 percent of GDP, and the debt-to-GDP ratio, consequently, continued to rise, although not as much as in western Europe and in Japan in particular (Figure 2.1). By 2016 it had reached 40 percent of GDP, mainly due to the increase in issuing deficit financing bonds, as an expansionary fiscal

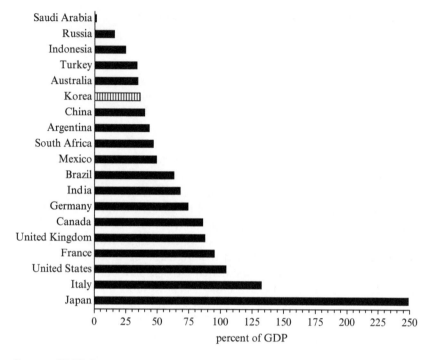

Source: OECD data.

Figure 2.1　Debt-to-GDP ratio in selected G-20 countries, 2016

policy implemented in response to slowing growth (Figure 2.2). Although the Medium-term Fiscal Management Plan (MFMP) for 2016–20 forecast gradual improvement in the operational budget balances, it was likely to be too optimistic, in that government revenue was expected to increase by 5 percent for these five years, despite weak economic growth. The projections were based on around 3 percent real growth and 2 percent inflation, which were well above recent trends. Moreover, the fact that the government for various reasons has postponed the efforts to achieve an equilibrium fiscal balance deepens concerns about narrowing fiscal deficits.

Structural Issues: Population Aging and Decline of Potential Growth

The annual population growth rate in Korea fell to 0.5 percent in 2015, and the aggregate population is forecast to begin to decrease from 2032 (Figure 2.3; National Statistics Office 2016).[2] The elderly dependency ratio (defined as population 65 years and older divided by population ages

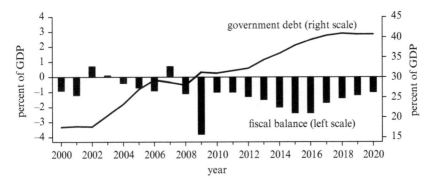

Note: Data after 2017 are projections of the plan.

Source: Ministry of Strategy and Finance, 2016-20 Medium-term Fiscal Management Plan data.

Figure 2.2   Fiscal balance and government debt in Korea, 2000–2020

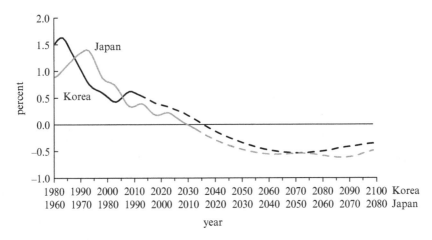

Note: Solid lines are historical data and dashed lines are projections.

Sources: National Statistics Office (2016) and Cho and Kwon (2014).

Figure 2.3   Population growth rates in Korea 1980–2100 and Japan 1960–2080

15–64) is expected to surge from around 15 percent in 2010 to 38 percent in 2030 (Figure 2.4). The population growth rate and the elderly dependency ratio of Korea are projected to follow a trend similar to Japan's, with a time lag of about 20 years. For example, it is expected that the population

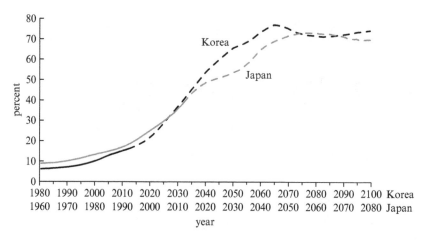

Note: Solid lines are historical data and dashed lines are projections.

Sources: National Statistics Office (2016) and Cho and Kwon (2014).

Figure 2.4   Dependency ratios in Korea 1980–2000 and Japan 1960–2080

growth rate of Korea will overtake Japan's from 2030, suggesting that the negative impact of population aging may be even larger than in Japan.

Rapid population aging aggravates the dynamics of the Korean economy from various perspectives. First, the slowdown in population growth results in a shortage of labor, the main cause of weakening potential growth. It also affects macroeconomic variables such as investment, consumption, interest rates and real estate prices. For example, a decline in the share of the young population, who are an investment-oriented cohort, leads to a decrease in the investment–output ratio. A slowdown of investment compared to savings accompanies a lower long-run real interest rate, causing surplus savings to be exported overseas. The population aging may cause a loss of competitiveness of labor-intensive industries, which have been the engine of growth since the 1970s. This suggests that Korea's manufacturing or export-oriented industries, which have taken Japan's industrial structure as a benchmark in the past decades, may gradually be replaced by other developing countries such as China. In addition, it is likely that the price of houses will decline, as the younger cohorts' demand for buying a house shrinks. It is not a coincidence that all these phenomena were witnessed in the Japanese economy more than 20 years ago, and now they are appearing in the Korean economy also.

According to long-term growth projections (Kim et al. 2016), Korea's growth rate is expected to decline from a 4 percent level in the 2000s to

Table 2.1 Economic growth forecast and growth contribution in Korea, 2001–40

Period	Real GDP (1+2+3, %)	Physical capital (1, %p)	Number of employees (2, %p)	TFP (3, %p)
2001–05	4.7	2.1	1.0	1.5
2006–10	4.1	1.8	0.5	1.8
2011–15	3.0	1.4	1.0	0.5
2016–20	2.8	1.1	0.6	1.0
2021–25	2.5	1.0	0.3	1.2
2026–30	1.9	0.8	−0.1	1.2
2031–35	1.5	0.6	−0.4	1.2
2036–40	1.2	0.5	−0.5	1.2

Note: Growth and contribution are simple averages over a five-year period and may differ slightly from the sum of contributions by factor. The growth accounting before 2016 is based on actual value. TFP = total factor productivity.

Source: Kim et al. (2016).

a 1 percent level in the 2030s (Table 2.1), mainly driven by the decrease in working population. The growth of capital stock is also forecast to slow down, contributing in part to weaker growth potential. However, the uncertainty in the economic growth projection is related to the long-term path of productivity growth. Because growth accounting considers productivity as residuals after subtracting the contribution of labor and capital stock, it cannot provide a clear basis for future prospects of productivity.[3] It is a stylized fact that productivity growth decelerated as the economy converged to a matured level, because the advantage of the catching-up stage gradually disappeared. In this regard, the projected productivity growth rate of around 1 percent in 2030s is not premised on a highly pessimistic scenario, as Japan's productivity growth already fell to less than 1 percent during 1990s (Table 2.2). This means that a decline in the potential growth rate is inevitable, and the speed of decline may be accelerated as productivity growth falls faster than assumed.

Improvement of productivity will be the most important factor to cushion the decline of the economic growth in the future. The increase in the labor participation rate for women and a more generous allowance of immigration to cope with the labor shortage will not be enough to cover the labor input reduction caused by population aging.[4] Likewise, it is difficult for the government to arbitrarily enforce capital accumulation through the expansion of investment. Considering Japan's productivity

Table 2.2   *Growth accounting and growth contributions in Japan,*
             1980–2009

Source and period	Real GDP (%)	Labor (%p)	Capital (%p)	TFP (%p)
IMF (1998)				
1980–90	3.9	0.6	1.9	1.4
1991–97	1.7	−0.3	1.4	0.6
Hayashi and Prescott (2002)				
1980–89	4.0	0.5	1.6	1.9
1990–99	1.3	−0.5	1.4	0.4
Conference Board (n.d., 2013 data)				
1990–99	1.0	−0.3	1.5	−0.3
2000–09	0.3	−0.2	0.5	0.0

Note: TFP = total factor productivity.

Source: Cho and Kwon (2014).

slowdown over 20 years, mainly due to inefficient resource allocation and delay of reforms, structural reforms are essential in Korea to prevent an abrupt slide of productivity, requiring increasing flexibility and efficiency in the production factor market and output market.

Weakening Tax Base

Such rapid decline of potential growth is expected to be accompanied by weaker government revenue growth. Given the historical elasticity of the tax revenue on GDP growth of 1.1, a decline in the potential growth rate of 1 percentage point will permanently lower the growth rate of the government tax revenue by 1.1 percentage points. That would mean a decrease in tax revenue of about 2.5 trillion won (1.6 percent of GDP in 2016), out of 2016 tax revenue of 242.6 trillion won. Moreover, a decline in the growth rate tends to be accompanied by lower inflation, as observed in most developed countries and also in Korea in recent years, meaning that the contraction of the revenue base is likely to be more serious than expected, because taxation has a nominal base. Meanwhile, Korea's tax burden is the lowest among the OECD countries, where the average tax burden is 25.1 percent (Figure 2.5). Given the long-term fiscal expenditure growth discussed below, the tax burden at its current level is unlikely to ensure fiscal soundness. This implies that an increase in the tax burden, corresponding to the increase in fiscal expenditure, is inevitable.

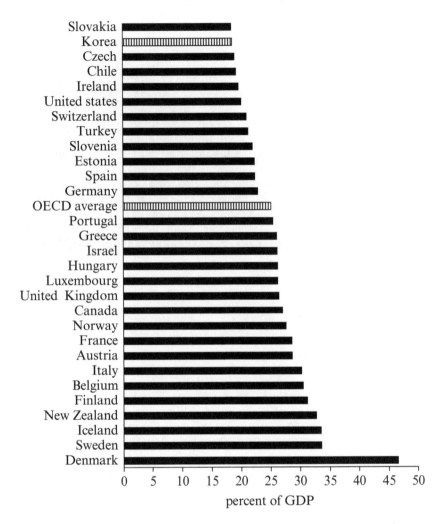

Source: OECD data.

Figure 2.5 Tax burdens in OECD countries, 2016

Increase in Mandatory Expenditure

The cost of social insurance and public assistance[5] is expected to increase from 3.8 percent of GDP in 2012 to 11.7 percent of GDP in 2060 (National Assembly Budget Office 2012), and this rapid increase in mandatory expenditure will reduce the discretionary fiscal buffer. According

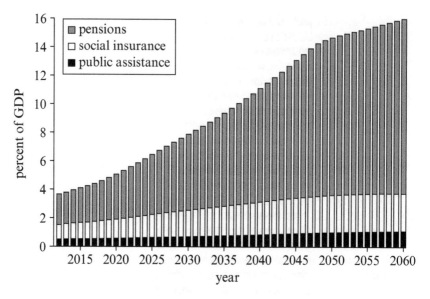

Source: National Assembly Budget Office (2012).

Figure 2.6   Pensions, social insurance and public assistance expenditure in Korea, 2012-60

to the government's 2016–20 Medium-term Fiscal Management Plan, the total expenditure in 2016 was 386.4 trillion won, comprising mandatory expenditure of 182.6 trillion won (46.8 percent) and discretionary expenditure of 203.8 trillion won (52.7 percent) (Figure 2.6). The proportion of mandatory expenditures in total expenditures was projected to increase from 46.8 percent in 2016 to 51.1 percent in 2020. The increase in social welfare expenditure restricts the role of counter-cyclical fiscal policy in response to the business cycle by reducing the room for discretionary stimulus measures. While the government should be able to reallocate resources temporarily in response to an economic downturn, the increase in mandatory expenditure means that only a small fraction of fiscal resources could be used in a discretionary manner. Meanwhile, fiscal policy to enhance growth potential needs to be expanded in various dimensions, such as improving the labor participation rate and increasing the national level of research and development (R&D) investment.

DEBT DYNAMICS IN KOREA

Discussion for Safe Level of Debt

To measure fiscal sustainability, some of the literature has used the concept of fiscal space, which refers to the availability of budgetary resources for a specific purpose without jeopardizing the sustainability of the government's financial position, or the stability of the economy (Ley 2009). Given this broad definition of fiscal space, the government budget constraint could provide useful insights for understanding fiscal sustainability in the context of debt dynamics, using the following equation:

$$d_{t+1} - d_t = (r_t - g_t)d_t - s_{t+1} \qquad (2.1)$$

where d is one-period debt as a share of GDP at the end of the period, g is the growth rate of GDP, s is the primary balance as a share of GDP and r is the interest rate on debt in period t and due in period $t+1$. To prevent an explosive debt-to-GDP ratio without bounds, the primary balance should be offset by effective interest payments (the interest rate–output growth differential multiplied by the debt-to-GDP ratio). The negative interest rate–output growth differential provides more room for primary balance adjustment to maintain a certain level of debt-to-GDP ratio. Given the interest rate–output growth differential, the fiscal space can be considered the distance between the current primary balance and the available primary balance that would not make the debt-to-GDP ratio explosive. In Korea, GDP growth still remains higher than the interest rate on government bonds, but it is expected to reverse around 2030, implying that a more aggressive adjustment of the primary balance is required to maintain the debt-to-GDP ratio at a certain level (Figure 2.7). This is because a sharp decline of labor input leads to a faster decrease of output growth than the marginal productivity of capital.

Based on insights from interest rates and growth differentials, Ostry et al. (2010) estimated fiscal space as the difference between the current levels of public debt and the debt limit implied by the countries' historical record of fiscal adjustment. Their estimates for 23 major countries found that Greece, Italy, Japan and Portugal have little fiscal space, whereas Iceland, Ireland and Spain had fiscal space of 50 to 70 percent of GDP. In particular, Korea is reported to have sufficient fiscal space of more than 100 percent of GDP, along with Australia, Denmark, Israel, New Zealand and Norway. Ostry et al. (2010) estimate that Korea's debt-to-GDP ratio will converge to zero eventually. These estimates, however, do not imply fiscal sustainability in the future, because the dynamic change of the economy

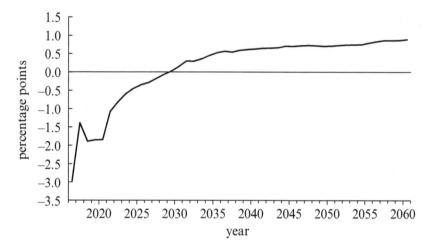

Figure 2.7   Interest rate–output growth differential in Korea, 2016–60

is not appropriately considered in calculating the debt limit. For example, the authors used the historical values of interest rates and output growth differentials, so that output growth was much higher than the interest rates. But in Korea, both the interest rate and the output growth are expected to decline, and the interest rate–output growth differential will revert to positive. In addition, the primary balance will deteriorate further mainly due to the increase in social welfare expenditure, given the interest rate–output growth differential. Looking forward, the fiscal space in Korea is likely to be depleted and may not be sufficient to guarantee sustainability.

What is the safe level of government debt without jeopardizing a government's solvency? The IMF (2014) estimated the safe level of government debt with a significantly lower probability of a fiscal crisis to be around 65–70 percent of GDP in Korea by using the definition of debt limit. However, it is difficult to estimate the debt limit and the safe level of debt, because both depend on the country-specific political and economic situation as well as external conditions. It is worth noting that countries with a low debt-to-GDP ratio could experience a solvency crisis (for example, Ireland and Spain).[6] Although these countries had sustainable debt levels, borrowing costs increased sharply, causing severe financing difficulties and undermining their solvency (Ghosh et al. 2013). Korea, located at the periphery of the world economy, had similar experiences in the Asian financial crisis in 1997 and the global financial crisis in 2008, in that rollover risk eroded during the crises.[7] In addition, the unification of South and North Korea will require large fiscal resources to reconstruct the economy.

Table 2.3 *Debt-to-GDP ratio and economic growth in developed and developing countries, 1946–2009*

Economic level	Debt-to-GDP ratio			
	Less than 30%	30–60%	60–90%	Over 90%
Developed countries				
Average value, 1946–2009	4.1	2.8	2.8	−0.1
Median value, 1946–2009	4.2	3.0	2.9	1.6
Developing countries				
Average value, 1946–2009	4.3	4.8	4.1	1.3
Median value, 1946–2009	5.0	4.7	4.6	2.9
Total				
Average value, 1970–2009	5.2	4.9	2.5	−0.2
Median value, 1970–2009	5.1	5.0	3.2	2.4

Source: Reinhart and Rogoff (2010).

Separately, there are various results of government debt level based on empirical analysis. Reinhart and Rogoff (2010) find that if the debt-to-GDP ratio in developed countries exceeded 90 percent, the economic growth declined significantly. In addition, the higher the share of foreign countries in the national debt, the greater the adverse effects, and this tendency is more prominent in emerging countries (see Table 2.3).[8] Cecchetti et al. (2011) estimate that a government debt threshold of 85 percent of GDP leads to a slowdown in economic growth, similar to Reinhart and Rogoff (2010). Also, they find that if the debt ratio rises 10 percentage points from its threshold, the economic growth rate declines by 0.1–0.2 percentage points. Kumar and Woo (2010) suggest that per capita GDP growth will fall by 0.2 percentage points if the government debt ratio rises by 10 percentage points.

Government Debt Trend to Anchor Fiscal Sustainability

Despite difficulties to measure safe levels of government debt, the discussion above suggests that it is important to prevent a continuing increase of the debt-to-GDP ratio amid population aging. To investigate how much fiscal adjustment is necessary under debt dynamics in Korea for the next decades, it is assumed that the Korean government will target its debt level at 50–70 percent of GDP in 2060. The existing long-term fiscal projection shows mainly how much the national debt ratio will be at a certain point in time, but these results can vary greatly depending on assumptions about economic growth and fiscal revenue and expenditure. For example, the National Assembly Budget Office (2012) predicted that the debt-to-GDP ratio would reach 183 percent in 2060, whereas Kim (2010) and Park and Jeon (2009) forecast 141 and 116 percent of GDP, respectively, in 2050.[9] These studies, however, paid little attention to the magnitude of fiscal adjustment required to stay at a certain level of government debt. Given a target level of government debt, this section examines how to maintain the government debt ratio every year to reach the level of 50–70 percent of debt-to-GDP ratio in 2060 by using the backward induction method. In other words, it is a method to determine the ratio of government debt to be maintained in the year t–1 in order to reach a specific government debt ratio in year t starting in 2060. In this case, the dynamic trend of the government debt ratio is estimated based on the result of the National Assembly Budget Office (2012). However, from 2017 to 2020, it is assumed that the figures in the National Financial Management Plan will be realized.

As shown in Figure 2.8, the debt-to-GDP ratio will gradually rise after reaching 40 percent of GDP in 2017, which is much slower than the previous forecast. Of course, the dynamic trend of the debt-to-GDP ratio could take various shapes. For example, until the mid-2020s, the scenario may be premised on a gradual decline in debt-to-GDP ratio and then a gradual rise. From this point of view, the dynamic trend of the debt-to-GDP ratio presented here is only one of the possible scenarios.

Figure 2.9 shows the dynamic trends of the fiscal balance to achieve a target debt-to-GDP ratio considered in Figure 2.8. This chapter uses

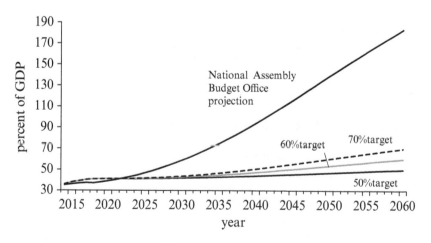

Figure 2.8   Government debt projections in Korea, 2014–60

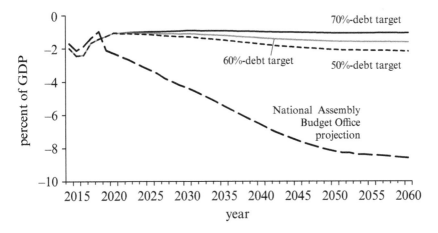

Figure 2.9   Fiscal balance projections in Korea, 2014–60

the operational fiscal balance, excluding the national pension, industrial accident insurance, unemployment insurance and the private pension fund, because the Korean government has no obligation to preserve the deficits of these social security funds. In other words, if a deficit occurs, it is assumed that the government will inject tax revenue or issue government bonds only when there is a legal obligation to finance it. Of course, when such funds are depleted, it is likely that the government will inject fiscal resources, even though there is no obligation. The operational fiscal balance should be reduced gradually by 2020, if the Medium-term Fiscal Management Plan is followed, and then maintained within a certain range depending on the target of government debt. For example, in order to achieve a debt-to-GDP ratio at 50 percent in 2060, the operational fiscal balance needs to maintain a deficit of only about 1 percent every year, whereas it is expected to approach 9 percent of GDP in 2060 (National Assembly Budget Office 2012). Given the pace of population aging and the growth rate of mandatory spending and the weakening of the revenue base mainly due to the potential growth rate decline, it will not be easy to maintain an operational fiscal deficit of 1–2 percent, which implies that overall fiscal reforms should be undertaken as soon as possible. Despite somewhat striking results, these are likely to be too optimistic given the recent increase in life expectancy. Choi (2016) points out that Korea's population estimates have been modified relatively broadly, mainly for those over 65 years of age, and shows that the effect of the unexpected increase in the elderly population on fiscal expenditure will rise from a mere 0.1 percent of GDP in 2020 to 2.8 percent 2060.

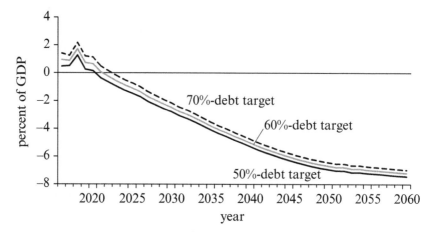

Figure 2.10   Fiscal sustainability gap in Korea, 2014–60

Fiscal Sustainability Gap

The fiscal sustainability gap captures the pressures on sustainability that emerge from fiscal balances accumulating over time to unsustainable debt stocks, even when initial debt stocks are modest (World Bank 2015). The fiscal sustainability gap is measured as follows:

$$\textit{fiscal sustainability gap} = b_t - \left(\frac{-g_t}{1+g_t}\right)d^* \qquad (2.2)$$

where g represents the growth rate of GDP, b is the fiscal balance as a share of GDP and d^* is the targeted debt-to-GDP ratio. A negative fiscal sustainability gap implies that fiscal adjustment is required to reach the ratio, given economic growth. As expected, the fiscal sustainability gap is expected to deteriorate gradually, showing that current fiscal soundness cannot be maintained unless fiscal reforms are implemented (see Figure 2.10). That is because the fiscal balance will worsen due to the increase in social welfare expenditure, while the economic growth rate will slow due to population aging. This result shows that a consensus on Korea's fiscal soundness could be different in a dynamic point of view. It should be noted that reducing the sustainability gap may make fiscal authorities confront a conflict of policies, because massive fiscal adjustment is likely to accompany a weakening of the growth potential. In other words, policy efforts to restore its sustainability could be partly offset by lower economic growth, hinting that fiscal adjustment should be implemented with a minimizing negative impact on economic growth.

Next, the magnitude of fiscal adjustment – the difference between the targeted and the projected debt-to-GDP ratio – is determined by the fiscal expenditure and revenue necessary to achieve each target of debt-to-GDP ratio. In addition, expenditure adjustment includes only discretionary spending given a fixed mandatory expenditure, because mandatory expenditure, including most of the social welfare program, is legally guaranteed. Three cases of sharing fiscal adjustment between the expenditure and revenue sides are considered: 5:5 distribution (Case I), 7:3 distribution (Case II) and 3:7 distribution (Case III). If fiscal adjustment is equally distributed (Case I), the tax burden ratio should rise from 18.4 percent in 2016 to about 23 percent, while discretionary expenditure should fall from 13.1 percent to about 9 percent of GDP in 2060, meaning that significant fiscal reforms are required.

Fiscal Reforms

The discussion so far shows that the current fiscal framework in Korea may no longer work effectively in maintaining fiscal sustainability amid population aging. In formulating fiscal reforms to anchor its sustainability, it needs to address the importance of fiscal transparency and accountability,[10] because they help to ensure that the government's decisions are informed by a shared and accurate assessment of the current fiscal position with government officers' responsibility. Thus, policymakers need to keep in mind fiscal transparency and accountability for fiscal framework and institutional reforms and actual changes in government budget practices, including effective resource reallocation and enhancing revenue. Fiscal reform issues will be discussed below, from the perspective of the government's fiscal transparency and accountability.

On the expenditure side, it does not seem easy to reduce discretionary expenditure to reduce GDP by more than 2 percentage points, because most discretionary expenditure consists of public servants' remuneration and defense spending, meaning preassigned expenditure. Furthermore, the restructuring would have to be in expenditures related to economic affairs, which are mostly discretionary, so that it is hard to expect more aggressive reforms except reallocations. Thus, it is desirable to gradually reduce the expenditure share of economic affairs, but simultaneously to prevent a rapid increase in social welfare expenditure. This suggests that expenditure restructuring in health, welfare, labor, education and general administration, which account for about two-thirds of total expenditure, is inevitable.[11]

On the revenue side, although there is enough room for an increase of the tax burden, considering the OECD average (25.1 percent), revenue policy should give first priority to expanding the tax base and to reinforcing the

Table 2.4   Tax exemption and reduction in Korea, 2014–17

	2014 (actual)	2015 (actual)	2016 (provisional)	2017 (outlook)
Tax exemption and reduction amount (A in trillion won)	34.3	35.9	36.5	37.0
Total tax revenue (B in trillion won)	205.5	217.9	232.7	241.8
Tax exemption and reduction rate ($\frac{A}{A + B}$ in %)	14.3	14.1	13.6	13.3

Source: Ministry of Strategy and Finance (various years), *Tax Expenditure Plan.*

growth potential. It is necessary to start a discussion on raising the rates of income tax, corporation tax and value added tax, which account for about 75 percent of tax revenue, and tax expenditures (notably exemptions and reductions) need to be restructured. Despite the recent reform of tax expenditures, their magnitude has not changed significantly for years. It is also important to expand the consensus about a heavier tax burden, by easing criticisms about inefficient expenditures, which in turn suggests another reason for more efficient and effective resource allocation.

The government introduced a Plan for Tax Expenditures to improve efficiency of tax exemption and reductions, and has implemented self-assessment of tax expenditure and in-depth evaluation from 2014 (see Table 2.4 for the initial plan). Preliminary feasibility studies on new tax expenditures are also conducted, to prevent in advance inconsiderate increases of tax expenditure.

These fiscal consolidations, however, do not necessarily mean undermining the economic growth potential. Recent studies have shown that the growth of countries with high sovereign debt is significantly slower. For example, Berkmen (2011) suggests that strengthening fiscal soundness may cause short-term costs, but it has a positive effect on growth potential in the long term. In particular, he emphasizes the need to improve the fiscal soundness of Japan, which has a very high government debt ratio, based on the analysis that its effects are strengthened when combined with structural reforms. Fiscal consolidation, also, is not synonymous with so-called "small government." As the population aging progresses, the government's expenditure will gradually increase. As long as welfare expansion is accompanied by restructuring in other sectors, such as economic affairs or broadening the tax base, it will not necessarily be in conflict with fiscal consolidation.

CONCLUSION

Korea, a small open economy, has been vulnerable to internal and external shocks. Fiscal policy as a last resort has played an important role in stabilizing the economy. Despite well-managed fiscal policy, concern about fiscal sustainability in Korea is expanding, as government debt continues to increase and the population structure is rapidly aging. In particular, population aging is expected to affect not only economic growth but also fiscal conditions. The potential growth rate is declining rapidly, mainly due to the decrease in labor input with slowed productivity growth. Consequently, revenue growth is forecast to slow gradually, driven by weak growth, while increasing demand for social welfare not only causes fiscal soundness to deteriorate, but also restricts the flexibility of fiscal policy. This suggests that Korea's fiscal space will be rapidly depleted and consequently may not be adequate to guarantee sustainability. The estimate of the fiscal sustainability gap based on interest rates and output growth is expected to deteriorate gradually, which shows that current fiscal soundness cannot be maintained, as the interest rate–output growth differential reverses amid the continuing increase in social welfare expenditure.

Simulation results for fiscal adjustment to anchor the debt-to-GDP ratio at 50–70 percent, despite difficulties in measuring sustainable or safe levels of government debt, show that the operational fiscal deficit, which is expected to reach 9 percent of GDP in 2060, needs to be maintained at about 1–2 percent over the next four decades. Given the magnitude of fiscal adjustment, if it is equally distributed between expenditure cuts and increased taxation, the tax burden ratio should rise from 18.4 percent in 2016 to about 23 percent, while discretionary expenditure should fall from 13.1 percent in 2016 to about 8 percent of GDP in 2060 (Table 2.5).

With rapid population aging, a fast-growing mandatory share of spending and a weakening revenue base, the operational fiscal deficit is unlikely to be maintained at around 1–2 percent, suggesting that overall fiscal reforms should be undertaken as soon as possible. On the expenditure side, it is desirable to gradually reduce the expenditure share of economic affairs, while preventing a rapid increase in social welfare expenditure. Expenditure restructuring of health, welfare, labor, education and general administration, accounting for about two-thirds of total expenditure, is an essential part of fiscal reform. On the revenue side, although there is enough room to increase the tax burden, considering the OECD average, revenue policy should give first priority to expanding the tax base and to reinforcing the growth potential. It is necessary to start a discussion on raising the rates of major tax components, together with reducing tax expenditures.

Table 2.5   Tax burden ratios and discretionary expenditures to achieve the national debt ratio target

Case	Tax burden ratio (% of GDP)	Discretionary expenditure (% of GDP)
In 2016	18.4	13.1
Case I		
Government debt 50%	23.5	8.7
Government debt 60%	23.1	9.0
Government debt 70%	22.9	9.2
Case II		
Government debt 50%	24.9	10.1
Government debt 60%	24.5	10.3
Government debt 70%	24.2	10.5
Case III		
Government debt 50%	22.2	7.2
Government debt 60%	22.0	7.6
Government debt 70%	21.9	8.0

NOTES

1. Under annual revenue appropriation, the expenditure should be adjusted to the revenue. This could lead to procyclical fiscal policy, deepening economic recession.
2. In 2015, the working-age population ages 15–64 accounted for 73.4 percent of the aggregate population, while the elderly population ages 65 and above were 12.8 percent of the total.
3. The contribution of labor input, which takes into account only the number of workers without consideration of their individual characteristics, is likely to be overestimated, while actual productivity growth identified by residuals is likely to be lower than estimated.
4. For example, from around 2020, even if the rate of women's economic activity increases gradually, the number of economically active people will decrease by 300 000 every year, which means that the number of employed people will decrease by about 180 000 every year.
5. In this study, the term "pension" means the four public pensions and the basic pension; "social insurance" means health insurance, long-term care insurance for the elderly, employment insurance and industrial accident insurance; and "public assistance" means the National Basic Livelihood Security System.
6. Government debt in Ireland and Spain in 2007 was only 25 and 36 percent of GDP, respectively, but rose to 118 and 84 percent in 2013.
7. It is unlikely that the Korean economy will experience a fiscal crisis such as rollover or liquidity risks, because Korea's external assets are steadily increasing, and the share of Korean government bond holdings by foreigners is very small, the same as in Japan.
8. On the other hand, Herndon et al. (2014) find that there is an error in the research data of Reinhart and Rogoff (2010), and that there is little difference in the growth rate between countries where the government debt ratio exceeds 90 percent.
9. The results of these studies were based on GDP in 2005. Since the national accounts

were reorganized in 2010, the following discussion will be based on 2010 GDP. In other words, the simulation was conducted by replacing the results of the National Assembly Budget Office (2012) with the 2010 GDP. The authors calculated 2010 GDP according to the method of Kim et al. (2016). On the other hand, if the budget is estimated by the National Assembly Budget Office (2012) based on 2010 GDP, it cannot be guaranteed that the levels of national debt and fiscal balance will be the same. However, the levels of key variables such as national debt, fiscal balance and health insurance revenues in the long-term fiscal estimation are expected to be very similar, because the difference between GDP in 2005 and GDP in 2010 was recognized as investment in knowledge production, including R&D, which had been treated as expenses.

10. The IMF (2012) defines fiscal transparency as the clarity, reliability, frequency, timeliness and relevance of public fiscal reporting and the openness to the public of the government's fiscal policymaking process. Accountability is defined as the degree to which public officials are held responsible for the way in which they conduct fiscal policy.
11. If Korea's national debt ratio is maintained at 50–70 percent, which is much lower than the previous forecast, as implied by studies by Reinhart and Rogoff (2010) and Cecchetti et al. (2011), it is highly likely that the macroeconomic stability will indirectly serve as a buffer against the decline in the growth rate. In this case, as the national tax revenues improve, the budget deficit will narrow and the national debt ratio will become even lower. This suggests that maintaining fiscal soundness at the appropriate level may not be difficult to achieve, as the virtuous cycle structure is settled.

REFERENCES

Berkmen, S. Pelin (2011), "The impact of fiscal consolidation and structural reforms on growth in Japan," IMF Working Paper WP/11/13, Washington, DC: International Monetary Fund.

Cecchetti, G. Stephen, M.S. Mohanty and Fabrizio Zampolli (2011), "The real effect of debt," BIS Working Paper 352, Basel: Bank for International Settlements.

Cho, Dongchul and Kyu-ho Kwon (2014), "20 years ago in Japan, today in Korea: population aging and economic downturn," in Dong-cheol Cho (ed.), "Dynamics of the Korean economy: focusing on comparison with Japan in the 1990s," Policy Research Series 2014-03, Sejong City: Korea Development Institute.

Choi, Yong-ok (2016), "Implication of rapid life expectancy increase," KDI-Focus 69, Sejong City: Korea Development Institute.

Conference Board (n.d.), *The Conference Board Total Economy Database*, available at www.conference-board.org.

Ghosh, A., J. Kim, E. Mendoza, J. Ostry and M. Qureshi (2013), "Fiscal fatigue, fiscal space and debt sustainability in advanced economies," *Economic Journal*, **123**, 4–30.

Hayashi, Fumio and Edward C. Prescott (2002), "The 1990s Japan: a lost decade," *Review of Economic Dynamics*, **5**(1), 206–35.

Herndon, T., M. Ash and R. Pollin (2014), "Does high public debt consistently stifle economic growth? A critique of Reinhart and Rogoff," *Cambridge Journal of Economics*, **38**(2), 257–79.

International Monetary Fund (IMF) (1998), *World Economic Outlook*, Washington, DC: International Monetary Fund.

International Monetary Fund (IMF) (2012), "Fiscal transparency, accountability, and risk," IMF Board Paper, Washington, DC: Fiscal Affairs and Statistics Departments, International Monetary Fund.

International Monetary Fund (IMF) (2014), *Republic of Korea: Staff Report for the 2013 Article IV Consultation*, Washington, DC: International Monetary Fund.

Kim, SeongTae (2010), "Study on the introduction of the fiscal rule: focusing on political zone pursuit and long-term financial estimation," Policy Research Series 2010-03, Seoul: Korea Development Institute.

Kim, SeongTae (2014), "Japan's fiscal policy and its implications since the 1990s," in Dongcheol Cho (ed.), "Dynamics of the Korean economy: focusing on comparison with Japan in the 1990s," Policy Research Series 2014-03, Sejong City: Korea Development Institute.

Kim, Seong Tae, Kyu-ho Kwon and Ji-woon Kim (2016), *Korea's Long-term Macroeconomic Projection*, Sejong: Korea Development Institute.

Kumar, S. Manmohan and Jaejoon Woo (2010), "Public debt and growth," IMF Working Paper WP/10/174, Washington, DC: International Monetary Fund.

Ley, E. (2009), "Fiscal policy for growth," PREM Note 131, Washington, DC: World Bank.

Ministry of Strategy and Finance (various years), *Medium-term Fiscal Management Plan*, Seoul: Ministry of Strategy and Finance.

Ministry of Strategy and Finance (various years), *Tax Expenditure Plan*, Seoul: Ministry of Strategy and Finance.

National Assembly Budget Office (2012), *2012–60 Long-Term Fiscal Outlook and Analysis*, Seoul: National Assembly Budget Office.

National Statistics Office (2016), "Population projections for Korea: 2015–2065," press release, December 8, Seoul: National Statistics Office.

Organisation for Economic Co-operation and Development (OECD) (n.d.). statistics cited from http://stats.oecd.org.

Ostry, D. Jonathan, Atish R. Ghosh, Jun I. Kim and Mahvash S. Qureshi (2010), "Fiscal space," IMF Staff Position Note SPN/10/11, Washington, DC: International Monetary Fund.

Park, Hyung-soo and Byeong-mok Jeon (2009), *A Study on the Development of a Mid and Long-Term Fiscal Model for Social Welfare Financial Analysis*, Seoul: Korea Institute of Public Finance.

Reinhart, C. and K. Rogoff (2010), "Growth in time of debt," NBER Working Paper 15639, Cambridge, Massachusetts: National Bureau of Economic Research.

World Bank (2015), *Global Economic Prospects: Having Fiscal Space and Using It*, Washington, DC: World Bank.

3.   Implications of delaying US Social Security financing reform: a look at the measurement, structural and generational issues

Sylvester J. Schieber*

INTRODUCTION

In the early 1800s, Jeremy Bentham (1824) wrote about common fallacies that plagued the society of his time. One of these fallacies was the deference that people paid to the wisdom of their ancestors and to old times. He noted that old times having occurred prior to current times ought to be thought of as "young or early time" and that with the passage of time, the phenomenon of accumulating knowledge was important. When considering individuals, the old person clearly had more experience than the young one, but considering generations, the opposite was true: the younger generation started with the collective learning that had been developed in prior generations and could build on it from there in the context of contemporary developments.

In public policy, Bentham saw that authorities often attempted to "tie up the hands of future legislators by obligations supposed to be indissoluble." He observed that at any point in time a governing ruler can use the tools available to assess the "exigencies of his own time" but, when it came to the future, "the sovereign has no such means of information; it is only by a sort of vague anticipation, a sort of rough and almost random guess drawn by analogy, that the sovereign of this year can pretend to say what will be the exigencies of the country" ten years hence. He lamented that lawmakers of the nineteenth century "shut their own eyes, and give themselves up to be led blindfold[ed] by the men of the 18th century" rather than being guided by their own judgment. Looking forward, he anticipated that "it will be equally right that the conduct of the 20th century should be determined not by its own judgment but by that of the 19th." Bentham did not prognosticate on the prospects of the twenty-first century but his "fallacy of wisdom" and the related "fallacy of immutable laws" have deep roots still controlling our plight in many regards.

More recently, Steuerle (2014) has written about a similar contemporary phenomenon, "Dead Men Ruling," controlling our modern political economy, which he describes as follows:

> In recent decades, both parties have conspired to create and expand a series of public programs that automatically grow so fast that they claim every dollar of additional tax revenue that the government generates each year. They also have conspired to lock in tax cuts that leave the government unable to pay its bills. The resulting squeeze deprives current and future generations of the leeway to choose their own priorities, allocate their own resources, and reach for their own stars. Those generations are left largely to maintain yesterday's priorities. (Steuerle 2014: 2)

The United States (US) Social Security pension system has been facing a widely recognized financing shortfall for at least the past quarter-century, and the program's trustees have repeatedly told policymakers in their annual trustees report that corrective legislation should be adopted to restore actuarial balance to the system. Despite the trustees' admonitions and similar ones from the Social Security Advisory Board (1998, 2001, 2005, 2010), policymakers have taken virtually no action to improve the system's financing outlook.

The system, largely financed on a pay-as-you-go (PAYGO) basis, has been running cash flow deficits since 2010, and the most recent projections suggest that the existing trust funds will be depleted by 2034. If that happens, benefit payments for all current and future beneficiaries at the time may be reduced by 20 to 25 percent relative to benefits provided under current law without corrective legislation. The prospect of such benefit reductions is unlikely, but the delay in adjusting the system's financing is shifting tremendous costs across generations in a way not generally understood.

The failure to take corrective action on the retirement program's financing is not a disclosure problem, as will be shown in the next section of this chapter. Rather, it has occurred because policymakers have shifted away from proactively managing the evolving benefit and tax trade-offs in the system, as they did over the first half-century's operation of the system, to passively letting the benefit side of the system evolve automatically under legislation adopted in the 1970s and 1980s based on mistaken assumptions about the future. The "Dead Men Ruling" the current evolution of the system failed to provide for the automatic governing balance between taxes and benefits that had persisted previously, with the implications that benefits now provided exceed legislated current costs and are shifting tremendous obligations to future participants in the system as discussed in the third section of this chapter. The chapter also explores measurement problems that are distorting policymakers' understanding of the role of Social Security in retirees' economic status. The final section discusses concluding observations.

THE LINK BETWEEN FINANCIAL DISCLOSURE AND POLICYMAKING

From the earliest days of Social Security's operations, the trustees with the input and support of the actuarial staff at Social Security have regularly reported on the actuarial status of the system. During the development of the annual reports, senior economists and other technical staff provide support to the system's trustees.[1] In the early years of the program, periodic advisory councils made up of members outside government were convened and provided policy recommendations and technical input to the plan administrators. As the program matured, these advisory councils generally convened technical panels of outside actuaries, demographers and economic experts to review the actuarial methods and assumptions being used to value the system. Since the mid-1990s, the Social Security Advisory Board has taken over the role of the earlier advisory councils and now convenes a new technical panel every four years or so.

The Office of the Actuary at the Social Security Administration has posted annual trustees reports for 1941 through 2017 on its website (Office of the Actuary). A quick scan of the reports indicates that the scope and depth of analysis in them has grown considerably over the years, with the evolution of actuarial science, with input of outside advisory groups, and with technical panels and the technological advances in computing capacity that have supported greater data analysis and understanding of the factors affecting the program's evolution.

In the early days of the program, policy debates focused on whether the system should be funded or operated on a PAYGO basis (Schieber and Shoven 1999). From the mid-1950s through the passage of legislation in 1983, the measuring stick for considering the financing adequacy of the pension system had been keeping projected Social Security revenues and expenditures in "close actuarial balance." John Wilkin, an actuary at Social Security during much of the 1970s and 1980s observed:

> Throughout the decades of the 1940s, 1950s and 1960s, financing decisions were based on the goal of obtaining a long-range actuarial balance of zero. Decisions in Congress and discussion between the administration and

Congress focused on the long-range costs of the program and of amendments to it. Changes were made only when adequate provision was made for the financing of those changes. Policymakers exercised financial discipline by adhering to specifying financing goals agreed upon, thus taking much of the arbitrariness out of the decision-making process (quoted in Schobel et al. 1989: 1702)

More recently, during the deliberations of the National Commission on Social Security Reform which led to the 1983 amendments, little progress could be made until agreement was reached on the financing goal, that is, to increase revenue and/or cut benefits by \$150–200 billion during the 1983–89 period and, in addition, to bring the system into long-range actuarial balance (Schobel et al. 1989: 1702).

The concept of "actuarial balance" has varied a bit over the years in both the measurement of Social Security's anticipated future operations and the development of financing policy. Generally, the system has been considered to be balanced if projected revenues are sufficient to cover projected program costs over the projection period. In recent years, the concept has been refined to assure that adequate projected resources are available in every year to cover the projected costs in that year.

The most recent valuation of Social Security's financing is reflected in Figure 3.1. The upper graphic shows the projection of the trust fund balances from the 2017 report, with the balance dropping to zero in 2034. The lower graphic shows the projected income and cost streams of the combined Old Age, Survivors and Disability Insurance pension systems (known together as OASDI), stated as a percentage of covered payroll taken from the "intermediate" projection – best estimate – from the 2017 trustees report. The picture shows only revenues attributable to tax collections and does not reflect the interest income generated by \$2.8 trillion held in the trust funds at the beginning of 2017. The financing shortfall reflected in the lower graphic of Figure 3.1 was equivalent to 2.83 percent of covered payroll or 0.95 percent of gross domestic product (GDP) over the 75-year projection period. In other words, if the payroll tax rate had been raised by 2.83 percent of covered payroll on 1 January 2017, the system would have been projected as being in "close actuarial balance,"[2] allowing benefits under current law to be paid in every year during the projection period at current tax rates with a remaining balance in the trust funds equivalent to one-year of benefit payments at the end of the projection period (Trustees 2017).

Over the years, the technical panels have called for greater documentation of Social Security's projection models, for modifications in developing and in setting various assumptions used in valuing the pension system, and for greater reliance on microsimulation models in developing their projec-

end-of-year trust fund balance in billions of dollars, 2017–34

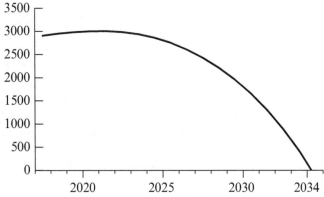

revenue and expenditure as percentages of covered payroll 2017–92

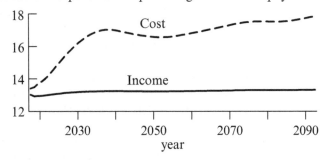

Source: Trustees, Social Security (2017: "Single-Year Tables"), accessed August 13, 2017 at www.ssa.gov/oact/TR/2017/lrIndex.html.

Figure 3.1 Projected US Social Security pension operations in the near and long terms

tions (Social Security Advisory Board 2017). Other analysts outside of Social Security have also been critical of Social Security actuaries' failure to use microsimulation, and the failure to capture realistic interactions of various economic and demographic assumptions in developing projections (Gokhale 2010).

In the late 1990s, the Congressional Budget Office (CBO) undertook the development of a separate Social Security microsimulation projection model (Meyerson and Sabelhaus 2000), which is now regularly used to provide an alternative set of projections on the system. In the latest projections for which results from both models were available at the time of this writing, the CBO projected that Social Security's financing shortfall was 4.68 percent of covered payroll compared with the trustees' projection of 2.66 percent. The CBO's projected shortfall relative to GDP over the 75-year projection period was 1.55 percent versus the 0.95 percent projected by the trustees. The trustees projected that the trust funds would be depleted under current law in 2034, and the CBO projected that they would be depleted in 2029. Hall (2016) summarized that two-thirds of the discrepancy between the two sets of estimates was related to four factors: (1) differences in the estimates of earnings subject to the payroll tax; (2) the trustees' assumptions of higher labor force participation rates, productivity growth and inflation than assumed by the CBO; (3) the trustees' projections of higher fertility rates and slower improvement in mortality than the CBO assumed; and (4) the trustees' higher projection of real interest rates than that projected by the CBO. The remaining one-third of the difference in the two projections is attributed to the different methodologies used in developing them. As an example of their different calculation approaches, Hall points to the CBO's use of projected payroll taxes and benefits calculated on individual persons from the microsimulation, versus the results for cohorts developed by the Social Security actuaries for the trustees (Hall 2016: 3).

The differences in projected operations of Social Security's pension system by its trustees and CBO might be important in the context of serious discussion about specific policy approaches to addressing the projected shortfalls, but they are immaterial in the context of current policy deliberations over securing the fiscal soundness of the system, because policymakers are not paying any attention to either set of projections in setting their policy agenda. For the general public, the argument over whether cell-based versus microsimulation projections are superior has no more relevance than a debate over how many angels can fit on the head of a pin. The Social Security trustees' projections, which suggest a smaller problem than those of the CBO, still imply that major adjustments to the pension's financing are in order, and have been so for the past quarter-century; yet policymakers have ignored the numbers that have been reproduced in formal documents presented to them repeatedly over that time. The lack of fiscal accountability in this case is more basically related to other factors.

FALLACY OF THE WISDOM OF THE DEAD MEN RULING

The US Social Security pension system has been largely operated on a PAYGO basis since the 1950s. Relative to PAYGO financing, there was some excessive build-up of assets in the early years of the program's operations and a larger build-up in assets resulting from the 1983 financing reform legislation. While the trust funds at the beginning of 2017 held $2.8 trillion, the assets represented only 7.7 percent of the estimated accrued obligations in the system at that time (Trustees 2017).

In a PAYGO-financed pension system, the cost of benefits paid each year is the product of two ratios: the ratio of the number of beneficiaries to the number of covered workers paying payroll taxes, multiplied by the ratio of average benefits paid to retirees to the average covered wages subject to the payroll tax.[3] The first of these ratios is frequently referred to as the dependency ratio, and the second is sometimes referred to as the wage-replacement ratio.

The 1972 Social Security Amendments introduced automatic indexation of Social Security benefits, although the first automatic adjustment of benefits did not occur until 1975. The automatic indexation was adopted in part to stem political gamesmanship between the administration and legislative branches of government. Congress had passed benefit increases for retirees of 15 percent in 1969, 10 percent in 1971, and 20 percent in 1972. In early 1969, before these three increments in benefits were granted, the ratio of average benefits to average covered wages was 0.270; by 1973, when the increments were imbedded in pensioners' benefits, the ratio had climbed to 0.338. These increases were adopted partly to reduce poverty rates among the elderly, from around three times the rate among the general population to something closer to parity. Partly, the increases were simply the result of political dynamics in which President Richard Nixon's administration would propose increases to keep up with inflation and the Democrats in control of Congress would "outbid" the recommendations (Derthick 1979: 346). The automatic indexation of benefits was intended to take the politics out of incrementing benefits.

It turned out that there was a major structural flaw in the 1972 legislation that resulted in initial benefits paid to new retirees growing much more rapidly than wages when realized price inflation exceeded wage growth rates. After the legislation passed, the next trustees report (Trustees 1973) reported that the ratio of benefit growth relative to wage growth between 1973 and 1980 would only be 0.940. However, if inflation exceeded wage growth under the 1972 legislation, initial benefits would grow more rapidly than wages or tax revenues. The underlying short-term economic assumptions, considered when automatic benefit indexation was adopted, turned out to be wildly wrong, as reflected in Table 3.1, and under the 1972 indexing provisions the ratio of benefits to wages would increase rapidly.

Policymakers realized fairly quickly after 1972 that benefits were going to grow more rapidly than wages and that corrective action was needed.

Table 3.1 *Comparison between five-year economic assumptions in the 1972 OASDI trustees report and actual experience (%)*

Period	CPI increases		Real wage increases		Unemployment rate[a]	
	Assumed[b]	Actual	Assumed[b]	Actual	Assumed[b]	Actual
1972	2.75	3.30	2.25	4.00	4.20	5.60
1973	2.75	6.20	2.25	7.00	4.20	4.90
1974	2.75	11.00	2.25	−3.60	4.20	5.60
1975	2.75	9.10	2.25	−2.50	4.20	8.50
1976	2.75	5.80	2.25	2.50	4.20	7.70
Cumulative	14.53	40.60	11.77	0.89	4.20	6.50

Notes:
a. The cumulative unemployment rate shown in this table is the average rate over the period.
b. The assumed rates shown here are taken from the mid-range assumptions.
CPI = consumer price index.

Sources: Trustees (1972) and Economic Report (1982).

By early 1974, however, the results of the United States' 1970 Decennial Census signaled the end of the high fertility rates that had occurred after the end of World War II, which also meant that ratio of beneficiaries to covered workers in the future would be different than previously anticipated. In 1970, the Social Security dependency ratio had been 0.269 and was projected to be 0.268 by 2010, when the early baby boom generation began retiring, and to grow to 0.325 by 2035, roughly when the baby boomers would be fully retired. By 2010, the actual dependency ratio was 28 percent higher than expected in 1972, and by 2017 the projection for 2035 was 43 percent higher than it was in 1972 (Trustees 1973, 2017).

It took Congress until 1977 to adopt new legislation to eliminate the excessive indexing of initial benefits resulting from the 1972 legislation, but the 1977 law included some grandfathering of benefits for workers close to retirement age. By 1982, the ratio of average benefits to average covered earnings had climbed to 0.372 from 0.338 in 1973. The 1977 legislation proved inadequate because of overly optimistic assumptions about inflation and wage growth. Inflation was expected to drive up prices by 28.2 percent from 1977 to 1981 while real wages were expected to increase by 12.9 percent (Trustees 1977). It turned out that prices rose by 60.0 percent over the period and real wages declined by 6.9 percent (Economic Report 1982).

Further corrective legislation was required in 1983 and addressed both the short- and long-term financing problems as they were understood at the time (see Schieber and Shoven 1999 for a history of these developments). Shortly after the 1983 legislation was signed into law, actuarial projections suggested that financing provisions then in place would cover benefits until at least 2063 (Ballentyne 1983). In 2063, the youngest members of the baby boom generation will be 99 years of age, so the implication at the time was that the 1983 legislation had secured the national pension through the baby boom generation's retirement period.

Despite growing trust fund balances after the adoption of the 1983 financing legislation, by 1987 the Social Security trustees were again concerned that the pension system was about to fall out of close actuarial balance. The system met that standard only in 1988, when the trustees changed the definition of the actuarial balance measure. In 1989, the trustees did not report at all on the financing relative to the close actuarial balance measure (Schobel et al. 1989). In 1990, there was again no mention of the financing status of the system relative to close actuarial balance in the trustees report, but Harry Ballantyne, the chief actuary at Social Security, wrote in his "Statement of Actuarial Opinion" appended to the report that "the OASDI program is not in close actuarial balance" (Trustees 1990: 149). By 1991, a new definition of close actuarial balance had been developed, and the trustees report that year indicated that current financing did not meet the new test (Trustees 1991: 99). In no year since 1991 has the system been judged to be in close actuarial balance.

The seeming solution to Social Security's long term financing imbalance adopted in 1983 proved to be a false promise. Three important developments since 1983, which account for the deteriorated financing prospects, have come to light (Chu and An 2017). The future prevalence of workers qualifying for Disability Insurance was underestimated in 1983, and important economic assumptions prove to have been overly optimistic. By far the largest factor accounting for the deteriorating outlook between 1983 and 2017, 70 percent of the total, has been the change in years considered in the 75-year valuation period favored by the trustees.

The 75 years considered in the 1983 projections spanned the period 1983 to 2057; the 2017 projections spanned 2017 to 2091. The period from 1983 through 2016, which was included in the first projection but not in the latter, had an average dependency ratio of 0.313 and a ratio of average benefits to average covered earnings of 0.304, suggesting an average cost of 9.5 percent of payroll to cover benefit costs. The period from 2058 through 2091 included in the second projection but not in the first has an average projected dependency ratio in the trustees' 2017 projection of 0.487 and a ratio of benefits to covered wages of 0.293, suggesting a cost of 14.3 percent over the period. So the 2017 projection has swapped out a low-cost set of years for a set with much higher costs not anticipated in 1983.

The problem with focusing on the marginal factors that generate a more pessimistic outlook on Social Security financing in 2017 than existed in 1983 is that it fails to identify the structural elements of existing legislation that lead to unanticipated financing deficits over time. Legislators cannot modify population demographics that drive dependency ratios, and have been reluctant to change program parameters, such as the age at which full benefits can be collected, beyond what was done in 1983. But there are other problems beyond growing dependency that should also be recognized.

The goal in tying evolving initial benefit levels to the rate of growth in average wages in the 1977 legislation was to create a relatively stable relationship between the growth in average benefits and average wages across generations. It was understood that raising the retirement age around the turn of the century would lead to a slight reduction in the ratio of average benefits to average wages, but that once that transition was complete, the ratio would stabilize again. The problem is that benefits are tied to the average wage index, which grows over time with the rate of growth in average wages in the total economy, while the payroll tax is applied only to covered wages. The concentration of wage growth at higher earnings levels since the mid-1970s means that this element of the current system's operation is not working as intended. In 2015, the ratio of average benefits to the average wage index was 0.311, exactly the same as it was in 1983, but the ratio of average benefits to average covered wages was 0.359 in 1983 and had risen to 0.389 by 2015.

This phenomenon of rising benefits relative to wages has been exacerbated by the behavioral phenomenon of higher labor force participation rates of women over the last half-century. In 1975, 59.8 percent of all OASDI beneficiaries were retired workers, and the residual were receiving some form of dependent or survivor benefits. By 2016, 82.2 percent of beneficiaries were receiving retired worker benefits (Trustees 2017) which are generally higher relative to pre-retirement earnings than the dependent and survivor benefits.

It is clear that the wisdom of policymakers who put in place the current benefit structure of the US Social Security pension system did not anticipate the developments that the program has faced since the benefit side of the system has been put on automatic pilot. Benefits have increased dramatically from what they anticipated, because of much higher ratios of beneficiaries to workers than they considered, and because they did not anticipate the benefit growth relative to wages inherent in seemingly immutable law. In their ignorance about future developments that would drive up benefits, they failed to consider how potential mistaken assumptions might affect future program costs.

Under the pre-1972 *modus operandi*, and even up until 1983, as the system moved out of actuarial balance from time to time, policymakers stepped in and negotiated a new financing equilibrium, mindful that growing benefits could be accommodated only by higher taxes on workers and that the costs of achieving a new equilibrium would have to balance the interests of both beneficiaries and taxpayers.

In the period since 1983, the temporary growth of the trust fund has meant that the governor that the tax rate imposed on a system historically financed on a PAYGO basis was no longer an immediate constraint on the unanticipated benefit growth. The system was formally recognized as being out of "close actuarial balance" in 1992, but it had been out of close actuarial balance in the prior five years, although not acknowledged as such by the trustees. In 1992, the 75-year unfunded PAYGO obligation was estimated to be $1.67 trillion: that is, if the trust funds had held additional funds in that amount, the existing payroll tax rate would have been sufficient to cover benefits provided in existing law over the next 75 years. But being out of close actuarial balance was of little immediate concern because, at the time, revenues were consistently greater than program expenditures. By 2010, the unfunded PAYGO obligations had climbed to $5.4 trillion, but continued to be masked by the trust fund that had climbed to $2.5 trillion. Despite program and administrative expenditures that exceeded tax revenues that year by $48.9 billion, the trust fund continued to grow (by $68.9 billion) because of interest credits on the trust fund balances. But by the beginning of 2017, the PAYGO unfunded obligations were up to $12.5 trillion. The trust fund was still growing with interest credits at an ever slower rate, and by 2022 the aggregate balance was expected to be in decline.

The structural problem in the financing equation for the pension system today is that current policymakers are not mediating the balance between taxpayers supporting the system and the benefit being paid to retirees. The cost drivers in the system – the dependency ratio and the ratio of average benefits to average covered wages – are on automatic pilot. The dependency ratio is growing in our aging society, and the ratio of benefits to covered wages is growing, because benefits are being indexed more rapidly than covered wages are growing, and because of changing behavioral patterns whereby women are more likely to be receiving retired worker benefits rather than dependents benefits. Because of the trust fund balances resulting from the 1983 financing legislation, policymakers have allowed the system to operate with the unanticipated growth in these two important cost factors for more than 30 years without addressing the long-term cost implications on future workers. The net result has been a tremendous cost shift from today's older participants in the system to younger workers and even those not yet old enough to be in the system (or even alive yet).

GENERATIONAL IMPLICATIONS OF DELAYED FINANCING REFORM

The Social Security Advisory Board[4] has published four reports (1998, 2001, 2005, 2010) in the past 20 years under the title "Social Security: why action should be taken soon." The first three of these reports gave a consistent set of reasons for taking prompt action:

> There are more choices available earlier; changes can be phased in more gradually; the cost of repairing Social Security can be spread more evenly over more generations of workers and beneficiaries; the longer change is delayed, the heavier the impact will be on each individual who is affected; there will be more advance notice for those who will be affected, so they can plan for their retirement; confidence in the ability of Social Security to pay benefits to future generations of retirees will be strengthened; there will be less disruption in labor market participation; there will be less disruption in decisions about consumption and saving. (Social Security Advisory Board 2005: 22–23)

The Social Security trustees have also been explaining to the public and policymakers the advantages of financing reform in the near term, which would allow program changes to be phased in gradually, giving "workers and beneficiaries time to adjust to them. Implementing changes sooner rather than later would allow more generations to share in the needed revenue increases or reduction in scheduled benefits and could preserve more trust fund reserves to help finance future benefits" (Trustees 2017: 24).

The problem with these and other similar charges for reform is that they are either so abstract that they do not clarify for policymakers or the public the measurable effects of delay, or they are so distant that they do not overcome human myopia. Without putting concrete measurements into the framework, it is hard for those being urged to adopt reforms to calculate the relative merits of more choices, gradual phase-in, ensuring confidence, and the like. Telling policymakers and current participants that failing to reform system financing now could have grave consequences in 2034, and expecting urgent action, fails to grasp one of the fundamental justifications of the program in the first place: namely that if workers are not required to save (contribute to the system) for their future retirement,[5] many of them will not do so adequately on their own, because they fail to understand when they need to start saving, how much to save, and so on.

Consider the situation we faced in 1994, two years after the trustees first included a statement in their annual report that Social Security was underfunded over the next 75 years, and what our situation would be today if we had implemented policy changes that year to bring the program back into close actuarial balance, the yardstick used for setting Social Security financing policy up through 1983. In 1994, the trustees estimated that the financing shortfall over the projection period was 2.13 percent of covered payroll. As with the situation today, that financing gap could have been closed by increasing future payroll tax rates, reducing benefits, or some combination of the two. For now, ignoring the relative implications of raising the payroll tax rate versus adjusting benefit levels, assume that Congress, having been forewarned two years earlier, adopted an increase in the payroll tax that was imposed in 1994 and thereafter equal to 2.13 percent of taxable payroll split evenly between employers and employees. The added accumulation of the trust funds at the end of 2015 would have been $3.77 trillion (an aggregation of annual amounts in Table 3.2). For simplicity, we have assumed that the policy change in 1994 would have been a payroll tax increase, but changes to aspects of the program that would have reduced benefits by an equivalent amount would have had the same effect on the trust funds.

Under this assumption, workers covered under Social Security from 1994 through the end of 2016 were exempted from paying the full estimated cost of the system during the period but ostensibly earned benefits as though they had paid taxes accumulated with interest equal to $3.77 trillion. The 2017 trustees report 75-year projection (Trustees 2017: 72) includes an estimate of the present value of future taxable payroll equal to $469.552 trillion over the projection period. The $3.77 trillion of foregone assets in the trust funds, because the financing of the system was not adjusted in 1994, was equivalent to 0.80 percent of the present value of future taxable payroll for the next 75 years as of 1 January 2017. The projected financing shortfall at the beginning of 2017, stated in the 2017 trustees report (Trustees 2017: 21) as a percentage of future taxable payroll, was estimated to be 2.83 percent, so the added trust funds, if taxes had been raised in 1994, would have reduced the 75-year shortfall to 2.03 percent of projected future taxable payroll in 2017. In other words, had policymakers increased the payroll tax by the projected shortfall in 1994, trust funds would have held $6.6 trillion instead of the $2.8 trillion actually held.

The question of whether or not we would have "saved" the added $3.77 trillion in the trust funds depends on whether additions to the trust funds represent added real savings; a matter of some controversy. The answer depends on whether additions in the trust funds lead to increased deficits elsewhere in the federal budget, and there is disagreement on that matter (Bosworth and Burtless 2004; Diamond and Orszag 2005; Nataraj and Shoven 2004; Smetters 2003).

At the end of 1993, federal debt held by the public equaled $3.2 trillion. By 2016, publicly held federal debt had climbed to $14.2 trillion. If the

Table 3.2   *Estimated added OASDI trust holdings at the end of 2016 if projected 75-year deficit in 1994 had been eliminated by payroll tax increase implemented in that year*

Year	Taxable payroll[a] ($ billion)	Added payroll tax rate[b] (%)	Added payroll taxes ($ billion)	Nominal interest rate[a] (%)	Added first-year trust fund accumulation[c] ($ billion)	EOY 2015 added trust fund balance[d] ($ billion)
1994	2780	2.13	59.21	7.1	61.32	202.39
1995	2913	2.13	62.05	6.9	64.19	193.02
1996	3065	2.13	65.28	6.6	67.44	189.50
1997	3276	2.13	69.78	6.6	72.08	175.99
1998	3516	2.13	74.89	5.6	76.99	194.75
1999	3737	2.13	79.60	5.9	81.95	210.18
2000	3992	2.13	85.03	6.2	87.67	192.03
2001	4158	2.13	88.57	5.2	90.87	186.23
2002	4238	2.13	90.27	4.9	92.48	162.32
2003	4343	2.13	92.51	4.1	94.40	163.18
2004	4540	2.13	96.70	4.3	98.78	163.71
2005	4747	2.13	101.11	4.3	103.28	172.99
2006	5023	2.13	106.99	4.8	109.56	173.42
2007	5250	2.13	111.83	4.7	114.45	157.35
2008	5413	2.13	115.30	3.6	117.37	147.53
2009	5255	2.13	111.93	2.9	113.55	137.77
2010	5290	2.13	112.68	2.8	114.25	131.73
2011	5466	2.13	116.43	2.4	117.82	126.93
2012	5685	2.13	121.09	1.5	122.00	131.54
2013	5888	2.13	125.41	1.9	126.61	135.54
2014	6156	2.13	131.12	2.3	132.63	137.99
2015	6370	2.13	135.68	2.0	137.04	140.33
2016	6610	2.13	140.79	2.4	142.48	142.48

Notes:

EOY = end of year. The total added 2015 EOY balance (right column) is $3768.90 billion.

a   Taxable payroll and nominal interest rates come from Social Security Office of the Actuary, based on Trustees (2016).

b   The estimated 75-year funding shortfall from 1994 comes from Trustees (1994: 22).

c   Estimate assumes contributions flowed into trust funds on a steady basis over the year and were invested at the current nominal interest rate until the end of the year.

d   Assumes estimated added assets available at end of year in which collected were invested at beginning of next year at that year's nominal interest rate for the following 15 years, and then reinvested in new 15-year bonds at the nominal interest rate prevailing in the year in which the original bonds were rolled over.

hypothetical accumulation in trust funds – had policymakers increased the payroll tax in 1994 by 2.13 percent of covered payroll – did not lead to added federal spending elsewhere in government operations during the years 1994 to 2016, the accumulated federal debt held by the public would have increased to only $10.4 trillion at the end of 2016, as the trust funds bought up an added $3.8 trillion of federal bonds. The increase in assets in the trust fund would have exactly offset accruing OASDI unfunded obligations, but would have also reduced obligations to outside bondholders by a similar amount. There was an opportunity to create real savings in this case. It is also possible – some believe probable – that policymakers would have run even larger deficits in general fund operations than they did, and would have offset the potential saving of the added payroll taxes. Given the size of the existing deficits in general fund operations during this period, it is plausible that policymakers would have resisted running even larger deficits in the general accounts, and the added trust funds would have been saved.

It is not just that the assumed higher payroll taxes in this scenario would have generated an additional $3.77 trillion in the trust funds at the beginning of 2017: the prospect of applying that higher payroll tax over the next 75 years would be expected to generate future added trust funds with a present value of $10 trillion. The added $3.77 trillion of "cash in the bank" plus the present value of added $10 trillion of "expected cash for the bank" would have equaled $13.77 trillion at the beginning of 2017, compared with the 75-year projected actuarial deficit of $13.28 trillion that existed at that time, because policymakers had refused to address the projected underfunding in 1994. Instead of being in a $13.28 trillion hole at the beginning of 2017, the system would have been sitting on a $0.45 trillion cushion from a 75-year perspective.

The thought of having a financing surplus in the system in 2017, versus the projected deficit in the trustees report, might appear to suggest that a 1994 fix would have resolved the long-term financing problems the system faces, but we must keep in mind the experience after the 1983 legislation closed the actuarial deficit then facing the program. In 2017, the OASDI programs were projected to have a financing shortfall of 0.38 percent of covered payroll for the year, compared with a shortfall of 4.57 percent of covered payroll for 2092.

The 1994–96 Social Security Advisory Council concluded that, under the valuation process used in estimating Social Security financing requirements in the future, it was not only important to have adequate financing over the 75-year projection periods, but to also assure that the system had "sustainable solvency" at the end of the projection period. The mere fact that there are sufficient resources to pay the benefits during a specific period does not mean that the system is sustainable over time. To be sustainably solvent, a system has to be able to pay benefits under assumed conditions in each anticipated future period of operations. Sustainable solvency in the context of the trustees' 75-year projection requires that the ratio of the trust fund balances has to be positive throughout the projection period and, further, that the ratio of trust fund balances to benefit claims is either stable or rising at the end of the projection period (Trustees 2017: 59).

In 2003, the Social Security trustees introduced a new measurement of future accruing obligations and revenues under the OASDI programs that takes account of annual balances beyond the 75-year projection period, assuming that "the current-law OASDI program and the demographic and economic trends used for the 75-year projection continue indefinitely" (Trustees 2016: 75). From 2004 through 2008, the future financing shortfall was estimated to be, on average, 3.5 percent of projected taxable payroll; from 2012 through 2016, the projected shortfall averaged 4.0 percent of future taxable payroll.

The new measurement was not introduced until some years after problems with the 75-year projection were recognized, but if the calculations had been done in 1994, the actuaries would have projected a financing deficit somewhat larger than the 75-year deficit of 2.13 percent of projected taxable payroll. One would expect that the longer the system was allowed to operate with financing shortfalls, the greater the shift in costs to later generations participating in the program. A crude extension of the difference in the 2004–08 to 2012–16 financing shortfalls to the 1994–98 period suggests that the sustainable solvency shortfall in 1994 would have been around 3.0 percent of payroll. Had the payroll tax been increased by 3.0 percent in 1994, the added accumulations in the trust funds at the end of 2016 would have been $5.31 trillion more than the actual balances, representing 0.65 percent of the estimated present value of future taxable payroll of $822.4 trillion. A higher payroll tax of 3.5 percent would have increased the trust fund balances at the end of 2016 by $6.19 trillion, the equivalent of 0.75 percent of the present value of future taxable payroll. With accumulations at these levels, the ability to save the added trust fund balances would be even larger than mentioned above.

Presentations of aggregate numbers amounting to trillions of dollars have little or no meaning to most of us. But the failure to impose taxes equal to the trustees' projected costs since 1994 has allowed workers subject to the lower tax rates to realize higher disposable incomes during their working careers than they would have achieved if the estimated actuarial cost of accruing Social Security benefits had been imposed on them. In order to give an idea of the magnitude of the benefits involved, Table 3.3 shows estimates of the added accumulations in the OASDI trust funds that would have arisen by the end of 2016 for a set of hypothetical workers, if they had been subject to: (1) a combined (employer and employee) increase in the payroll tax of 2.13 percent of covered payroll in 1994 and subsequent

Table 3.3   *Estimated OASDI trust fund shortfalls arising because of*
failure to increase the payroll tax by 2.13 or 3.5 percentage
points in 1994 on selected hypothetical workers ($)

Birth year	2.13% tax increase in 1994			3.50% tax increase in 1994		
	Medium earner	High earner	Maximum earner	Medium earner	High earner	Maximum earner
1956	30736	49188	71528	51999	83216	121287
1966	28759	46023	71528	49177	78699	121287
1976	18174	29084	58914	31707	50741	101004

years to cover the 75-year projected deficit; or (2) a 3.50 percent of covered payroll to cover the upper estimate of the sustainable solvency deficit that existed then. The values shown in the table include both the foregone taxes and the added interest the trust funds would have accrued over the years if the added contributions had been made. The hypothetical workers' earnings histories were developed to be consistent with the "medium" and "high" earners developed by Social Security's actuaries (Clingman and Burkhalter 2016) and a worker who was assumed to have earnings at or equal to the maximum subject to the OASDI payroll tax in each year. Workers from three different birth cohorts were considered. In the calculations presented here, the workers were each assumed to begin their careers and paying taxes at age 21, to work through age 66, and to retire at age 67.[6]

The workers born in 1956 and 1966 had earnings in each year from 1994 through 2016, while the workers born in 1976 did not begin work until 1997. The medium and high hypothetical earners born in 1956 accounted for slightly larger losses to the trust funds than their counterparts born in 1966, because the former were further along in their careers and had somewhat higher earnings in each calendar year than those born later. The maximum earners from the 1956 and 1966 birth cohorts would have generated identical losses because their earnings were identical each year. The 1976 maximum earner generated a somewhat smaller loss than those born earlier because the youngest earner had no earnings in the first three years of the period.

In aggregate, workers with higher earnings accounted for bigger losses to the trust funds than those with lower earnings, and older workers who worked steadily since 1994 did somewhat better than younger ones, unless they were consistently at the maximum earnings levels subject to the OASDI payroll tax. Clearly, the failure to tax covered payroll at known costs allowed some workers to avoid a significant share of the burden of the costs accruing under the program, or to escape benefit adjustments that could have generated similar improvements in system financing.

The aggregate analysis in the earlier section suggested that not taking up financing reform in 1994 means that Social Security participants in the future are facing higher payroll tax obligations or larger benefit reductions of 0.6 to 0.8 percent of covered payroll than they would have faced if the financing problem had been addressed earlier. What this means is that a worker starting their career today will face a future increase in taxes or loss of benefits equal to that amount, on average, on career annual earnings. This would equal about one-third of a total year's earnings over a 45-year career, equal to more than $17 000 for an average earner today, and more than $42 000 for an earner at maximum covered earnings.

Most reform proposals that have been put forward in recent years would largely exempt current retirees and those near retirement from bearing much, if any, of the burden of restoring financing balance to the system. This means that the financing reforms that have been delayed over the past quarter-century would effectively shift the costs of the delay to younger workers and those not yet in the workforce.

Schieber (2017) reviews a recent proposal put forward by a Commission on Retirement Security and Personal Saving organized by the Bipartisan Policy Center (2016) in Washington. The proposal was intended to restore solvency to Social Security not just for the next 75 years, but into the indefinite future beyond that. One of the constraints in formulating the components of the proposal was that the adjustments be roughly half on the benefit side of the program and half on the revenue side. In the final scoring of the package, the estimates suggested that over the next 75 years, 56 percent of the adjustment would be on the revenue side. The final proposal was endorsed by 18 out of 19 members of the commission.

Table 3.4 shows the timing of the changes in revenues and costs under the commission reforms as projected by Social Security's actuaries over a 75-year period. For example, the results for 2025 indicate that 8.4 percent of the present value of revenue increases over the 75-year period would be realized by that year, but that only 0.5 percent of the cost reductions. By 2045, nearly 30 years after the reforms were in place, 40.8 percent of the increase in present value of revenues would have been realized while only 25.7 percent of the adjustments on the benefits side. These results make it clear that the payroll tax revenue aspects of the reform proposals are relatively front-loaded while the benefit reductions are more back-loaded.

The right-hand column in the Table 3.4 shows the total improvements attributable to the revenue increases as a percentage of total improvement

Table 3.4   Improvement in the funding balance attributable to added non-interest revenues

Year	Cumulative percentage of 75-year present value accrued from:		Percent of cumulative improvement in trust fund balance attributable to added revenues
	added revenues	reduced costs	
2025	8.4	0.5	95.8
2035	25.1	10.9	75.1
2045	40.8	25.7	67.5
2055	55.8	40.1	64.5
2065	69.7	56.4	61.7
2075	82.5	74.1	59.3
2085	94.4	91.5	57.4
2090	100.0	100.0	56.7

Note: The percentage of the cumulative 75-year projected present value of increases in OASDI non-interest revenues or reductions in costs and the cumulative percentage improvement in the funding balance attributable to added non-interest revenues by specified dates under the BPC Commission's Social Security reform proposals (%).

Source: Schieber (2017: Exhibit 2) derived from Social Security Administration, Office of the Actuary, estimates of the financial effects on Social Security of the reform plan released on 9 June 2016 by the Bipartisan Policy Center's Commission on Retirement Security and Personal Saving, Table 1d, accessed on February 9, 2017 at www.ssa.gov/oact/solvency/BPCCRSPS_20161011.pdf.

in trust fund balances for specified years under the actuaries' assumption that implementation of the proposal would have taken place in 2016. By their estimates, in 2025, 95.8 percent of the improved financing balance would be attributable to tax increases, overwhelmingly payroll tax increases. Forty years under the package, nearly two-thirds of the financing improvement still would be attributable to increased revenues. A worker in the early years of their career at the time of the reform would bear the brunt of the added revenue burdens under reform, while someone retiring at the time of the reform would bear hardly any at all. But by the time the young worker reached retirement age, the effects of the reform measures would be nearly fully matured. Although the proposal would roughly balance benefit and revenue adjustments, there would be no rough equity across generations. For the most part, older generations in the system would be off the hook for bearing the adjustment costs: younger generations would bear the brunt of both ends of the adjustments.

INCOME STATUS OF OLDER AMERICANS

There are two reasons generally given for why older generations should be exempted from any significant adjustments in restoring Social Security's financing balance. The first is that they played by the program's contribution rules during their working lives and should not face changes to the rules of the game in or near retirement. The second is that retirees and those near retirement generally live on lower incomes than they had during their working careers and have less flexibility to adjust to changes in their income sources than younger generations.

When policymakers suggest that it would be unfair to adjust benefits of retirees and those near retirement when we take up Social Security financing reform, they virtually always ignore the added burden imposed on future taxpayers that has resulted because those now retired or near retirement have been exempted from paying the full cost of program participation over the past 25 years. I am unaware of a single policymaker ever making reference to the net beneficial effects of delaying Social Security financing reform on the lifetime income of current retirees and older workers, as shown above in Table 3.3. Comments about the economic vulnerability of the elderly are fairly common and appropriate for some, but not nearly to the extent often implied.

The Social Security Administration regularly publishes information on the prevalence and the relative magnitude of various income sources received by the elderly. The source of the information used in developing the publications is the Census Bureau's Annual Social and Economic Supplement (ASEC) to the Current Population Survey (CPS), a cross-sectional survey of a nationally representative sample of US households that is used to measure the levels and distribution of income and poverty levels across the population over time.[7] The CPS-ASEC results are used by the government to track the economic status of various segments of the population and to assess the existing effectiveness of various public policies and the potential for new policies to address issues revealed by the survey results.

From 1976 through 2014, the percentage of elderly households reported to be receiving Social Security benefits was relatively constant, varying from 87 to 91 percent and accounted from 36 to 40 percent of their total income through 2012 and then dropping to 33 percent in 2014 (see Table 3.5 for a summary of the various reports). Receipt of income from other pensions and retirement accounts grew modestly over the period. In 1976, only 31 percent of the elderly reported such income, and it amounted to only 16 percent of total income. The effects of the Employee Retirement Income Security Act of 1974 was apparent in the data as pension receipt

Table 3.5   *People ages 65 and older receiving income from specified sources and aggregate income from each source, 1976–2010 (%)*

Year	Social Security	Assets	Pensions	Earnings	Public assistance
Share receiving income by source					
1976	89	56	31	25	11
1980	90	66	34	23	10
1984	91	68	38	21	9
1988	92	68	42	22	7
1992	92	67	45	20	7
1996	91	63	41	21	6
2000	90	59	41	22	5
2004	89	55	41	24	4
2008	87	54	41	26	4
2010	89	52	40	26	4
2012	89	51	39	28	4
2014	87	62	44	29	4
Share of aggregate income from each source					
1976	39	18	16	23	2
1980	39	22	15	19	1
1984	38	28	15	16	1
1988	38	25	18	17	1
1992	40	21	20	17	1
1996	40	18	18	20	1
2000	38	18	18	23	1
2004	39	13	20	26	1
2008	37	13	19	30	1
2010	37	11	19	30	1
2012	36	11	17	34	1
2014	33	10	21	32	1

Sources:
Data for 1976–2000 are from the Social Security Administration, *Trends in the Economic Status of the Elderly, 1976–2000,* accessed July 2, 2013 at www.socialsecurity.gov/policy/docs/ssb/v64n3/v64n3p12-text.html#chart4.
Data for 2004 are from Lynn Fisher and Nicole Pascua, *Income of the Population 55 or Older, 2004*, Social Security Administration (2006), accessed at www.ssa.gov/policy/docs/statcomps/income_pop55/2004/.
Data for 2008 are from Lynn Fisher and Brad Trenkamp, *Income of the Population 55 or Older, 2008*, Social Security Administration (2010), accessed at www.socialsecurity.gov/policy/docs/statcomps/income_pop55/2008/incpop08.pdf.
Data for 2010, 2012 and 2014 are from Brad Trenkamp, *Income of the Population 55 or Older, 2010*, *Income of the Population 55 or Older, 2012*, *Income of the Population 55 or Older, 2014*, Social Security Administration (2012, 2014 and 2016), accessed at www.socialsecurity.gov/policy/docs/statcomps/income_pop55/2010/incpop10.pdf., www.ssa.gov/policy/docs/statcomps/income_pop55/2012/incpop12.pdf and www.ssa.gov/policy/docs/statcomps/income_pop55/2014/incpop14.pdf.

increased to 42 percent of the elderly accounting for 18 percent of their income by 1988. Receipt of pension income continued to rise to 45 percent of the elderly by 1992 but then dropped slightly and was at only 44 percent in 2014. From 1988 through 2014, it accounted for 18 to 21 percent of the elderly's income. Social Security as a share of total elderly income had dropped slightly in recent years because of increased earnings by the elderly.

According to Social Security's latest estimates, in 2014, nearly 17 percent of family units with a member older than 65 relied solely on Social Security for income, 29 percent received 90 percent or more of their income from the program, and 34 percent received 80 percent or more of total income from Social Security (Trenkamp 2016: 222). Not everyone aged 65 and over receives Social Security, and among those in the lowest quintile of the income distribution in 2014, only 75 percent received benefits, but 14 percent received means-tested cash assistance and 31 percent received non-cash public assistance. In the second income quintile, 94 percent received Social Security benefits; in the third quintile, 93 percent received them; in the fourth quintile, 89 percent did; and in the top quintile, 82 percent (Trenkamp 2016: 69). Above the bottom quintile, many households not reporting Social Security income were still relying on earned income and some were receiving public pensions from career employment not covered under Social Security.

Among those aged 65 and older in 2014 receiving Social Security benefits in the first income quintile, on average, the benefits accounted for 94 percent of the unit income. Social Security accounted for 86 percent of income, on average, for those in the second quintile, 68 percent of income for those in the third quintile and 46 percent of the income of those in the fourth quintile (Trenkamp 2016: 290).

The series of Social Security reports (summarized in Table 3.5) have taken on the mantle of official documentation of the vital importance of Social Security in providing retirement income security over the past four decades. Policymakers have taken note. For example, at a hearing before the Social Security Subcommittee of the US House of Representatives House and Ways Committee, Xavier Becerra (Becerra 2014), a Democratic Representative from California and ranking minority member of the subcommittee, observed:

> Social Security is the heart of retirement security. Six out of ten seniors rely on Social Security for more than half of their income. For almost half of Americans over 80, nearly all of their income comes from Social Security. Without Social Security nearly half of women over the age of 65 would be poor. Americans have earned that vital retirement security. Over 160 000 000 Americans today pay into Social Security with their paycheck tax

contributions every week in exchange for economic security for themselves and their families.

Now, only the highest income earners, 25% of retirees, receive any significant income from something other than Social Security, like an IRA [individual retirement account] or work-based retirement plan. And that's even despite the substantial subsidies that are provided for retirement savings through the tax code.

So, Mr. Chairman, the best way for Congress to improve retirement security for all Americans is by protecting Social Security from benefit cuts and making sure it is as strong for future generations as it was for their parents and grandparents.

Representative Becerra's statement was based directly on numbers out of the most recent Social Security report on income of the elderly.

Other prominent players in discussions about retirement and Social Security policies often rely on the Social Security analysis of the Current Population Survey (CPS) or develop their own analysis from the CPS. The National Academy of Social Insurance summarized the data: "About nine in 10 American aged 65 and older receive Social Security. For nearly two out of three of those beneficiaries (65 percent), Social Security was more than half their total income, and for one in three (36 percent), it is all or nearly all of their income" (National Academy 2013). Selena Caldera, writing for the American Association of Retired People, tallied the CPS herself to show that 13.7 percent of older Americans live on Social Security alone, 9.9 percent rely on Social Security for 90 to 99.9 percent of their income, and 25.5 percent receive between 50 and 89.9 percent of their income from the program (Caldera 2012). Many other interest groups offer similar renditions on this theme.

There is one basic problem with the series of Social Security reports on the sources and levels of the elderly's income and similar analyses of CPS evidence. The results do not reflect the actual prevalence or importance of asset and pension income accruing to the elderly. In 1990, the pension and IRA income reported by elderly federal income tax filers was 21 percent more than income reported on the CPS (Schieber 1995). The CPS estimate supposedly reported pension income of all the elderly in 1990, whereas the IRS filings included only a subset of the elderly, because those with low incomes were not required to file tax forms, so the CPS totals should have been equal to or larger than the reporting on the tax forms. By 2000, the pension income paid to Social Security beneficiaries reported on the CPS was $172 billion short of IRS reporting of pension income that year, a shortfall of 54 percent. In 2007, the CPS shortfall climbed to $357 billion relative to tax filings by Social Security beneficiaries, with at least 63 percent of the income not being captured on national survey (Miller and Schieber 2014: 19).

Recently, Bee and Mitchell (2017) have explored whether underreporting of pension income has been concentrated among retirees with higher incomes or more broadly distributed. They did this by comparing survey responses on the survey, about the amounts of five kinds of income potentially received by elderly households in 2012, with administrative record values gathered from the Internal Revenue Service (IRS) and Social Security Administration. The five sources of income for which administrative data were matched to CPS respondents' survey records were: earnings, Social Security benefits, Supplemental Security Income benefits, interest and dividend income, and retirement income (not including any Social Security benefits). The retirement income included benefits received from defined benefit pension plans, including survivor and disability benefits, plus any distributions from individual retirement accounts (IRAs) or employer-sponsored defined contribution plans. The subsequent discussion here will refer to this grouping of "retirement income" as pensions or pension income. The comparison of the pension income reported for 2012 on the CPS-ASEC and the reporting of the matched respondents to the survey on the administrative files is presented in Table 3.6.

Overall, 50 percent more of the units reported receiving pension income on tax forms than in response to the CPS questions for 2012. At the bottom of the CPS income distribution, the rate of pension receipt was more than five times higher on tax records than on the survey. In the second CPS income decile, 3.4 times as many units received pensions as reported on the CPS and, across the income distribution, the receipt of pension income was underreported. Among all units in the bottom decile, the average amount of pensions reported on tax forms was 29 times the average reported on the CPS; the difference was a multiple of 10 in the second decile and 9 times in the third; overall, the average pensions reported on tax forms was twice what was reported on the CPS. Even among units that reported receiving pension income on the CPS, the amounts reported overall on the CPS were only 73 percent of the amount reported on tax filings. The implications of this underreporting of pension income were significant in the larger context of total income:

> Replacing survey income responses with administrative record values leads to several striking findings. First, relative to the 2012 number derived from the CPS ASEC alone, the median income for households aged 65 and over is 30 percent higher in the linked sample (rising from $33 800 to $44 400). Second, the poverty rate for persons aged 65 and over is 2.1 percentage points lower in the linked sample (falling from 9.0 to 6.9 percent). Third, across most of the income distribution, we find that retirement income underreporting is mainly responsible for the overall income discrepancy, while self-reported earned income and Social Security benefits correspond well with administrative records. (Bee and Mitchell 2017: 2–3)

Table 3.6 *Receipt and average amounts of pension income*

CPS income decile	Mean CPS income ($)	Reported pension recept (%)		Mean pension income, all CPS respondents ($)		Mean pension income of those receiving pensions ($)	
		CPS respondents	Administrative records	CPS respondents	Administrative records	CPS respondents	Administrative records
1	5032	7	36	216	6177	3109	17202
2	11620	12	41	467	4812	3903	11810
3	15381	22	57	966	8685	4455	15249
4	19604	35	66	2058	13617	5852	20610
5	25075	47	76	3933	16335	8340	21410
6	31757	59	81	7046	20027	11914	24631
7	40793	65	84	10601	21357	16276	25569
8	54286	68	81	15290	24745	22376	30587
9	76677	66	80	21446	28998	32328	36189
10	172800	60	78	26858	42539	45110	54528
Average	45288	44	68	8886	17727	20138	27550

Note: Receipt and average amounts of pension income received across the income distribution in 2012 by family units with at least one person age 65 or older as reported on the CPS-ASEC or on federal income tax forms.

Source: Derived from Bee and Mitchell (2017: 57).

Bee and Mitchell also tracked the trend in underreporting of pension income back to 1990. They did this by linking historical versions of the Survey of Income and Program Participation (SIPP), another nationally representative sample of the population, and the CPS-ASEC to administrative records.[8] In 1990, both the survey and administrative records indicated that 91 percent of the sample units were receiving Social Security benefits; and in 2012, the respective rates were 84 and 86 percent. On the pension side, the survey results in 1990 indicated that 40 percent of the units were receiving this income, but the administrative data indicated that 45 percent were; by 2012, the respective differences were 36 and 61 percent (Bee and Mitchell 2017: 69). (Note: these differences are not the same as those in Table 3.6 because the table focuses on household benefits, and these are based on individual persons.) The problem of not reporting pension income on the national surveys has clearly got worse over time.

The results from the CPS-ASEC and similar surveys have been used widely to analyze the effectiveness of the retirement security system, and as the basis for policy proposals to modify various aspects of the existing components of the system. Generally, the survey evidence suggests that individual and family income falls when workers retire. But the failure to properly measure retiree income distorts public perceptions about the economic status of the elderly in comparison with their economic status prior to retirement. Bee and Mitchell show this by tracking individual income in the years leading up to and after claiming Social Security benefits by the segment of the individuals in the CPS-ASEC sample who claimed the benefits from 2003 to 2007. A portion of their results is presented in Table 3.7. For couples, their pooled income is equivalence-adjusted using a scale described in Short (2015) to account for economies of scale in living costs relative to persons living alone.

The results in Table 3.7 show income levels in the year Social Security is claimed, labeled t in the table, compared with income in the year prior to claiming, $t-1$; in the year after, $t+1$; and five years after claiming, $t+5$. The income in the year that Social Security benefits are claimed is often misleading as an indicator of pre-retirement income or earnings, because it is not clear when during the year benefits are claimed. If they are claimed early in the year in conjunction with retirement from work, earnings may be a slight fraction of typical annual earnings. Using the income from the year prior to claiming as the comparative measure of pre-retirement earnings, Table 3.7 indicates that income after Social Security claiming does not fall nearly as much relative to pre-retirement income as the CPS-ASEC results imply.

Brady et al. (2017a, 2017b) have brought another set of federal income tax filing data augmented with Social Security data on birth dates, gender

Table 3.7 Equivalence-adjusted income

Years from claiming Social Security	25 percentile by income		Median income		75 percentile by income	
	CPS reporting	Administrative data	CPS reporting	Administrative data	CPS reporting	Administrative data
Income ($) at:						
t−1	24 117	27 906	42 508	46 997	69 203	73 841
t	22 396	29 631	41 518	48 143	67 658	75 388
t+1	21 613	27 987	38 116	45 982	64 344	71 898
t+5	20 105	26 533	33 443	42 334	54 904	64 346
Change in income (%)						
t−1 to t+1	−10.4	0.3	−10.3	−2.2	−7.0	−2.6
t−1 to t+5	−16.6	−4.9	−21.3	−9.9	−20.7	−12.9

Note: Equivalence-adjusted income in 2012 dollars at specified quartile points by years from initial Social Security claiming as measured by the 2013 CPS-ASEC and matched administrative data.

Source: Derived from Bee and Mitchell (2017: 62).

and date of death (if applicable) to explore what happens to workers' income levels as they transition into retirement. The data used in the study were from the IRS's Statistics of Income 1999 Edited Panel, a longitudinal sample of individual income tax returns with information from 1999 through 2010. The study uses a subsample of the nationally representative sample drawn in 1999. The subsample includes individuals aged 55 to 61 in 1999 who were working and not receiving Social Security benefits at the time.

The analytical results presented by Brady et al. (2017a, 2017b) are extensive, but the pension receipt rates and levels compare favorably with those estimated by Bee and Mitchell's administrative data linked to CPS respondents. Brady et al. focus on individuals who were not receiving Social Security benefits in 1999, who subsequently claimed their retirement benefits by 2010, while excluding those claiming Social Security Disability Insurance benefits. Brady and his colleagues consider the extent to which income in the period prior to Social Security claiming is replaced in subsequent years, and look at income replacement on two levels: first, the replacement of total income; and second, the replacement of work-related income by the combination of earnings, Social Security and pensions in the post-claiming period.

Table 3.8 shows average income levels in 2016 dollars in the year prior to individuals claiming Social Security benefits in each of the bottom four quintiles and among those in specified percentile groupings in the top quintile. The table also shows how income reported in the year prior to Social Security claiming compares to that reported in the year Social Security benefits were claimed and each of the next three years. Total income replacement is highest at the bottom of the distribution and tends to decline at higher points in the distribution. Income in the three years after Social Security claiming (that is, income in year t+3) is at least equivalent to income in the fourth quintile of year t–1 and somewhat higher in the lower three quintiles. The table also reflects the results in median terms and is similar to the results considering the averages.

The results in Table 3.8 suggest that the structure of the US retirement system is working as policymakers have intended. Since the inception of Social Security, the benefit structure has been tilted to provide higher earnings replacement at lower earnings levels than further up the earnings distribution. It has also been well understood that Social Security benefits would be increasingly inadequate at higher career-average earnings levels to provide sufficient retirement incomes to allow retirees to maintain pre-retirement living standards at career-average earnings levels, and because of that, higher earners would be more likely to accrue retirement wealth through supplemental retirement plans favored under the federal

Table 3.8 Income and taxes of retired workers in year t−1

Item	1999 per capita total income category						
	Lowest quintile	Second quintile	Middle quintile	Fourth quintile	80–95th percentile	95–99th percentile	Top 1 percent
Average per capita income and taxes reported in year t−1 ($)							
Work-related income	17 123	28 234	39 022	50 423	76 424	101 291	281 127
Total income	18 161	30 773	41 862	55 011	87 670	187 300	896 128
Income and payroll taxes	1710	4013	6315	9419	17 170	41 555	200 986
Total income net of taxes	16 452	26 761	35 547	45 592	70 499	145 745	695 142
Average total per capita income net of taxes relative to income net of taxes in year t−1 (%)							
Year SS benefits claimed	117.9	105.3	106.1	102.4	96.2	92.0	92.4
Year after SS benefits claimed	123.4	106.2	104.4	100.0	93.3	95.9	81.4
2 years after SS benefits claimed	129.6	105.6	101.3	107.1	92.1	80.5	72.9
3 years after SS benefits claimed	127.4	103.0	102.0	99.1	87.3	79.2	62.5
Median per capita income and taxes reported in year t−1 ($)							
Work-related income	16 400	28 000	39 100	49 500	72 100	86 600	88 100
Total income	17 100	29 100	40 200	52 100	78 200	122 800	297 900
Income and payroll taxes	1200	3700	5900	8400	14 500	25 400	59 500
Total income net of taxes	15 800	25 400	34 600	43 500	63 000	95 300	238 700
Total per capita income net of taxes relative to income net of taxes in year t−1 (%)							
Year SS benefits claimed	116.5	105.5	102.0	100.2	98.9	95.9	95.3
Year after SS benefits claimed	122.2	105.9	101.7	97.5	88.9	92.8	86.8
2 years after SS benefits claimed	122.2	104.3	100.0	95.2	86.5	89.8	79.1
3 years after SS benefits claimed	120.3	103.1	98.6	94.0	85.6	79.9	74.3

Note: Average and median incomes of retired workers in year t−1 (the year before claiming Social Security benefits) and relative income in the year benefits are claimed and each of the subsequent three years.

Source: Brady et al. (2017b: Tables S5a and S6a).

Table 3.9   Distribution of inflation-adjusted net work-related income

Quintile or percentile ranking by total income in 1999	Rank in the distribution of income replacement for those who no longer worked after claiming Social Security (%)				
	10th	25th	Median	75th	90th
Bottom quintile	47	69	103	148	_a
Second quintile	51	74	96	124	166
Middle quintile	58	77	99	124	167
Fourth quintile	55	74	92	115	149
80–95th percentile	42	64	90	118	155
95–99th percentile	23	42	65	101	150
Top 1 percent	15	35	100	192	_a

Notes:
Distribution of inflation-adjusted net work-related income three years after claiming Social Security retirement benefits as a percentage of net work-related income in the year before claiming Social Security among individuals by income ranking in 1999.
a.   The calculated replacement of work-related income in year t–1 by work-related income in year t+3 was truncated at 200 percent and the cell value for this case exceeds that amount.

Source: Brady et al. (2017a, pp. 37–39).

income tax code. But the potential tax benefits accorded higher earners have been limited almost from the inception of the income tax. Low levels of retirement income may persist for retirees who were at the bottom of the earnings distribution during their careers, but replacement rates well in excess of 100 percent suggest that many of the low-income retirees are better off after their careers than they were when working.

The results in Table 3.8 are based on total income reported by Social Security beneficiaries in their post-claiming years, and include some earnings. Brady et al. also consider what they call "work-related income," which provides a narrower focus on the effectiveness of the retirement income security system. In the pre-claiming period this includes earnings and pension income; in the post-claiming period it includes earnings, pension income and Social Security benefits. Table 3.9 shows the extent to which pre-retirement work-related income in the year before Social Security benefits were claimed was replaced by work-related income in the third year after Social Security benefits were claimed for individuals who no longer reported earnings. At the median, replacement of work-related income close to 100 percent net of federal taxes through the middle income quintile suggests the majority of Social Security retirees should be able to maintain their pre-retirement consumption expenditure levels to the extent that they were living on work-related income prior to retiring.

Schieber (2017) uses the CPS-ASEC to show that many of the elderly have realized much greater income growth over the past 30 to 40 years than their younger counterparts. The evidence from Bee and Mitchell and from Brady et al. suggest that Schieber's results dramatically understate the extent to which elderly incomes have grown relative to those of younger segments of society. The notion that the elderly segment of society is uniquely vulnerable because of reduced incomes in retirement relative to when they were employed does not comport with the evidence that is now available. There are segments of the elderly population that remain economically vulnerable because of low absolute incomes even though their retirement income may be higher than while working. The work of the Bipartisan Policy Center's Commission on Retirement Income Security and Personal Saving suggests that this economic vulnerability cannot be resolved by higher saving, and helps to explain why one of the goals of many recent Social Security reform proposals is to increase the income redistribution in the current benefit structure. To the extent that Social Security financing reform becomes partly about greater income redistribution through the national pension, exempting current elderly participants from sharing the burden of those changes would raise further generational equity issues.

DISCUSSION

This chapter has argued that Social Security's financing imbalances have not arisen or persisted because of the failure to measure the expected future revenues and costs of the system. The persistent financing problem over the past quarter-century has been the result of policymakers' unwillingness to act on the information given them, and to follow the approach that policymakers did prior to putting the system on automatic pilot under the legislation adopted in 1972, 1977 and 1983. When policymakers finally consider legislation to restore financing balance, they should reconcile the discrepancies between the trustees' and the CBO's outlooks of the future, and develop legislation that will most likely assure long-term sustainable solvency.

A more critical problem than picking the right projections of revenues and expenditures is to find a mechanism that will create a structural balance in the system's financing equation that is sensitive to the income security needs of retirees, while also constraining the costs on workers supporting the system. The dependency ratio in the system is now rising rapidly because the baby boom generation is transitioning into retirement, and the benefits-to-covered wages ratio is trending upward because the index used to determine benefits is rising more rapidly than average covered earnings. The automatic pilot features that drive the ratio of average benefits to average covered wages were put in place because policymakers concluded that the periodic process of political negotiation of benefit levels and tax rates was leading to unsustainable costs. They thought they were fixing this problem in a way that would stabilize future cost rates somewhat around the rates put in place in the mid-1980s. But they were wrong.

What is needed to restore equilibrium to the system's cost–benefit balance is either: (1) a return to the periodic negotiation and setting of benefits and supporting tax elements of the system; or (2) the automation of benefit adjustments to keep cost rates in line with what is deemed to be acceptable. In mathematical terms, taxes are limited to 100 percent of workers' earnings, but the political limit is much lower. Even countries that are much more accepting of higher tax rates than the United States have moved to cap the tax claims of their PAYGO national retirement systems.

Sweden has eliminated a number of risks in its pension by converting workers' accruing benefits from a promised annuity at retirement to an accumulating defined contribution account that increments over time by contributions based on workers' earnings and annual interest credits. The system is still financed on a PAYGO basis, so the accounts are notional rather than holding capital instruments. When the system is deemed to be adequately financed, the individual accounts are incremented annually by the rate of growth of average wages. At retirement, a worker's accumulated cash balance is converted to an annuity that is determined on the basis of the life expectancy of that worker's birth cohort and their age at the time of claiming. Individuals can claim as early as age 61, but deferring claiming until later, up to age 70, results in higher benefits actuarially adjusted to actual claiming age. The system is monitored over time to assure that there is a balance between expected benefits and the assets – that is, the value of future contributions – to cover them. If a deficit arises, the interest rate used to increment account balances and determine annuities at retirement is adjusted to bring the system back into balance with expected revenues under the existing guaranteed statutory tax rate of 16 percent of covered wages supporting the system.

Toward the end of the twentieth century, Germany's national pension costs were rising rapidly due to population aging following from improving life expectancies and low fertility. By the turn of the century, the cost of its system had risen to around 19.5 percent of covered payroll, and was projected to approach 30 percent by 2040. Shortly after the beginning of the new millennium, government officials began to pursue policies to limit the contribution rates to no more than 20 percent in 2020 and 22 percent in 2030. Initially unsuccessful in creating a mechanism to achieve this goal, the parliament adopted reforms in 2004 that introduced a sustainability factor to pension determinations under the national defined benefit system. This modification resulted in reductions of the replacement of pre-retirement earnings as the beneficiary-to-worker ratio in the system increases over time.

The pension changes in both Sweden and Germany suggest that pension replacement of earnings will decline, a result that has not been universally embraced. One of the members of the Swedish National Social Insurance Board concluded: "What was said to be a weakness of conventional PAYG [pay-as-you-go] schemes, i.e., that all financial problems were met by raising the rate of contribution, has now gone into reverse: All financial problems are met by reducing benefits" (Settergren 2003). At the same time, Honekamp (2007) argues that neither the Swedish nor German systems can be fully successful, because nominal benefits for current beneficiaries are protected against reductions when the demographic safety valves are employed.

It is nearly certain that US policymakers would never adopt changes to Social Security that would reduce current retirees' nominal benefits, so including them under financing reforms would require other approaches. The application of the federal income tax to benefits is one way to include existing beneficiaries, and flat dollar caps on annual cost-of-living adjustments, or scaled percentage limits on the adjustments, could limit future growth of benefits for current retirees. Other countries have adopted policies along these lines. For example, Austria, Greece, Portugal and Slovenia have frozen automatic adjustment of benefits for all but their lowest earners; Luxembourg has scaled back its expected increases by 50 percent (OECD 2013); pension indexation in Belgium was frozen in 2015; Italy shifted to a "cost-of-life" indexation, where benefits above a specified level were only to be increased by a fixed amount; and Spain based indexation, in part, on the ratio of pension contributions to expense and, in part, on changes in life expectancy (OECD 2015: 24–25).

The generational implications of recent policy proposals which contend that they would balance financing reforms between benefit adjustments and revenue increases should not be overlooked. If both ends of the stick are to strike current younger and future workers, the balancing of benefit and revenue adjustments may be an improper way to consider the implications of reform. In the current financing mechanism of the US system, it is not clear that added revenues collected from higher tax rates in the next few decades can be saved. Other countries have adopted policies to save accumulating trust funds by investing them in capital assets in the local economy or internationally; Canada is a prime example. In the United States, the politics of government investment in private equity is a contentious political issue that would further complicate an already difficult policy problem. If policymakers cannot agree on a way to save the revenues collected if higher tax collections are part of the rebalancing, young workers might be better off with gradual reductions in Social Security replacement of earnings, coupled with added opportunities to save through supplemental, tax-favored retirement plans.

No matter what direction the deliberations on Social Security reform take in the next few years, they need to be taken up in the context of a realistic view of the economic capacity and benefits being provided by the other elements of the national retirement system in the United States. The recent work by Bee and Mitchell (2017) and Brady et al. (2017b) indicate that the supplemental elements of the existing system are far more robust than have been considered in previous discussions about Social Security policy. They also indicate that the means are available to develop far more realistic measures of the economic status of the elderly in the United States than the CPS or other similar surveys have provided over the past 40 or more years.

NOTES

*   The author thanks Stephen Goss for reviewing the Social Security trust fund estimates of foregone revenues presented, Shai Akabas for providing background data used in developing the final report of the Bipartisan Policy Center's Commission on Retirement Income Security and Personal Saving, and Liang Wang for comments on an earlier draft of the chapter.

1.   The trustees include the Secretaries of the US Departments of Health and Human Services, Labor and Treasury, plus the Social Security Commissioner and two public trustees nominated by the President and approved by the Senate.

2.   The actuarial balance is the difference between the income rate and cost rate for a period. A balance of zero for a period indicates that the cost for the period can be met by contributions with a remaining (contingency) trust fund reserve at the end of the period equal to 100 percent of the next year's cost. The test of close actuarial balance requires both that the system is sufficiently financed in the short run and that the trust fund ratios are positive throughout the 75-year projection period under the intermediate assumptions used to value the system.

3.   In a retirement plan financed on a PAYGO basis, *revenues = expenditures*. Revenues equal the payroll tax rate (t) times the average earnings (W) subject to the payroll tax times the number of covered workers (NW). Expenditures equal the average benefit loaded to include administrative costs (B) times the number of beneficiaries (NB). So: $t \times W \times NW = B \times NB$. Restating the equation to solve for the tax rate needed to balance the system: $t = B/W \times NB/NW$.

4.   The Social Security Advisory Board, established in 1994 legislation, is supposed to monitor developments affecting the programs and their participants in order to make recommendations to the President and Congress on matters deserving attention by policymakers or administrators.

5.   The argument here is not that contributing to a PAYGO-financed retirement system is real savings in a macroeconomic context but, from an individual perspective, contribut-

ing to Social Security is required for workers to qualify for benefits and will ultimately determine their benefit entitlements. To the extent that Social Security is one of the assets in the retirement portfolio, contributions to the program are equivalent to other forms of retirement saving, whether more or less efficient than those other forms of saving.
6. The hypothetical worker examples developed by the Social Security actuaries are assumed to work through age 64 and retire at age 65. In this example, their earnings during ages 65, 66 and 67 were assumed to equal their earnings at age 64.
7. The CPS is done monthly to track various measures of labor force activity. The monthly surveys have periodic supplements gathering information on other characteristics and activities of the population. The ASEC is a regular supplement to the basic survey administered each March, in which information is gathered on the sources and levels income of individuals in sample households over the prior year.
8. The SIPP linkage is important because they did not have administrative data linked to the CPS-ASEC prior to 1995, but could compare reporting rates of pension and Social Security income on the CPS-ASEC and SIPP from 1995 through 2008 to show nearly identical reporting of these sources of income on the two files. Thus, for the 1990 comparison of survey versus administration reporting rates, the SIPP match results were used in lieu of a match with the CPS-ASEC.

REFERENCES

Ballentyne, Harry C. (1983), "Long-range projections of Social Security Trust Fund operations in dollars," Actuarial Notes 2017.1, Washington, DC: Social Security Administration, available at www.ssa.gov/oact/NOTES/pdf_notes/note117.pdf.

Becerra, Xavier (2014), Opening statement at "Hearing on what workers need to know about Social Security as they plan for their retirement," before the Subcommittee on Social Security, Committee on Ways and Means, US House of Representatives (July 29), available at https://waysandmeans.house.gov/hearing-on-what-workers-need-to-know-about-social-security-as-they-plan-for-their-reti rement.

Bee, Adam and Joshua Mitchell (2017), "Do older Americans have more income than we think?", SESHD Working Paper 2017-39, Washington: US Census Bureau, available at www.census.gov/library/working-papers/2017/demo/SEH SD-WP2017-39.html.

Bentham, Jeremy (1824), *The Book of Fallacies*, London: John & H.L. Hunt.

Bipartisan Policy Center (2016), *Report of the Commission on Retirement Security and Personal Saving*, available at https://cdn.bipartisanpolicy.org/wp-content/uploads/2016/06/BPC-Retirement-Security-Report.pdf.

Bosworth, Barry and Gary Burtless (2004), "Pension reform and saving," paper presented at a conference of the International Forum of the Collaboration Projects, Tokyo, Japan, February 17–19.

Brady, Peter J., Steven Bass, Jessica Holland and Kevin Pierce (2017a), "Using panel tax data to examine the transition to retirement," paper presented at the 2016 NTA Annual Conference, Washington, DC, November 12, available at www.irs.gov/pub/irs-soi/17rptransitionretirement.pdf.

Brady, Peter J., Steven Bass, Jessica Holland and Kevin Pierce (2017b), "Supplemental tables," available at www.irs.gov/pub/irs-soi/17rpbbhptables.xls.

Caldera, Selena (2012), "Social Security: who's counting on it?," Washington, DC: AARP Public Policy Institute, available at www.aarp.org/content/dam/

aarp/research/public_policy_institute/econ_sec/2012/Social-Security-Whos-Cou
nting-on-It-fs-252-AARP-ppi-econ-sec.pdf.

Chu, Sharon and Seung H. An (2017), "Disaggregation of changes in the long-range
actuarial balance for the Old Age, Survivors, and Disability Insurance (OASDI)
Program since 1983," Actuarial Note Number 2017.8 (July), Social Security
Administration, available at www.ssa.gov/oact/NOTES/ran8/an2017-8.pdf.

Clingman, Michael and Kyle Burkhalter (2016), "Scaled factors for hypothetical
earnings examples under the 2016 Trustees Report assumptions," Actuarial Note
Number 2016.3, Washington, DC: Social Security Administration, available at
www.ssa.gov/oact/NOTES/ran3/an2016-3.pdf.

Derthick, Martha (1979), *Policymaking for Social Security*, Washington, DC:
Brookings Institution.

Diamond, Peter A. and Peter R. Orszag (2005), *Saving Social Security*, Washington,
DC: Brookings Institution.

Economic Report (1982), *Economic Report of the President 1982*, available at www.
presidency.ucsb.edu/economic_reports/1982.pdf.

Gokhale, Jagadeesh (2010), *Social Security: A Fresh Look at Policy Alternatives*,
Chicago, IL: University of Chicago Press.

Hall, Keith (2016), "Comparing CBO's long-term projections with those of the
Social Security Trustees," testimony before the Subcommittee on Social Security,
Committee on Ways and Means, US House of Representatives (September 21),
available at www.cbo.gov/publication/52154.

Honekamp, Ivonne (2007), "PAYG in an ageing society: the case of Sweden versus
Germany," *Pensions*, **12**(3), 138–53.

Meyerson, Noah and John Sabelhaus (2000), "Uncertainty in Social Security Trust
Fund projections," *National Tax Journal*, **53**(3), Part 1, 515–30.

Miller, Billie Jean and Sylvester J. Schieber (2014), "Contribution of pension and
retirement savings to retirement income security: more than meets the eye,"
Journal of Retirement, **1**(3), 14–29.

Nataraj, Sita and John B. Shoven (2004), "Has the unified budget destroyed the
federal government trust funds?," paper presented at a conference sponsored by
the Office of Policy, Social Security Administration and Michigan Retirement
Research Consortium, Washington, DC, August 12–13.

National Academy of Social Insurance (2013), "The role of benefits in income and
poverty," available at www.nasi.org/learn/socialsecurity/benefits-role.

OECD (2013), "Pensions at a glance 2013: OECD and G20 indicators," Paris:
Organisation for Economic Co-operation and Development, available at http://
dx.doi.org/10.1787/pension_glance-2013-en.

OECD (2015), "Pensions at a glance 2015: OECD and G20 indicators," Paris:
Organisation for Economic Co-operation and Development, available at http://
dx.doi.org/10.1787/pension_glance-2015-en.

Schieber, Sylvester J. (1995), "Why do pension benefits seem so small?", *Benefits
Quarterly*, Fourth Quarter, 57–70.

Schieber, Sylvester J. (2017), "Generational equity and Social Security financing
reform," *Journal of Retirement*, **5**(1), 12–31.

Schieber, Sylvester J. and John B. Shoven (1999), *The Real Deal: The History and
Future of Social Security*, New Haven, CT: Yale University Press.

Schobel, Bruce D., Roland E. King, Robert J. Myers and John C. Wilkin (1989),
"Current issues in US Social Security and Medicare programs," *Record of
Society of Actuaries*, **15**(3B), 1699–1713.

Settergren, Ole (2003), "The reform of the Swedish pension system: initial results," *Revue Française des Affaires Sociales*, **4**, 369–98.

Short, Kathleen (2015), "The supplemental poverty measure: 2014," *Current Population Reports P60-254*, available at www.census.gov/library/publications/2015/demo/p60-254.html.

Smetters, Kent (2003), "Is the Social Security Trust Fund worth anything?," unpublished paper, University of Pennsylvania.

Social Security Advisory Board (1998, 2001, 2005, 2010), "Social Security: why action should be taken soon," Washington, DC: Social Security Advisory Board, available at www.ssab.gov/Advanced-Search-Results?sb-search=why+action+should+be+taken+soon&sb-inst=0_dnn_avtSearch1&sb-logid=4559-wsqtgeo8ezcwme2p.

Social Security Advisory Board (1999, 2003, 2007, 2011, 2015), "Technical Panels of the Board," available at http://ssab.gov/About-the-Board/Technical-Panels; and

Social Security Advisory Board (2017), "Technical Panel on Labor Force Participation," June, available at http://ssab.gov/Details-Page/ArticleID/1180/Technical-Panel-on-Labor-Force-Participation-A-Report-to-the-Board-June-2017.

Steuerle, C. Eugene (2014), *Dead Men Ruling: How to Restore Fiscal Freedom and Rescue Our Future*, New York: Century Foundation Press.

Trenkamp, Brad (2016), "Income of the population 55 or older, 2014," Washington, DC: Social Security Administration, available at www.ssa.gov/policy/docs/statcomps/income_pop55/2014/incpop14.pdf.

Trustees, Social Security (1972), "The 1972 annual report of the Board of Trustees of the Federal Old-Age and Survivors Insurance and Federal Disability Insurance Trust Funds," available at www.ssa.gov/oact/TR/historical/1972TR.pdf.

Trustees, Social Security (1973), "The 1973 annual report of the Board of Trustees of the Federal Old-Age and Survivors Insurance and Federal Disability Insurance Trust Funds," available at www.ssa.gov/oact/TR/historical/1973TR.pdf.

Trustees, Social Security (1977), "The 1977 annual report of the Board of Trustees of the Federal Old-Age and Survivors Insurance and Federal Disability Insurance Trust Funds," available at www.ssa.gov/oact/TR/historical/1977TR.pdf.

Trustees, Social Security (1990), "The 1990 annual report of the Board of Trustees of the Federal Old-Age and Survivors Insurance and Federal Disability Insurance Trust Funds," available at www.ssa.gov/oact/TR/historical/1990TR.pdf.

Trustees, Social Security (1991), "The 1991 annual report of the Board of Trustees of the Federal Old-Age and Survivors Insurance and Federal Disability Insurance Trust Funds," available at www.ssa.gov/oact/TR/historical/1991TR.pdf.

Trustees, Social Security (1994), "The 1994 annual report of the Board of Trustees of the Federal Old-Age and Survivors Insurance and Federal Disability Insurance Trust Funds," available at www.ssa.gov/oact/TR/historical/1994TR.pdf.

Trustees, Social Security (2016), "The 2016 annual report of the Board of Trustees of the Federal Old-Age and Survivors Insurance and Federal Disability Insurance Trust Funds," available at www.ssa.gov/oact/TR/historical/2016TR.pdf.

Trustees, Social Security (2017), "The 2017 annual report of the Board of Trustees of the Federal Old-Age and Survivors Insurance and Federal Disability Insurance Trust Funds," available at www.ssa.gov/oact/TR/2017/tr2017.pdf.

PART II

Improving fiscal accountability

4. Enhancing accountability of Korea's government funds system through consolidated management of surplus money in budget-type funds

Yongok Choi

INTRODUCTION

Government funds are an important pillar of Korean central government finances. In 2016 they accounted for 36.1 percent (141.1 trillion won) and 31.7 percent (122.5 trillion won) of total revenue and expenditure, respectively. The number of government funds increased continuously to 114 in 1993, after the first three were established in 1960 under the Budget and Accounts Act. As the number of government funds increased, the opacity and inefficiency due to separately operated funds were pointed out. In 1993, the Framework Act on Fund Management was enacted to consolidate funds of similar nature and to abolish unnecessary funds. Constant efforts led to the reduction in the number of funds to 46 in 2004. After that year, however, they began to increase again, and 65 funds were being managed by 2016.

The government funds system allows flexible financial management, supplementing rigid budget accounting in ways that can increase expertise and efficiency. Funds undertake specific policies and projects, and increase the welfare of the society as a whole by operating with relative independence from the influence of political circles. However, amid the rapidly expanding numbers and sizes of funds, it is true that they are exposed to several issues in terms of transparency and efficiency.

The purpose of this chapter is to analyze and search for methods to overcome the problems of the government funds system from the perspective of fiscal accountability. The justification for the existence of a fund is that it is for a "specific purpose." The most important obligation of a fund is therefore answerability regarding its expenditures, and it should be possible to impose sanctions based on its performance. There is a need to precisely and transparently disclose information for each expenditure, to conduct retention evaluations based on this information, and to close funds if the results warrant it.

In addition, as the funds system acts as an important pillar of government finances, it is obligated to improve its efficiency. Increasing the efficiency is more important in the current times of increasing ratios of mandatory expenditure due to a rapidly aging population and as the economy shifts to a state of low growth. The goal of "improvements in efficiency" is a goal of integrated finances – including general accounts, special accounts and interactions between overall funds – rather than demanding efficiency at the level of each separate fund.

As a method to improve the financial accountability of the funds system, this chapter proposes integrated management of surplus money from budget-type funds. Surplus money can be defined as the liquid assets in the accounts that are not spent during the fiscal year. If the surpluses were managed together, the current principal agents of fund management could be freed from their obligation of efficient asset management. In addition, by unifying the windows of accounting for fund expenditures, comparable information can be generated, and this information can be used in fund retention evaluations. Also, integrated management of surplus funds can contribute to the improvement of fiscal soundness of national finances. Efficiency would be improved through economies of scale and a reduction in liquidity risks.

The next section examines the current status of the government funds system in Korea. It summarizes the positive aspects of the system as well as the problems that have been exposed so far. The third section discusses the accountability that the fund system should possess, and examines the impediments to accountability and methods for improvement. The fourth section deals with the expected effects of the proposed improvement method – the consolidated management of surplus money from budget-type funds – followed by conclusions and implications.

OVERVIEW OF THE GOVERNMENT FUNDS SYSTEM IN KOREA

Significance of the System

Government funds can be established only according to the law (under Article 5 of the National Finance Act) and in limited cases where there is a need for the government to flexibly manage funds for a specific purpose, and where they can be managed without relying on a budget of revenues and expenditures. They are similar to special accounts, as the relation between revenue and expenditure is clear: each fund is used for a specific purpose, drawing from specific sources of revenue such as government and private contributions, and not general taxes. However, while the regular annual government budget is strictly controlled according to specific laws, government funds operate with a relative guarantee of autonomy and enjoy flexibility in terms of their purpose. Funds differ from the budget in another way, because changes in expenditure plans of major items of up to 20 percent can be made without a vote from the National Assembly.

As such, flexible management is possible, and the funds system is deemed to have various positive functions by supplementing rigid budget accounts. First, the government can provide intensive support through the funds for targeted sectors to trigger economic growth more effectively. The government can secure a support system through a government fund in sectors that have strong external economic effects or in cases where there is a political determination to provide support. Examples include funds to support a certain industry, funds to support small and medium-sized enterprises, funds to support farmers and fishermen, and funds to expand social overhead capital.

In cases where the private financial market is not yet mature, government funds have been used as a window for policy financing by lending capital to the private sector at low interest rates. In other words, they have also undertaken the functions of quantitative expansion and supplementing private capital.

In cases where the national order of priority is likely to change due to political diversions, the funds system allows certain industries to operate with relative independence from the influence of politics, which in turn can increase social welfare. Social insurance funds are particularly relevant in this case.

In addition, as the relationship between income and expenditure of funds is clear, government funds can solve challenges caused by a discordance in timing. One examples of this is the Radioactive Waste Management Fund, which continuously accumulates fees for the management of spent nuclear fuel, in order to prepare for over 100 years of future expenditure. Another is the National Pension Fund, where the mode of paying benefits is operated in a partially funded system over the long term.

Current Status of Government Funds

The first three government funds were established in 1960 under the Budget and Accounts Act, and by 2016 a total of 65 funds were being

Table 4.1 *Total revenue of the central government in Korea, 2016 (trillion won)*

Item	Budget			Funds	Total
	Tax	Non-tax	Subtotal		
Revenue	222.9	27.2	250.1	141.1	391.2

Source: National Assembly Budget Office (2016: 16).

Table 4.2 *Total expenditure of the central government in Korea, 2016 (trillion won)*

	Budget				
	General accounts	Special accounts	Subtotal budget	Funds	Total
Total gross expenditure	268.4	62.3	330.7	620.0	950.7
Total net expenditure	214.6	49.3	256.6	122.5	386.4

Note: "The size of total expenditure is the total of budget and funds (excluding exchange stabilization funds in the financial sector and account funds), excluding not only internal trading between accounts/funds, but also accommodating transactions such as the issuance of government bonds or borrowing, which preserve financial earnings and expenses" (National Assembly Budget Office, 2016).

Source: National Assembly Budget Office (2016: 38).

managed by 22 government departments. They can be categorized into 46 budget-type funds, 8 financial sector funds, 6 social insurance funds, and 5 account funds. In addition to the increasing number of funds, the capital being managed has also increased significantly, almost doubling from 312.3 trillion won in 2004 to 620.0 trillion won in 2016.

Tables 4.1 and 4.2 provide summaries of the total revenue and total expenditure, respectively, of the central government in 2016. According to these data, government funds accounted for 36.1 percent (141.1 trillion won) of the total revenue and 31.7 percent (122.5 trillion won) of the total expenditure of the central government. The funds accounted for approximately 8 percent of gross domestic product (GDP) and therefore can be considered to play an important role in public finance.

ACCOUNTABILITY OF THE SYSTEM

Accountability of Government funds

Accountability of government funds can be divided into those where accountability is assigned to each fund managing entity, and those where it is required as a component of public finance. The most important duty of the fund managing entity is to manage the funds that have been raised in a manner that is appropriate to the objectives in creating each fund. In addition, the principal agents of fund management should manage the assets transparently and efficiently, according to Article 79 of the National Finance Act. The accountability that is required at this stage comprises answerability, transparency and openness. The first component involves answering whether the funds have been lawfully raised, whether they have been spent appropriately according to the goal of the fund, and whether those financial actions have brought the expected results. This accountability is safeguarded by requiring the fund managing entity to establish fund management plans, to undergo a National Assembly review and vote in relation to the management plans and results, and to submit performance reports and asset management guidelines for the relevant financial activities.

In addition, transparency is required more than efficiency in asset management. As such, as the assets of each fund are managed according to stipulated rules and regulations, decision-making by a majority and with independence are required in the management and supervision system. This is possible by securing transparency and the principle of information disclosure. The primary purpose of budget-type funds is the effective operation of the "proper purpose business," and while considering the public nature of a fund it is acceptable that more emphasis may be placed on transparency than on efficiency for the secondary task of asset management.

As a component of public finance under the government funds system, each fund is under obligation to justify its expenditure and should be subject to closure when its performance is low. Enforcing these provisions in particular is a prerequisite to maintaining openness in management for the nation. In many cases, budget-type funds are created to promote something specific, and the existence of such funds is observably the result of interest groups pursuing gain for themselves. Therefore, only by evaluating funds – and being able to dissolve them if the results justify it – can such interest groups be effectively prevented from abusing their power. In this regard, Article 82 of the National Finance Act requires an evaluation of existing funds to be reported every three years to the National Assembly and disclosed to the public.

In addition, the government funds system, which plays an important role in public finance, is obligated to maintain fiscal soundness in its handling of national finances. After a fund has been established by a government grant, it may raise additional revenue by borrowing, which in turn increases public debt, although this increment of the debt does not appear in the annual government budget. This aspect of fund management should be taken into consideration because of its potential effects on the soundness of national finances. Increasing the efficiency of national finances is even more important in the current times of fiscal slack in the economy due to the rapidly aging population and state of low growth. The efficiency improvement goal at this level should be understood differently from the goal aimed at the level of each individual fund. The goal of improving efficiency required at the individual fund level derives from the obligations of asset management to smoothly conduct the "proper purpose business," which is the primary duty of the fund. Due to the public nature of the fund, the obligation of transparency is given priority over efficiency improvement. However, efficiency enhancement in terms of being core to government finances is a more fundamental problem, and must be defined by taking into consideration the interactions between general accounts, special accounts and funds. The act of improving efficiency from the perspective of each individual fund is not always the same as improving the efficiency of national finances as a whole. For example, when surplus funds accrue in individual funds, it may be desirable from an efficiency standpoint to manage them to create profit, whereas from the standpoint of the entire nation it may be more efficient to make use of the surplus by depositing the money in other accounts or funds.

Problems in Accountability

The first among the current problems in the accountability of government funds is that the obligations are improperly formulated. The principal entity managing an individual fund is required to manage the assets, particularly surplus funds. In addition to any lack of expertise in asset management on the part of the managing entity, transparency is given priority over efficiency, and therefore the tasks of installing an asset management council, creating asset management guidelines, conducting the asset management evaluation and managing the risk are all executed separately within each budget-type fund; a procedure that is significantly inefficient.

Second, the enforcement of restrictions based on performance is not effective. A fund retention evaluation is the sole device that can impose restrictions based on the results of fund management. Across the six decades since the first funds were created, however, the only ones that have been dissolved as a result of retention evaluation are the Defense Industry Fosterage Fund and the Culture Industry Promotion Fund (in 2003) and the National Scholarship Fund (in 2009), which shows that the system lacks effectiveness. Even if a retention evaluation were to recommend integration or dissolution of a fund, no means are available to enforce the action.

Third, surplus funds of the government tend to be regarded as "pocket money" or vested rights of the relevant departments, which means that answerability related to accountability does not always function properly. The principal entity managing a fund during the budget formulation process is asked to create a fund management plan. It appears that 12 of the 46 budget-type funds have consistently created their fund management plans with overstatements in their expense plans, and the accumulated surplus money appears in plans to cover these expenses, although it is rarely used.

It would be challenging to try to solve all these problems with the introduction of only one or two policies or regulations. This chapter aims to show that consolidated management of surplus money from budget-type funds can weaken the inappropriate vested interests created by funds, encourage an environment where the obligations of answerability and enforcement function well, and contribute to the efficiency of national finances as a whole.

The following section examines the expected effects of integrating surplus money from budget-type funds, which is proposed as a method to strengthen accountability in the government funds system. The expected effects in improving transparency qualitatively are discussed, together with the expected effects in improving efficiency through quantitative analysis.

EXPECTED EFFECTS OF THE PROPOSED METHOD

Improvements in Transparency

If surplus money from government funds were integrated and managed as a single entity, rather than as individual funds, transparency would improve significantly, because the expenditure details from each fund could then be generated on a level comparable with all the others. This proposed change can be compared with the improvement in transparency that was attempted by unifying the operating channels of government by the Ministry of Strategy and Finance. Efforts are being made to generate details about expenditures from the funds and to decrease arbitrariness on the part of the fund managing entities, by utilizing a digital budgeting and accounting system (known as d-Brain) and designating expenditure items via guidelines for budgeting and fund management plans. Nevertheless, each fund still separately manages its own revenues and expenditures, and it is difficult to believe that 46 different funds are all able to apply the same standards uniformly to generate information.

If the accounting management window were unified with integrated management of surplus money, information and knowledge to appropriately sort the expenditure could be accumulated, and in the long term, more objective and comparable expenditure data across funds could be constructed. By being able to analyze expenditure details between funds item by item, information to verify the appropriateness of purchases of goods and services would easily be obtained, which would contribute to preventing lax management, and aid in improving efficiency. In addition, the comparable information that would be generated could be used to increase the accuracy of fund retention evaluations.

Improvements in Efficiency

The integrated management of surplus money from budget-type funds is also expected to have a direct positive effect on improving efficiency. Currently, some surplus money of each government fund is invested in the Investment Pool for Public Funds (IPPF). The decision to do so is based on each fund's strategic asset allocation. However, to exploit potential economies of scale, it would be better to make the strategic asset allocation decision once the surplus money from all budget-type funds has been integrated. Also, the consolidated management of government funds would decrease the liquidity risk to improve efficiency as a whole.

Determining the Magnitude of Surplus Money

As observed from Table 4.3, at the end of 2015, the asset size of budget-type funds reached approximately 205 trillion won. Of this amount, approximately 169 trillion won (82.1 percent) were held as financial assets, the amount deposited in the Public Capital Management Fund (PCMF) was approximately 10 trillion won (5.1 percent), real estate assets accounted for 7.7 trillion won (3.7 percent), and other assets 18.7 trillion won (9.1 percent).

Table 4.3 also summarizes the change in the assets of budget-type funds. From the end of 2012 to the end of 2015, the assets increased by approximately 51.6 trillion won, since revenue was greater than expenses, including project expenses and fund management expenses. Examined in more detail, the increase in the deposits in the private sector (approximately 15.3 trillion won) was used as project expenses, and the sum of the deposits in monetary and nonmonetary financial institutions and the internal

Table 4.3   *Changes in budget-type fund assets in Korea, 2012–15 (100 million won)*

Assets	Year ending 2012 (A)	Year ending 2015 (B)	Change (B–A)
Total assets (C+D+E+F+G)	1 536 753	2 053 247	516 494
Financial assets (C+D)	1 276 019	1 685 253	409 234
Deposit in monetary and non-monetary financial institutions (C)	191 498	447 579	256 081
Deposit in private sector (D)	1 084 521	1 237 674	153 153
Internal transactions (deposit in PCMF) (E)	17 700	104 064	86 364
Other assets (uncollected revenues) (F)	192 611	186 573	−6038
Real estate (G)	50 423	77 357	26 934

Sources: Ministry of Strategy and Finance (2014, 2016).

transactions (34.2 trillion won deposited in the PCMF) can be considered as the increase in surplus funds. Of this increase, approximately 8.6 trillion won was deposited in the PCMF and approximately 25.6 trillion won was deposited in monetary or non-monetary financial institutions or the Bank of Korea.

Through the assets of budget-type funds, we can roughly calculate the amount of surplus money in those funds. This estimate may vary, however, depending on how surplus funds are defined. In the narrowest definition, if we exclude "deposits in the private sector," which are being used as financing expenses for conducting business purposes, we can estimate approximately 44.8 trillion won in surplus money at the end of 2015. If we add the 10.4 trillion won deposited in the PCMF, the amount increases to 55.2 trillion won, and if we include uncollected revenues, it increases further to 73.8 trillion won. If we include "deposits in the private sector," thus using the widest definition of the word, it makes a significant jump to 198 trillion won.

In order to scrutinize the amount of and changes in surplus funds, this study utilizes daily revenue and expenditure details from each fund to analyze the trend of surplus money. For this analysis, all transaction data for revenue and expenditure actions that occurred from January 1, 2013 to December 31, 2015 were used. All revenue transactions from each fund were recorded with information on revenue source, income amount, transaction date and a detailed description of each transaction. Also, all transactions of expenses from each fund were recorded with information about the expenditure item, amount, date and revenue source.

Using these data, it was assumed that each fund would not actively manage its surplus funds but instead would retain them in the integrated fund. Then the sample path of the cash flow was calculated. In order to do so, the following procedure was adopted:

1. The initial cash holdings (surplus money at the end of 2012) was set at total financial assets excluding the "deposits in the private sector."
2. On the revenue side, it was assumed that some transactions did not occur. These include collections from deposits in monetary financial institutions, deposits in non-monetary financial institutions and deposits in the PCMF, which can be considered as management of surplus money.
3. On the expenditure side, it was assumed that transactions related to the management of surplus money and internal transactions between funds did not occur.

Figure 4.1 shows the estimated total surplus money by integrating the surpluses from 31 of the budget-type funds using this procedure. At the end

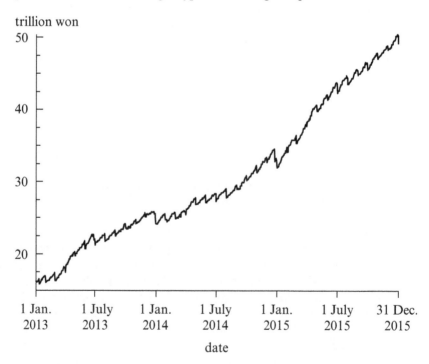

Figure 4.1   Trend of surpluses of 31 budget-type funds in Korea, January 1, 2013 – December 31, 2015

of 2012, the total surplus was 16.2 trillion won, and if these budget-type funds continued to hold idle money after project-related expenditures as cash, by the end of 2015 the total would have increased by approximately 33.1 trillion won to 49.3 trillion won. Note that approximately only 27 percent (8.8 trillion won) of the increase in surplus money during this period was deposited in the PCMF and used for public purposes to improve the efficiency of national finances.

Economies of Scale and Reduction in Liquidity Risk

The direct effects of efficiency improvement through the integrated management of surplus money can be analyzed largely in terms of two factors. The first is the improvement in the rate of return due to the effects from economies of scale. The surplus of each fund is managed after passing through an asset management council vote. Decisions, such as the strategic asset allocation, are taken by the council, and this allocation is retained in the IPPF. As asset allocation at present is predetermined for each fund before deposit in the IPPF, it is challenging to exploit economies of scale. Second, each fund is required to maintain cash reserves to carry out its operations, and the appropriate amount of the reserves is calculated based on asset management guidelines from the Ministry of Strategy and Finance. However, the appropriate amount of cash reserve for budget-type funds can be significantly reduced even at the same risk level. By having less cash holdings, we can increase efficiency.

The economies of scale effect was analyzed using data for the asset management performance of each fund for three years. Such data are recorded separately under the categories of short-term assets and mid- to long-term assets. Short-term assets are subdivided into cash assets (less than three months) and liquid assets (over three months and less than one year).

Table 4.4 shows basic statistics on the balance and the rate of return by investment for each fund during 2013–15. Most funds (128 observations) appear to deposit their surplus money in the money market fund (MMF) managed by IPPF, and in addition there are large differences between funds in the selection of investment products. Furthermore, the fact that the standard deviation of the balance is larger than the average shows that there are large differences between funds.

To estimate the economies of scale effect, the following regression model was used for each type of investment asset, utilizing data from the fund level:

$$RI_{i,t} = \mu_t + \beta \log(AB_{i,t}) + \varepsilon_{i,t} \tag{4.1}$$

Table 4.4 Basic statistics on asset management performance in Korea

Investment product	Obs.	Balance (100 million won)		Return (%)	
		Mean	SD	Mean	SD
Cash assets					
Deposits for fixed interest rates	33	118.5	144.5	1.8	1.1
MMF, MMDA	64	775.8	3295.7	1.5	0.9
Cash assets – other	44	1273.7	4295.4	0.6	1.2
MMF managed by IPPF	128	363.5	550.8	2.2	0.4
Liquidity assets					
Deposits for fixed interest rates (less than 6 months)	39	141.4	220.0	2.6	0.4
Deposits for fixed interest rates (less than 1 year)	42	215.9	325.6	2.7	0.6
Government bonds managed by IPPF	37	516.4	1151.6	2.7	1.1
Liquidity assets – other	29	342.6	710.4	2.5	0.7
Commercial bonds	5	1801.3	2212.3	2.6	0.7
Commercial bonds managed by IPPF	11	688.8	1231.7	2.9	0.8
Mid- to long-term assets					
Deposits for fixed interest rate (over 1 year)	53	1080.4	2739.0	2.9	0.6
Government bonds	9	5057.7	12913.8	3.1	4.8
Government bonds managed by IPPF	49	810.2	1147.9	3.3	1.3
Commercial bonds	15	14282.9	29791.2	-6.7	27.8
Commercial bonds managed by IPPF	34	333.1	541.8	3.3	1.0
Domestic stocks and bonds	6	30261.7	45894.3	1.6	1.1

	Obs.				
Domestic stocks and bonds managed by IPPF	40	3633.8	9839.5	2.5	1.1
Active	9	1136.2	2391.7	-4.1	10.6
Active by IPPF	6	258.4	272.7	0.1	9.8
Alternative investments	12	342.4	479.6	7.0	22.0
Real estate (domestic)	12	335.3	482.3	-1.1	15.2
Real estate (foreign)	7	3.0	3.1	32.0	86.5
Derivatives	5	328.6	644.0	0.5	1.0
Traditional foreign assets	7	60.3	45.8	13.8	12.6

Note: SD = standard deviation. Obs. = number of observations.

Source: Internal data (asset management evaluation by funds) of the Ministry of Strategy and Finance.

RI and *AB* refer to the return on investment and average balance, respectively, for fund i (= 1, . . ., 45)[1] in the year t (= 2013, 2014, 2015). μ_t is a dummy variable to control for the year fixed effect. A positive value for β can be interpreted to mean that a positive effect of economies of scale does exist. The reason that we can expect a positive effect in the performance is that the bigger funds have more options from which to choose products, even in the same category.

β and the *t*-value are summarized in Table 4.5. Short-term and cash assets and mid-to-long-term assets at fixed interest rates (over one year), which account for a large portion of asset distribution, are shown to have positive effects of economies of scale. Moreover, short-term assets have economies of scale in all cases.

Table 4.5   Estimation results on the economies of scale effect in Korea

Investment product	Estimate	t-value
Cash assets		
Deposits for fixed interest rates	0.00182	1.70
MMF, MMDA	0.00158	3.67
Cash assets – other	0.00244	5.13
MMF managed by IPPF	0.00003	0.56
Liquidity assets		
Deposits for fixed interest rates (less than 6 months)	0.00021	1.00
Deposits for fixed interest rates (less than 1 year)	0.00026	0.69
Government bonds managed by IPPF	−0.00017	−0.23
Liquidity assets – other	0.00169	4.25
Commercial bonds	−0.00019	−0.44
Commercial bonds managed by IPPF	−0.00232	−2.44
Mid- to long-term assets		
Deposits for fixed interest rates (over 1 year)	0.00346	9.39
Government bonds	−0.00241	−0.21
Government bonds managed by IPPF	0.00039	0.56
Commercial bonds	0.03318	1.31
Commercial bonds managed by IPPF	−0.00100	−1.68
Domestic stocks and bonds	0.00129	0.54
Domestic stocks and bonds managed by IPPF	0.00050	0.48
Active	0.02958	1.62
Active by IPPF	−0.00552	−0.33
Alternative investments	−0.05210	−1.47
Real estate (domestic)	0.00893	0.34
Real estate (foreign)	−0.50565	−0.95
Derivatives	−0.00057	−0.12
Traditional foreign assets	0.09590	0.86

Though the estimated economies of scales are positive overall, the magnitude of their effects is quite small. However, it is worth noting that the effect could be increased by reducing administrative costs, once the surplus money is pooled. Moreover, if the strategic asset allocation is made after pooling the surplus money, then many more investment opportunities will be accessible.

While there are several methods to estimate appropriate cash reserves to cope with liquidity risk, most funds use the cash flow at risk method, the concept of which is to calculate and prepare for the worst cash flow that can occur during a specific time at a given confidence level. The value can be estimated by repeated sampling with replacement of daily net expenditure data. A sample path for the cash flow of a certain period is repeatedly generated and determined to be the percentile value that is the lowest at the given confidence level.

Table 4.6 is a summary of the basic statistics on the daily net expenditure of the 31 targeted budget-type funds. In the majority of the funds, the average has a positive value, which means that, on average, the revenues of funds were greater than their business expenditures. While the standard deviation of net expenditures varies from 310 million won (for the Government Fund for Patriotic Martyrs and Independence Fighters) to 101.9 billion won (for the National Housing and Urban Fund), the differences were smaller than the differences in the amounts of surplus money. The columns for 1 and 5 percentiles provide information about the lower limits of the amount of net expenditures that can occur in one day for each fund. The fact that should be highlighted is that the estimated value of the autocorrelation coefficient of net expenditures in most funds has a value near zero. This means that the serial dependence of net expenditures, which are defined as the differences between the revenues and expenditures of funds, is negligible.

Table 4.7 shows the estimation results for the appropriate cash reserve size based on the cash flow data from the 31 budget-type funds. If we calculate the required cash reserve for one week at the 95 percent confidence level, then 939.1 billion won are required when each fund is managed separately. By contrast, in the case where they are integrated, the required cash holding level decreases by approximately 74 percent to 239.8 billion won. As for the one-month case, the integrated management (0.4 trillion won) decreases by 82 percent from individual management (1.9 trillion won), which shows that the longer the duration, the greater the effect of integrated management.

Table 4.6 *Basic statistics on daily net expenditures by fund in Korea (100 million won), 2013–15*

Fund	Mean	SD	1 percentile	5 percentile	Autocorrelation
National Housing and Urban Fund	518.8	1018.6	−2618.8	−130.5	0.06
Electric Power Industry Basis Fund	26.0	229.7	−693.4	−112.6	−0.02
Radioactive Waste Management Fund	12.8	152.4	−126.3	0.0	−0.01
Farmland Management Fund	8.1	143.9	−266.1	−74.6	0.00
Korea Sports Promotion Fund	−0.3	325.4	−425.5	−127.2	0.00
Agricultural and Fishery Disaster Reinsurance Fund	1.3	18.8	−1.9	0.0	0.00
Inter-Korean Cooperation Fund	−1.9	29.1	−102.2	−15.4	0.15
Livestock Development Fund	0.6	129.5	−499.0	−82.8	0.02
Broadcasting and Communications Development Fund	−1.5	119.9	−317.0	−85.4	0.00
Wage Claim Guarantee Fund	4.5	30.8	0.0	0.0	−0.02
Economic Development Cooperation Fund	0.2	129.6	−204.2	−76.5	−0.05
Korea Foundation Fund	−0.2	7.0	−9.5	−5.0	−0.04
Nakdong Rivers Watersheds Management Fund	0.0	35.1	−170.0	−11.8	−0.02
The Korean Culture and Arts Promotion Fund	−1.3	28.0	−66.7	−20.8	0.04
Heritage Protection Fund	0.4	17.3	−35.8	−12.0	−0.03
Fund for the Promotion of Private Schools	0.2	49.4	−182.8	−27.4	−0.01
Asbestos Damage Relief Fund	0.2	3.9	−6.8	−1.1	0.00
Fisheries Development Fund	2.0	54.2	−187.1	−28.7	−0.05
Government Fund for Patriotic Martyrs and Independence Fighters	0.3	3.1	−0.5	−0.1	−0.01
Korea Press Fund	−0.2	4.2	−10.9	−2.9	−0.01
Gender Equality Fund	0.1	5.2	−9.6	−1.7	0.00

Fund for Management of Yeongsan and Sumjin Rivers	0.0	11.7	−54.8	−2.1	−0.12
Atomic Energy Fund	−0.3	68.3	−280.3	0.0	0.00
Emergency Medical Fund	0.1	56.2	−177.3	0.0	−0.02
Agricultural Fund for Performance of Free Trade Agreement	−0.6	104.4	−338.6	−57.4	0.02
Local Press Commission Fund	−0.1	3.6	−7.4	−1.3	0.00
Youth Fostering Fund	−0.1	11.4	−29.1	−7.8	0.00
Fund for Management of Han River	0.4	86.5	−411.2	0.0	−0.02
Direct Payment for Farm Income Support	1.5	40.8	−7.6	0.0	0.00
Fund for Advancement and Commercialization of Technology	1.2	45.6	−102.3	0.0	0.07
Micro Enterprise and Market Promotion Fund	1.8	435.4	−689.1	−281.8	−0.05
Total	571.8	1248.8	−2680.9	−514.9	0.05

Table 4.7   Appropriate cash reserves by fund in Korea (100 million won)

Fund	One week		One month	
	95%	99%	95%	99%
National Housing and Urban Fund	1956	5561	2965	10748
Electric Power Industry Basis Fund	790	1335	1474	2170
Micro Enterprise and Market Promotion Fund	172	342	390	575
Radioactive Waste Management Fund	399	616	838	1178
Farmland Management Fund	635	1130	1544	2161
Korea Sports Promotion Fund	4	74	48	78
Agricultural and Fishery Disaster Reinsurance Fund	142	224	321	704
Inter-Korean Cooperation Fund	595	1035	1315	2289
Livestock Development Fund	384	664	983	1501
Broadcasting and Communications Development Fund	–	–	–	41
Wage Claim Guarantee Fund	326	643	868	1271
Economic Development Cooperation Fund	18	91	64	124
Korea Foundation Fund	179	292	374	546
Nakdong Rivers Watersheds Management Fund	106	209	269	366
The Korean Culture and Arts Promotion Fund	47	81	117	167
Heritage Protection Fund	235	454	513	785
Fund for the Promotion of Private School	8	27	32	55
Asbestos Damage Relief Fund	256	480	505	785
Fisheries Development Fund	1	5	3	16
Government Fund for Patriotic Martyrs and Independence Fighters	14	27	36	48
Korea Press Fund	17	31	35	51
Gender Equality Fund	61	96	119	175
Fund for Management of Yeongsan and Sumjin River	458	553	605	1024
Atomic Energy Fund	287	490	512	785
Emergency Medical Fund	481	1091	1114	1640
Agricultural Fund for Performance of Free Trade Agreement	9	14	20	28
Local Press Commission Fund	39	67	88	121
Youth Fostering Fund	455	758	879	1261
Fund for Management of Han River	24	229	133	408
Direct Payment for Farm Income Support	156	399	399	554
Fund for Advancement and Commercialization of technology	1136	1580	2750	3481
Total of Individual Funds	9391	18602	19313	35135
Consolidated Management	2398	6507	3531	12566

CONCLUSION AND POLICY IMPLICATIONS

This chapter attempts to understand the accountability required in the government funds system to maintain fiscal soundness in public finance, to propose an institutional strategy to help in enhancing the fiscal accountability and to measure the economic effects of that strategy. The most important obligation that should be placed on each fund managing entity is answerability concerning the expenses of the funds. And it is also important to be able to enforce provisions to close a budget-type fund when its performance is low. As a main component of public finance, there is an obligation to improve the efficiency of national finances. The chapter argues that integrated management of surplus money from budget-type funds will contribute to strengthening the fiscal accountability of the government fund system. By unifying the accounting channel of fund revenues and expenditures, accurate information related to the obligation of answerability can be generated, and fund retention evaluations can be carried out more effectively based on such information. In addition, by consolidating surplus money in budget-type funds, a significant efficiency improvement in public finance can be expected through economies of scale in asset management and a reduction in liquidity risk.

At the end of 2015, the surplus money from budget-type funds was estimated to be at least 45 trillion won, and up to a maximum of nearly 200 trillion won. The analysis of asset management performance shows that positive economies of scale do exist and that their effect is particularly strong in short-term investments. In addition, through integrated management, liquidity risk can be significantly reduced. In each scenario, liquidity risk can decrease by 70–80 percent when integrated management is used rather than individual management. Thus, when using integrated management, much smaller cash reserves are required, and therefore improvement in efficiency can be expected.

For integrated management of surplus money from budget-type funds, more thorough analysis on the assets and expenditures for each fund should be conducted, and related regulations and laws need to be reviewed. There is a need to establish a system that can monitor, in real time, the incomes and expenditures of government funds. At the same time, an institutional strategy is needed, to ensure that individual funds do not encounter any obstacles in carrying out their operations, even without discretion in using their surplus money.

NOTE

1. At the end of 2015, the number of budget-type funds was 45. In 2016 the new Judicial Service Promotion Fund, which is a budget-type fund, was established.

REFERENCES

Ministry of Strategy and Finance (2014), *Fund Status 2014*, Seoul: Ministry of Strategy and Finance (in Korean).
Ministry of Strategy and Finance (2016), *Fund Status 2016*, Seoul: Ministry of Strategy and Finance (in Korean).
National Assembly Budget Office (2016), *Public Finance of Korea 2016*, Seoul: National Assembly Budget Office (in Korean).

5. The long-term impact of aging on the federal budget

Louise Sheiner*

The United States (US) is in the midst of a demographic transition. In 2007 the share of the population that was aged 65 or older was only 12.5 percent. In 2017 it was 15 percent, and in 2037 it is projected to reach 21 percent. These demographic changes have aroused considerable concern about our fiscal future, as much of the budget of the federal government is allocated to old-age entitlement programs. In particular, Social Security, which provides public pensions, and Medicare, which provides health insurance to the aged, will rise as a share of gross domestic product (GDP) as the baby boom generation moves further into retirement.

Although we often talk about aging as arising from the retirement of the baby boomers, that is somewhat misleading. The retirement of the baby boomers represents the beginning of a permanent transition to an older population, reflecting the fall in the fertility rate that occurred after the baby boom, and continued increases in life expectancy. Because aging is not a temporary phenomenon, we cannot simply smooth through it by borrowing. Instead, it is clear that population aging will eventually require significant adjustments in fiscal policy: either cuts in spending or increases in taxes; or, most likely, some combination of the two.

Demographic change is relatively easy to forecast, and economists have been studying and debating the budgetary pressures associated with aging for a long time now. But, in addition to the expected consequences of demographic change, it is possible that some other changes that we have been experiencing in the economy may also be linked to aging: in particular, low interest rates and lower productivity growth. These too have important consequences for our long-term fiscal outlook.

In the following section, I discuss the effects that aging has on federal spending on entitlement programs and the implications for the overall debt burden. In the third section, I review the evidence on the effects of aging on interest rates and productivity, and show how these factors affect the long-term budget picture. In the fourth section, I discuss some potential policy responses to aging. In particular, I examine the role that increasing labor force participation may play, and discuss the issues that policymakers need to consider when choosing the composition and timing of changes in spending and revenue. The final section draws conclusions.

DIRECT EFFECTS OF AGING ON THE FEDERAL BUDGET

Table 5.1 presents Congressional Budget Office (CBO) projections of revenues and spending that show how spending and taxes will evolve assuming that current laws remain unchanged, with a few exceptions that I will discuss later.[1] As the table shows, federal spending is projected to increase from just under 21 percent of GDP in 2017, to almost 30 percent of GDP in three decades; tax revenues are projected to creep up slowly over time. The resulting continued imbalances between spending and revenues give rise to an unsustainable fiscal future, as seen in the rising projected debt.

Table 5.1　　*US federal government revenues and spending 1987–2007 with Congressional Budget Office projections for 2017–47 (% of GDP)*

	1987	1997	2007	2017	2027	2037	2047
CBO baseline							
Revenues	17.9	18.6	17.9	17.8	18.4	19.0	19.6
Spending	21.0	18.9	19.1	20.7	23.4	26.3	29.4
Discretionary spending	9.3	6.5	7.3	6.3	5.3	5.3	5.3
Social security and health	6.4	7.6	8.0	10.4	12.9	14.6	15.6
Other spending	5.3	4.8	3.8	4.0	5.2	6.4	8.5
Deficit	3.1	0.3	1.1	2.9	5.0	7.3	9.8
Federal debt	40	44	35	77	81	81	87
Scenario 1: No aging							
Deficit	–	–	–	2.9	3.1	3.3	4.1
Debt-to-GDP	–	–	–	79	81	83	87
Scenario 2: No aging or excess cost growth							
Deficit	–	–	–	2.6	2.3	1.5	0.8
Debt-to-GDP	–	–	–	78	77	67	55
Scenario 3: Revenues and non-entitlement spending constant share of GDP							
Deficit	–	–	–	4.6	7.0	10.8	15.3
Debt-to-GDP	–	–	–	85	99	144	210

Source:　Data from Congressional Budget Office (2017b).

Table 5.2   US debt-to-GDP ratio under different interest rate assumptions, 2017–47 (%)

Interest rate assumption	2017	2027	2037	2047
Baseline	77	89	113	150
Remain low	77	87	101	121
Rise immediately to historical level	77	103	136	179

Source: Data from Congressional Budget Office (2017b).

Federal debt, already historically high in 2017 at 77 percent of GDP, is projected to increase rapidly over time, reaching 150 percent of GDP by 2047 (Table 5.2).

These rapid increases in deficits and debt are driven by two primary factors: aging and healthcare costs that grow much faster than the economy. In addition, years of primary deficits (deficits not including interest on the debt) lead to rapid increases in interest on the debt as well, providing a third reason for escalating debt levels.

Understanding Aging

Population aging is the product of two important forces: a decline in fertility and an increase in life expectancy. From 1926 to 1965, fertility averaged 2.75 children per woman; since 1965, fertility has hovered around 2 children per woman. This large change, which at first increased the ratio of working-age adults to children, is now translating into a decrease in the ratio of working-age adults to the elderly.

There also have been substantial gains in longevity. In the 1960s, average US life expectancy was 67 years for males and 73 years for females. In 2015, the averages were 76 and 81, respectively. Although longer life generally improves well-being, it also increases the number of Americans who are aged 65 and older, and extends the time period during which certain program benefits must be paid. Of these two factors – lower fertility and increased life expectancy – lower fertility is by far more important, accounting for about two-thirds of the expected increase in the ratio of elderly to working-age Americans over the next three decades.[2]

Aging imposes significant challenges on our old-age entitlement system: Social Security, which provides cash pensions, and Medicare, which provides health insurance. Because spending programs depend on the number of dependents and on real wages, and tax revenues depend on the number of workers and real wages, the ratio of dependents to workers is a key parameter in determining the sustainability of a pay-as-you-go entitlement system.

Social Security is an entitlement program that provides annual payments to beneficiaries aged 62 years or older. Initial benefits per beneficiary are tied to average wage growth in the economy, so Social Security would remain constant as a share of GDP if there were no demographic changes, policy changes, or other major structural changes in the economy. Instead, over the next 30 years, the CBO projects that Social Security outlays will increase by almost 30 percent, from 4.9 percent of GDP in 2017 to 6.3 percent in 2047.[3] Virtually all of this rise is driven by population aging.[4]

Medicare is a public health insurance program that provides health insurance primarily to Americans aged 65 and older, although some non-elderly disabled individuals are eligible as well. Medicare expenditure growth is driven by two forces: population aging, which increases the share of Medicare beneficiaries in the population, and growth in health spending per beneficiary. These two factors reinforce each other: aging without per-beneficiary spending growth would be easier to finance, as would per-beneficiary spending growth without aging. Together, these two factors are projected to lead to a doubling of Medicare spending as a share of GDP over the next 30 years, from 3.1 percent of GDP to 6.1 percent of GDP.

How much would Medicare spending increase without aging? Assuming that age-adjusted health spending per beneficiary continues to increase at its expected pace,[5] Medicare spending would still increase by a substantial 40 percent or so, far lower than the doubling of spending projected by the CBO.

Taken together, population aging is projected to increase entitlement spending over the next 30 years by 4.3 percent of GDP. Scenario 1 of Table 5.1 also shows what the fiscal outlook would be without aging. Even without aging, the United States would still face significant deficits (the difference between spending and revenues), but they would increase slowly over time – from about 3 percent of GDP today to 4 percent in 30 years – rather than widening substantially as in the baseline. Furthermore, assuming that interest rates and productivity growth are invariant to demographic change (a point to which I return later), these deficits are close to being sustainable, in the sense that debt does not explode.

How can that be, given the significant increase in health costs that increase spending on Medicare, as well as other non-age-related health programs? To see what is happening, look to Figure 5.1 (and Scenario 2 of Table 5.1: "no aging or excess cost growth"), which shows the projected debt-to-GDP ratios under the assumption that: (1) there is no aging; and (2) health spending per person grows in line with GDP per person. In this

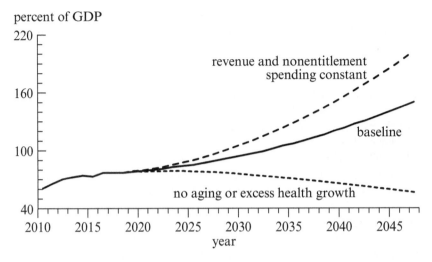

percent of GDP

Source: Data from Congressional Budget Office (2017b).

Figure 5.1 US debt-to-GDP ratios under various assumptions, 2010–47

scenario, shown as the lower dashed line, the debt-to-GDP ratio actually declines, reaching just above 50 percent by 2047.

Do CBO projections understate the fiscal challenges faced by the US?
As noted above, the CBO's projections are intended to represent spending and revenues under the assumption that Congress does not change laws. They are not meant to forecast what Congress will actually do or what will actually happen, but are instead an exercise that provides a baseline to Congress that shows the magnitude of the policy changes that will be necessary. But there are two difficulties with this approach: projecting discretionary spending and projecting revenues.

Projecting discretionary spending
First, it is hard to know what a current law approach means when it comes to discretionary spending, that is, annually appropriated spending that funds many of the basic functions of government, including national defense, transportation, education and tax collection. Unlike entitlement spending such as Social Security and Medicare, discretionary spending is not dictated by benefit and eligibility formulas. Instead, Congress decides annually how much to appropriate. In recent years, such appropriations have often been governed by legislation that set limits on total discretionary spending. For example, the Budget Control Act of 2011 set caps on

discretionary spending through 2021. But, for 2022 and forward, CBO projections do not reflect current law (because they cannot) and instead, reflect budget conventions that assume that discretionary spending rises with inflation from 2022 to 2027, and with GDP thereafter.[6] The net result of the recent declines in discretionary spending and the tight caps over the next few years is that discretionary spending in the CBO projection is expected to decline by 1 percent of GDP over the next ten years, reaching a level lower than seen over the past 50 years. It is projected to remain at that level throughout the remainder of the projection period (see Table 5.1, CBO baseline). If, instead, discretionary spending were to return to something closer to a historical average, spending and projected deficits would be higher in each year of the long-term forecast.

Projecting revenues
The second area where the CBO projections might be understating the budgetary challenges is revenues. The US income tax system is indexed for inflation, but not for real GDP growth. Because the tax system is progressive, as average incomes rise over time, more and more taxpayers are pushed into higher tax brackets, a phenomenon known as "real bracket creep." This means that, without changes in law, tax revenues automatically rise over time. In practice, tax laws are changed frequently – often in response to the perception that taxes are "too high" – and there has been no upward trend in revenues as a share of the economy over time (see Table 5.1, CBO baseline).

Thus, the assumptions about future taxes and discretionary spending in the CBO's long-run projection may not reflect the most likely or plausible path. Indeed, there is continuing pressure in Congress to raise spending – particularly defense spending – above the levels dictated by the legislated caps. The administration and Congress are also putting together a tax reform plan that will likely include some significant cuts in tax rates. If legislation is enacted in a way that is not deficit-neutral, then the long-run projections could show much larger deficits and debt.

For example, imagine that, instead of falling over the next ten years as a share of GDP, discretionary spending were to remain at today's level; a level still low by historical standards. And imagine that, instead of allowing real bracket creep to push revenues up over time, revenues instead remained constant as a share of GDP at 2017 levels. The upper dashed line in Figure 5.1 (and Scenario 3 of Table 5.1: "revenues and non-entitlement spending constant share of GDP") shows what the trajectory of the debt would look like in this scenario. Without the fiscal benefits of lower discretionary spending and higher revenues, the fiscal picture looks much more daunting, rising to 210 percent of GDP in 2047. If an actual tax cut were assumed, the picture would look even worse.

Of course, it is possible that Congress will allow spending to drift down and revenues to drift up, given the long-run fiscal picture. In that case, the important lesson from these projections is that they already assume increases in taxes on future taxpayers – revenues in 2047 are about 10 percent higher than in 2017 – and already assume that future taxpayers are living with much lower discretionary spending than the historical norms.

INDIRECT MACROECONOMIC EFFECTS

Aging and interest rates

The very low real rates of interest that have been observed here and abroad since the Great Recession after 2007 have led researchers to think more carefully about the determinants of interest rates. Figure 5.2 shows the government's borrowing costs over time, adjusted for inflation. As noted by Carvalho et al. (2016), the fact that these low interest rates have been trending down for more than two decades suggests that forces other than accommodative monetary policy must be at play.

Several studies have argued that demographic trends, specifically aging, may have played a significant role in the decline in interest rates (Elmendorf and Sheiner 2017; Gagnon et al. 2016; Ikeda and Saito 2012; Carvalho et al. 2016). The reasoning is as follows. As the growth rate of

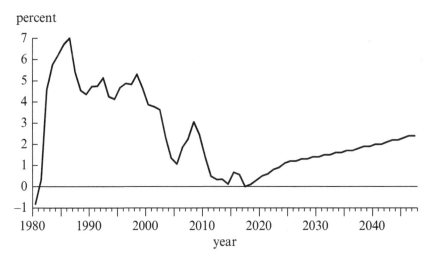

Source: Data from Congressional Budget Office (2017b).

Figure 5.2   Real interest rates on federal debt, 1980–2047

the labor force slows, capital per worker increases, leading to a reduction in the marginal product of capital and the real interest rate. If, at the same time, workers are also trying to increase their saving to accommodate their longer life expectancy and increased years of retirement, this can put further downward pressure on interest rates.

Fujita and Fujiwara (2016) estimate that demographic change in Japan can account for about 40 percent of the 2.3 percentage point decline in real rates between 1996 and 2013. Looking at a sample of Organisation for Economic Co-operation and Development (OECD) countries, Carvalho et al. (2016) find that changing demographics led to a reduction of the equilibrium interest rate by at least 1.5 percentage points during 1990–2014, about one-third to one-half of the overall decline in the real interest rate. Gagnon et al. (2016) conclude that demographic shifts alone can account for a 1.25 percentage point decline in the US equilibrium real interest rate since 1980, which by their estimates is nearly all of the permanent decline in real interest rates over that time period. Their model also suggests that interest rates are likely to remain low over the foreseeable future.

The impact of low interest rates on the fiscal outlook
The federal government is a net borrower. With federal debt already equal to more than 75 percent of GDP, reductions in borrowing costs have sizable effects on interest payments and deficits. In their projections of the federal government's borrowing costs, shown in Figure 5.2, the CBO assumes that interest rates remain low for a few years, but then gradually rise to their historical average. If Gagnon et al. are correct, then interest rates are likely to remain low over the foreseeable future, rather than increase. On the other hand, if these low interest rates are really the result of the Great Recession and other temporary factors, interest rates might increase much more rapidly than expected by the CBO and other forecasters.

Table 5.2 shows the impact on the debt-to-GDP ratio of these different assumptions. If interest rates remain low (I assume that the real interest rate is a constant 0.5 percent for this simulation), then the debt-to-GDP ratio rises much more gradually, but still hits 121 percent of GDP by 2047. If, on the other hand, interest rates rise immediately to their historical average (2.5 percent), then the fiscal situation is more challenging, with the debt-to-GDP ratio rising to 179 percent in 30 years.

Effect of aging on productivity and productivity growth
Productivity growth has also been slow both in the United States and abroad since the financial crisis of 2007. But, as Fernald (2014) notes, the slowdown appears to have begun a few years before the financial crisis, and

productivity remains low even now, suggesting that something structural, rather than cyclical, is at work.

One hypothesis is that population aging is behind the slowdown in productivity growth. There are a number of channels through which aging may affect productivity growth. First, the average age of the labor force could have an effect on productivity. On the one hand, older workers are more experienced and so might be more productive. On the other hand, older workers may not have the skills to keep up with new technologies and so might be less productive. Furthermore, declining physical health and cognitive abilities associated with aging may result in lower productivity. If the mechanisms through which aging affects productivity growth is through changes in the average age of the labor force (that is, if the average age of the workforce affects the level of worker productivity), then the effect should be tailing off, because, as shown in Figure 5.3, most of the aging of the labor force is behind us.[7] For example, the median age of the workforce started declining as the large baby boom cohort began entering the labor force in around 1960, and bottomed out at around 35 in the early 1980s. It has been rising sharply since then, reaching 42.2 in 2016. Although the average age of the workforce is expected to continue increasing, that increase is expected to be quite slow, with the average increasing from 42.4 in 2017 to 43.4 in 2047.

But the age of the workforce might also have an effect on the growth rate

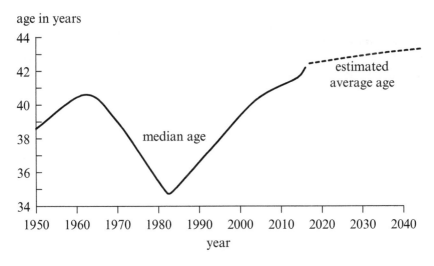

Source: Data from Congressional Budget Office (2017b).

Figure 5.3   Median and average ages of US workforce, 1950–2047

of productivity. Research suggests that the prime age for producing scientific inventions, patents, publications and other creative material peaks between 30 and 40, and declines through later years (National Academy 2015). As a smaller share of the labor force is in these peak creative years, the rate of technological progress may slow.

Another channel through which aging might permanently affect the rate of productivity growth is through the effect of a reduction in labor force growth on investment. The rate of labor force growth has slowed sharply over the past three decades, a product of both the reduction in fertility and the plateauing of women's labor force participation (discussed below). Looking forward, the rate of labor force growth is expected to remain low. As described in Elmendorf and Sheiner (2017), one possible response to this slowdown is an increase in the capital–labor ratio, as firms substitute machines for increasingly scarce labor.[8] This increase in the capital–labor ratio will raise the level of labor productivity.

But the slowdown in labor force growth means that investment growth will also slow (even if it does not initially slow as much as labor while firms increase the capital intensity of their operations). As noted by Cutler et al. (1990), this slowdown in investment could restrain growth in total factor productivity (TFP): the productivity growth that comes from technological change rather than from changes in the capital intensity of work. Because innovation may consist largely of fixed costs – the fixed costs of research and development (R&D), for example – slowing investment means that fixed costs are spread over a smaller pool of capital, making it less profitable. Thus, the rate of technological progress might slow when labor force growth slows.

Thus, the theoretical implications of aging on productivity growth are ambiguous. Empirical research also reaches conflicting conclusions. Using panel data on OECD and low-income countries, Feyrer (2002, 2008) concludes that productivity growth decreases when the proportion of workers who are over 49 years old rises. However, a report by the National Research Council (2012) notes that Feyrer's effects are sensitive to specification, so his results should be taken with caution. Upon re-estimating Freyer's model, the National Research Council concludes that there will be a negligible effect of an aging labor force on aggregate US productivity growth over the next two decades: between–0.1 and +0.1 percentage points each year.

More recent papers (Liu and Westelius 2016; Aiyar et al. 2016) find that aging in Europe and Japan reduced annual TFP growth. In Japan, Liu and Westelius estimate that the aging workforce reduced Japan's annual TFP growth by as much as 0.7–0.9 percentage points between 1990 and 2005. Aiyar et al. find that, for 28 countries in Europe, the growing number of workers aged 55 and older decreased annual TFP growth by an average of 0.1 percentage point over the past two decades. Similarly, Maestas et al. (2016) find that a 10 percent increase in the fraction of the population older than 60 years leads to a 3.7 percent decrease in productivity growth. However, Cutler et al. (1990), find that a 1 percentage point decrease in the annual labor force growth rate actually raises productivity growth by 0.62 percentage point a year.

More recently, Acemoglu and Restrepo (2017) find no evidence of a negative relationship between population aging and slower GDP per capita growth across countries. On the contrary, the relationship is positive and significant, whether aging is measured by the change in the average age of the adult population or by the change in the ratio of old to young workers. They argue that countries with aging populations might be more likely to adopt automation technologies and thereby increase worker productivity.

Effect of productivity on the federal budget

While the link between demographic change and productivity growth is much more uncertain than that between demographic change and interest rates – in both direction and magnitude – it is worth at least exploring what the implications of such a link might be for our fiscal future.

Productivity growth can affect the federal budget through many different channels (see Sheiner 2018). First, slower productivity growth will lower revenues as a share of GDP, because there will be less "real bracket creep," a concept explained above. Second, slower productivity growth – if distributed broadly – will lead to increases in poverty, which will boost spending for federal anti-poverty programs such as Medicaid and food stamps. Third, slower productivity growth will raise the GDP share of spending programs that are not fully indexed to wages, including Social Security (in which only initial benefits are indexed to wages, and subsequent benefits are indexed to inflation) and food stamps (which are indexed to the price of food). Finally, slower productivity growth may also lead to lower interest rates, which would partially offset the negative effects of slower productivity growth on the fiscal outlook. (See Hamilton et al. 2015 for a discussion of the effects of productivity growth on interest rates.)

In a 2016 report, the CBO calculated the effects of slower productivity growth on the federal debt. It found that a permanent 0.5 percentage-point decrease in productivity growth would raise the ratio of debt to GDP in 30 years from 141 percent (its baseline in 2016) to 173 percent.

POLICY RESPONSES TO AGING

The fundamental challenge of population aging is that it increases the ratio of non-workers to workers. Thus, one potential pathway to address aging is to increase the size of the labor force. This can be accomplished through increased immigration or increased labor force participation.

Increasing immigration

About three-fourths of immigrants are adults between the ages of 20 and 54 (Migration Policy Institute 2017). Thus, increasing immigration can lower the age of the workforce and increase the ratio of workers to retirees. The CBO assumes the rate of immigration (the number of immigrants in a year as a share of the US population) will average 0.32 percent over the next 30 years; the Social Security Administration assumes a slightly higher number, about 0.37.[9] Although the CBO does not provide information about the sensitivity of its long-run outlook to immigration assumptions, it has produced cost estimates of legislation that would increase immigration. In particular, the CBO (2013) found that the Border Security, Economic Opportunity, and Immigration Modernization Act (S. 744) would increase the labor force by about 5 percent by 2033, and lower the deficit from 2023–24 by 0.2 percent of GDP (with a smaller impact in the first ten years). The Social Security Administration (Board of Trustees 2017) does provide sensitivity analyses about the effects of immigration.[10] They show that a 25 percent increase in immigration rates from their baseline would lower the 75-year imbalance (the difference between average Social Security outlays and average Social Security income over 75 years) by about 10 percent, from 2.8 percent of payroll in its baseline to 2.6 percent in its high-immigration alternative. Thus, both the CBO and the Social Security trustees find increased immigration to have beneficial, but small, effects on the budget outlook.

Increasing labor force participation

Another way to increase the number of workers is to increase labor force participation; by those either over or under 65. Increased labor force participation will likely lead to some small increases in Social Security benefits, because benefits are tied to earnings histories, but would have no effect on Medicare benefits, which do not rise with earnings.[11] Increased labor force participation is also a useful response to aging from a household perspective. Increasing work effort – by working more during the normal working years, or by delaying retirement – can help to adjust to longer life expectancy, to lower returns on saving arising from population aging, and to any benefit cuts enacted in response to the fiscal challenges of aging.

Table 5.3 Labor force adjustments to undo aging, 2017 versus 2047

Item	Workers (millions)	Beneficiaries ages ≥62 (millions)	Ratio of workers to beneficiaries	Share of ages ≥62 in labor force (%)	Overall participation rate (%)
Baseline					
2017	171	46	3.7	25	63
2047	188	73	2.6	25	59
Changes in 2047 to get ratio to 2017 level					
Increased labor force participation, unchanged benefits	270	73	3.7	25	85
Delayed retirement with benefit cuts	205	56	3.7	43	65
Effects of 3 "plausible" scenarios					
Assume benefits do not change					
Delay retirement	193	73	2.6	29	61
Increase women's LFP	202	73	2.8	30	64
Do both	209	73	2.9	35	66
Assume increased work effort is offset by lower benefits					
Delay retirement	193	69	2.8	29	61
Increase women's LFP	202	68	3.0	30	64
Do both	209	63	3.3	35	66

Source: Data from Congressional Budget Office (2017b).

Table 5.3 presents some simple calculations of the magnitude of the changes in labor force participation required in order to completely offset population aging. Of course, in reality, assessing the effects of policies that change labor force participation on the budget is much more complicated than what is shown here. Such an analysis would require knowing the wages of those whose participation changes, the effects of their increased participation on Medicare and Social Security outlays, and any offsetting effects from changes in the take-up of other programs, such as Medicaid and health subsidies in the Affordable Care Act. Nevertheless, this simple exercise helps to gauge orders of magnitude.

The table uses the CBO's projections of population and labor force participation (CBO 2017a, 2017b). The first row of the table shows the data for 2017; with 171 million workers and roughly 46 million retirees (which I define as those 62 or older who are not in the labor force), the worker-to-retiree ratio is 3.7. By 2047, the CBO projects that the worker-to-retiree ratio will decline to just 2.6.

Two different types of adjustments can raise that ratio back to 3.7. The first increases the size of the labor force – the numerator in the worker-to-retiree ratio – through either delayed retirement or increased labor force participation of younger Americans, but makes no adjustment to benefits. So, people get the same Social Security and Medicare benefits despite working longer. This leaves the denominator in the worker-to-retiree ratio unchanged. This assumption is largely in keeping with current law.[12] The second type of adjustment assumes that people delay retirement but lose the benefits they would have received. This means they no longer count as beneficiaries, putting them in the numerator and taking them out of the denominator in the worker–retiree ratio calculation. Such a change should be viewed as a benefit cut and would require legislation.

The bottom two sections of Table 5.3 show the implications of these adjustments. When benefits are unchanged, overall labor force participation (defined as the share of the population 16 and over who are in the labor force) would have to increase dramatically – from 59 percent to 85 percent – in order to fully offset the effects of aging. In the second scenario, when all of the increase in labor force comes from delayed retirement and that delayed retirement also reduces benefits, overall labor force participation increases much less, but the participation of Americans 62 or older increases much more, from 25 percent to 43 percent. At the same time, the number of beneficiaries falls about 25 percent, from 73 million to 56 million.

These are very large changes, and most likely impossible to achieve. Figure 5.4 (and Table 5.4, upper panel) shows the CBO's projections of labor force participation rates by age and sex. They anticipate only minor changes in participation over time, with some small reductions among prime-age men, a continuation of a trend that has been ongoing for some time (Executive Office of the President 2014). They also anticipate some continued increases in participation at older ages, particularly for women. The labor force participation of women, which plateaued in the late 1990s (Lee 2014), is expected to remain well below that of men.

To get a sense of what types of increases might be achievable, I consider three scenarios. (For a similar analysis for Japan, see Clark et al. 2010.) First, I consider what would happen if years of work increased with life expectancy. As shown in Table 5.5, the CBO projections assume that life expectancy at 62 increases by 2.4 years for men and 2.2 years for women between now and 2047, but expected years of work increase only 0.4 years for men and 2 years for women.[13] Imagine instead that, in response to this increased longevity and presumably better health, people delay retirement

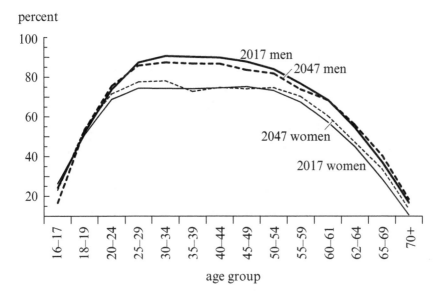

Source: Data from Congressional Budget Office (2017b).

Figure 5.4   US labor force participation by age group and sex, 2017 and 2047

by adopting the labor force participation of those two years younger (so that a 70-year-old has the same participation as what CBO projects a 68-year-old will have).[14] Under this assumption, as shown in column 3 of Table 5.5, the expected time in the workforce at age 16 increases by 1.6 years for men and 3.1 years for women between 2017 and 2047; expected time in the labor force at 62 (assuming survival until age 62) increases by 1.8 years and 2 years for men and women, respectively.[15]

As a second scenario, suppose that women's labor force participation climbed over the same 30-year period to equal that of men. As shown in column 4 of Table 5.5, this would boost the change in women's expected years of work by 6.6 years at age 16 and by 2.5 years at age 62. Finally, as a third scenario, assume both of these changes occur simultaneously. The lower panel of Table 5.4 shows what participation rates would be under scenarios 2 and 3.

The results are shown in the bottom panel of Table 5.3. Consider, at first, the effects of the increases in the labor force, while keeping benefits the same. Under this assumption, these increases in labor force participation only undo a small part of the decrease in the ratio of workers to beneficiaries. If workers act as if they are two years younger, the labor

Table 5.4 Labor force participation rates by age, 2017 versus 2047 (%)

Item	Age range in years													
	16–17	18–19	20–24	25–29	30–34	35–39	40–44	45–49	50–54	55–59	60–61	62–64	65–69	70+
CBO projections														
Men (2017)	24	52	74	87	91	90	90	88	84	77	69	55	37	17
Men (2047)	17	53	76	86	87	87	87	84	82	74	68	56	41	18
Women (2017)	26	51	69	74	74	74	75	75	73	68	57	45	29	11
Women (2047)	23	54	72	78	78	73	75	74	75	70	60	47	34	14
Scenarios														
Baseline comparison	20	53	74	82	83	80	81	79	78	72	57	37	16	–
Women's rate = men's rate	17	53	76	86	87	87	87	84	82	75	65	44	20	–
Women's rate = men's rate and 2 year retirement delay	17	53	76	86	87	87	87	86	83	79	71	54	22	–

Sources: Fullerton and Tschetter (1983), Toossi (2015), Congressional Budget Office (2017b) data and author's calculations.

Table 5.5   Changes in life expectancy and years of work, 2017–47

Age and sex	CBO baseline		Alternate LFP scenarios		
	Life expectancy (1)	Years of work (2)	Shift LFP schedule 2 years for 45+ (3)	Women LFP increases to men's (4)	Shift younger and change women's LFP (5)
At age 16					
Men	3.6	0.4	1.6	0.4	1.6
Women	3.0	2.0	3.1	6.6	7.9
At age 62					
Men	2.4	0.9	1.8	0.9	1.8
Women	2.2	1.1	2.0	2.5	3.5

Sources: Congressional Budget Office (2017b) projections and author's calculations.

force increases by 5 million workers; not enough to significantly change the ratio of workers to beneficiaries. Increasing the labor force participation of women so that it is equal to that of males has a bigger effect, increasing the ratio to 3.0. Doing both of these helps a little bit more.

On the other hand, if the generosity of the system is assumed to decrease alongside the labor force changes, the effects are more significant. Even so, cutting benefits, increasing the labor force participation of women, and delaying retirement for all only brings the ratio up to 3.3, still well below the 3.7 ratio in 2017. Of course, to the extent that benefits will be trimmed in the future, increasing labor force participation is a helpful way to mitigate the effects on living standards.

Cut spending or raise taxes
Increased labor force participation clearly has a role to play in addressing the challenges of aging, but on its own solves only a small part of the problem. It is clear that government spending eventually will have to decline, or taxes will have to increase. There are two policy questions that need to be answered: first, when should these changes take place? and second, what should the composition of the tax increases and spending cuts be: which programs, which taxes?

Timing of policy changes
With about two-thirds of the demographic transition still ahead of us, it is still possible to smooth consumption over time by enacting tax increases and spending cuts now that allow for smaller changes in the future. The

Table 5.6   Take action to stabilize debt-to-GDP ratio, 2017–67

Action	2017	2027	2037	2047	2057	2067
Take action to stabilize debt-to-GDP ratio						
Panel A: debt-to-GDP ratio						
Adjust now	77	53	41	39	39	39
Adjust in 20 years	77	89	109	105	105	105
Panel B: required deficit reduction (as a share of GDP)						
Adjust now	3.8	3.8	3.8	4.0	4.0	4.0
Adjust in 20 years	0.0	0.0	4.1	4.1	4.1	4.1
Assume debt-to-GDP ratio must be 77% in 2047, then stabilize debt-to-GDP ratio						
Panel C: debt-to-GDP ratio						
Act now	77	68	67	77	77	77
Act in 20 years	77	89	113	77	77	77
Panel D: required deficit reduction (as a share of GDP						
Act now	2.5	2.5	2.5	4.0	4.0	4.0
Act in 20 years	0.0	0.0	7.6	4.0	4.0	4.0

Note: All projections assume revenues and noninterest spending are a constant share of GDP after 2047.

Source: Data from Congressional Budget Office (2017b).

question is whether we should. As noted by Elmendorf and Sheiner (2017), the optimal response to aging is probably not to complete the smoothing of consumption, because the rates of return on that saving are not likely to be large enough to be worth it. Indeed, with government borrowing costs extremely low by historical standards, the benefits of higher saving now appear quite small.[16]

Panels A and B of Table 5.6 show two scenarios that are based on an extended CBO baseline where I assume that, after 2047, taxes and non-interest spending are constant as a share of GDP. In one scenario, I assume that policymakers take action today to stabilize the debt in perpetuity. In the second, I assume that policymakers allow the debt to increase for 20 years as in the CBO baseline, and then take action to stabilize the debt. Panel A shows what happens to the debt in each case. If policymakers take action today, the debt eventually stabilizes at about 40 percent of GDP; if they wait 20 years, the debt-to-GDP ratio is much higher, ending up at 105 percent of GDP.

Panel B shows the changes in the deficit required under each scenario. What is striking about the numbers is how little long-run benefit is derived from taking action today and reducing the debt-to-GDP ratio. If action is taken today, the deficit needs to be reduced by 3.8 percent of GDP. If no action is taken for 20 years – that is, there are no cutbacks in spending or increases in taxes for 20 years – then, when action is eventually taken, the change in the deficit needs to be 4.1 percent of GDP, or just 0.3 percentage points more than if we take action today. This very small benefit is a direct result of the very low interest rates that are expected to prevail over the next few decades. With borrowing rates projected to be just 0.5 percentage point above GDP growth by 2047, debt is not very costly and reducing it is not very beneficial.

Analysts often do a different calculation that shows a much larger benefit to acting sooner, shown in Panels C and D of Table 5.6. They compare the reductions in the deficit (through tax increases or spending cuts) that would be necessary at different points in time if the goal is to ensure a particular debt-to-GDP ratio at the end of the period. For example, if the goal is for the debt-to-GDP ratio in 2047 to be 77 percent, the same as in 2017, the deficit would have to decrease by 2.5 percent of GDP starting in 2017, and 7.6 percent starting 20 years later. But these changes are not intended to stabilize the debt-to-GDP ratio; they just make sure they hit 77 percent in 2047. To stabilize debt at 77 percent of GDP from 2047 on, the deficit cut relative to the current baseline would have to be 4 percent of GDP. So, in the "act now" case, additional deficit decreasing measures would have to be taken in 2047, whereas in the "act in 20 years" case there could be large spending increases or tax cuts. These comparisons tend to overstate the benefits of acting sooner rather than later because they compare temporary changes, not permanent ones.

Of course, interest rates are extremely hard to predict, and the larger the debt-to-GDP ratio, the more vulnerable the budget is to unexpected interest rate increases. Thus, prudence requires us to aim for a lower debt-to-GDP ratio than we otherwise would. Furthermore, changes to entitlements are often best made years in advance in order to give people time to adjust their spending and work decisions. Thus, it makes sense to start making small adjustments to spending and taxes, and to start thinking about what kinds of changes we will want to make in the future.

Composition of spending cuts and tax increases

Of course, decisions about which programs to keep and what taxes to raise will depend on preferences, which belong in the sphere of politics, not economics. But economics does have a valuable contribution to make. I highlight two important issues: the difference between spending on investment and spending on consumption, and the implications of the growing disparities in life expectancy by income.

Investment versus consumption

Cutting valuable investments to lower the debt makes little sense from an economic perspective. So long as the risk-adjusted social return on the investments exceeds the government's borrowing costs, future well-being improves when the government borrows to invest. Investments need not "pay for themselves" in the narrow sense that the return is so large that just the tax revenues arising from the investment are sufficient to pay off the cost of borrowing: this is too high a bar, that would preclude the government from making many extremely valuable investments. Instead, the social rate of return needs to be adjusted (downward) for any deadweight loss that arises out of any increases in taxes that might be necessary to pay off the debt.[17]

Deciding what is investment and what is consumption is not straightforward. Unlike state and local governments, the federal government does not have a separate capital account. And, even if it did, it would likely not adequately capture spending that, from an economic perspective, represents investment or has investment-like features. Of course, spending on infrastructure and equipment should be counted as investment, but so too should some social spending; particularly transfers to low-income children, which have been shown to have impacts that last well beyond the childhood years. Butcher (2017) provides a nice summary of the research on the long-run effects of government spending, which suggest that cash transfers through the Earned Income Tax Credit or other programs, and in-kind transfers such as food stamps, housing assistance and health insurance, have significant effects on adult outcomes such as educational attainment, earnings and health. Thus, spending on education, infrastructure and transfers to low-income families should be viewed as essential to future well-being and should be protected.

Increasing disparities in life expectancy

While life expectancy has increased over time in the United States, recent research shows that the gains have occurred mostly in the top half of the income distribution. For example, according to a recent report from the National Academy of Sciences (2015), for the cohort born in 1930, life expectancy at age 50 was 76.6 years for men in the bottom quintile of lifetime earnings, and 81.7 for men in the top quintile, a gap of 5.1 years. For the cohort born in 1960, if recent trends continue, they estimate those life expectancies will be 76.1 and 88.8, a gap of 12.7 years.

The policy implications of such rising disparities are profound. Medicare and Social Security are annuities, which means that people get them for as long as they live; as the rich live longer and longer, they get more and more of the benefits of entitlement programs. The National Academy report calculates, for example, that increased life expectancy for those born in 1960 relative to those born in 1930 will boost the present value of lifetime benefits from Social Security and Medicare by almost 50 percent for those in the top income quintile, whereas those in the bottom income quintile receive no benefit at all. In addition, differential life expectancy is likely associated with differential health, meaning that lower-income workers are likely less able to delay retirement. Changes to entitlement programs need to take account of this rising disparity if they are to maintain fairness. Policies that cut benefits more for high earners, or base retirement ages on years of contribution, should be preferred over policies that cut benefits across the board. Perhaps more importantly, addressing the reasons for this rising disparity, which are still unclear, needs to be a priority for the federal government.

CONCLUSION

Population aging will put significant pressure on the federal budget in the coming years, and policy changes are inevitable. With a permanently older population, and with health spending continuing to rise faster than GDP, it seems likely that overall government spending will have to be higher. Remembering that some government spending is actually investment, and taking into consideration the widening disparities in life expectancy, tipping the balance a bit more toward higher taxes rather than cuts to spending is preferred. But, given the size of the challenge, some combination of spending cuts and tax increases will likely be required.

It is difficult to find policies to lighten the future burden. Increases in labor force participation can help, but without concomitant cuts in benefits they are not likely to make a large dent. Similarly, policies to lower the debt now have only small effects on the changes required in the future, because the interest savings from such policies are small. Measures to improve the efficiency of health spending are one exception: such policies could help address fiscal imbalances without requiring much sacrifice. Continuing to experiment with payment reforms should be an important priority for the government.

Of course, all of these projections are subject to a great deal of uncertainty, and prudence requires that we consider the downside risks, including faster-than-anticipated increases in interest rates and further declines in productivity growth. Acting to slow the increase in the debt-to-GDP ratio a bit more than we otherwise would, makes sense given these risks. Furthermore, changes to entitlements are often best made years in advance, in order to give people time to adjust their spending and work decisions. Thus, a reasonable policy is to begin to make small adjustments to spending and taxes and to start planning the kinds of changes we will want to make in the future.

NOTES

*   I am grateful to Vivien Lee for excellent research assistance and Bill Gale, Ron Lee, Andy Mason, David Wessel, and participants at seminars at the East–West Center and the Nomura Foundation for helpful comments.

1.   All of the data in this chapter are based on the CBO's March 2017 Long-Term Budget Outlook (CBO 2017a, 2017b).

2.   Calculation based on numbers in Goss (2014).

3.   One policy change that is included in these projections is the gradual increase in the normal retirement age, from its current 66 to 67 over the next decade. While workers are still allowed to begin drawing benefits at age 62, an increase in the normal retirement age lowers the benefits they receive (see CBO 2018).

4.   Indeed, several structural factors in the economy would likely lower the ratio of Social Security spending to GDP in the absence of aging, including a reduction in the share of GDP going to labor, and continued increases in health spending and increased wage inequality, all of which lower taxable Social Security wages and hence lead to lower future benefits.

5.   When health spending per beneficiary increases faster than GDP per capita – as it has over the past five decades – health spending increases as a share of GDP even in the absence of aging. The difference between health spending growth – adjusted for the age distribution of beneficiaries – and per capita potential GDP is called excess cost growth. In addition, the age of the Medicare population also has an impact on Medicare spending. In the next decade, as the baby boomers retire, the average age of a Medicare beneficiary will decline, leading to lower Medicare spending; but over time, as the baby boomers get old and as life expectancy continues to increase, the average age of a Medicare beneficiary will increase, boosting spending. The effect of the change in the age distribution of the population on per beneficiary spending is properly called an effect of aging, not of rapid health spending growth.

6.   Different conventions apply during the first ten years (the so-called budget window) and in the long run (from year 10 to year 30).

7.   Table 5.3 plots the median age of the workforce from Fullerton and Tschetter (1983) and Toossi (2015) and my (rough) calculations of the average age of the workforce in the CBO projections. Because the CBO reports labor force participation rates only by age group, as opposed to single years of age, I needed to make assumptions about the average age within each group to calculate the overall average.

8.   In the model in Elmendorf and Sheiner (2017), the increase in the capital labor ratio is eventually reversed, but the process is slow: the capital labor ratio increases over the 15 years from 2017 to 2032, and then slowly drifts back to its initial level. The reversal is not complete for 60 years or so.

9.   Author's calculations based on the single year tables associated with the trustees report.

10.   Social Security assumes declining rates of immigration over time, whereas the CBO assumes constant rates, so the sensitivity of the CBO projections to changes in assumptions could be somewhat different.

11.   Reznik et al. (2009) estimate that, on average, the present value of increased Social

Security benefits offset about half of the payroll taxes paid when a worker ages 62 to 65 delays retirement. Increases in income taxes are not offset at all.

12. Under current law, when people below the normal retirement age (66 now, but rising to 67) work and claim benefits, Social Security applies an earnings test that automatically delays benefits. Workers older than the normal retirement age do not face an earnings test – so can work and still receive benefits – but can delay claiming if they choose. When benefits are delayed, they are adjusted upward in an actuarially fair manner, on average, so that the present value of benefits is unchanged. Medicare does not apply an earnings test – everyone who reaches 65 is eligible – but it does require that Medicare be the secondary payer for beneficiaries who have employer-provided health insurance. Thus, under current law, Medicare could save money when workers delay retirement past 64.

13. The larger increase for women represents cohort effects, because women turning 62 in 2047 have higher labor force participation at all ages than women who turn 62 in 2017.

14. I start this shift at age 45. That is, I do not change participation rates of those younger than 45, but shift participation for those 45 and older to those projected for those two years younger.

15. The expected years of work at a given age are conditional on actually attaining that age. Thus, increasing participation at older ages has a larger effect on work years at 62 than at 16.

16. Elmendorf and Sheiner (2017) discuss the impact of low interest rates on optimal fiscal policy.

17. Imagine, for example, that a $1 investment today will increase wages by 5 cents per year every year, and imagine that the government's borrowing cost is 2 percent and the average tax rate is 20 percent. Without changing tax rates, the government will gain an additional 1 cent per year from the additional wages, which is not enough to pay the 2 cents per year interest cost. Assume that there is deadweight loss, so that when the government raises taxes on wages to collect the additional cent, work effort falls so that the increment to wages is now just 4.5 cents per year. This is still a good deal. Tax revenues go up enough to pay the additional interest costs, and workers are left with an additional 1.5 cents per year after tax.

REFERENCES

Acemoglu, Daron and Pascual Restrepo (2017), "Secular stagnation? The effect of aging on economic growth in the age of automation," NBER Working Paper 23077, Boston, MA: National Bureau of Economic Research.

Aiyar, Shekhar, Christian Ebeke and Xiaobo Shao (2016), "The impact of workforce aging on European productivity," Working Paper 16/238, Washington, DC: International Monetary Fund.

Board of Trustees, Federal Old-Age and Survivors Insurance and Federal Disability Insurance Trust Funds (2017), *The 2017 Annual Report of the Board of Trustees of the Federal Old-Age and Survivors Insurance and Federal Disability Insurance Trust Funds*, Washington, DC: Social Security Administration.

Butcher, Kristin (2017), "Assessing the long-run benefits of transfers to low-income families," Hutchins Center Working Paper 26, Washington, DC: Hutchins Center on Fiscal and Monetary Policy at Brookings Institution.

Carvalho, Carlos, Andrea Ferrero and Fernanda Nechio (2016). "Demographics and real interest rates: inspecting the mechanism," Working Paper 2016-05, San Francisco, CA: Federal Reserve Bank of San Francisco, available at www.frbsf. org.

Clark, Robert, Naohiro Ogawa, Makoto Kondo and Rikiya Matsukura (2010),

"Population decline, labor force stability, and the future of the Japanese economy," *European Journal of Population*, **26**(2), 207–27.

Congressional Budget Office (CBO) (2013), Online report of the CBO to the Senate, July 3, with a cost estimate of S. 744 (the Border Security, Economic Opportunity, and Immigration Modernization Act), available at www.cbo.gov/system/files/113th-congress-2013- 2014/costestimate/s744aspassed.pdf.

Congressional Budget Office (CBO) (2017a), Online CBO long-term budget projections in "The 2017 long-term budget outlook," available at www.cbo.gov/publication/52480.

Congressional Budget Office (CBO) (2017b), Online CBO Excel file with data supplementing the CBO's "2017 long-term budget outlook," available at www.cbo.gov/system/files/115th-congress-2017-2018/reports/52480-2017projectionsunderlyingsocialsecurityestimates.xlsx.

Congressional Budget Office (CBO) (2018), "Raise the full retirement age for Social Security, mandatory spending option 31 in *Options for Reducing the Deficit: 2019 to 2028*," available at www.cbo.gov/system/files/2019-06/54667-budgetoptions-2.pdf.

Cutler, David, James Poterba, Louise Sheiner and Lawrence Summers (1990), "An aging society: opportunity or challenge?", NBER Working Paper 1559, Boston, MA: National Bureau of Economic Research.

Elmendorf, Douglas and Louise Sheiner (2017), "Federal budget policy with an aging population and persistently low interest rates," *Journal of Economic Perspectives*, **31**(3), 175–94.

Executive Office of the President of the United States, Council of Economic Advisers (2014), *The Labor Force Participation Rate since 2007: Causes and Policy Implications*, Washington, DC: Executive Office of the President of the United States.

Fernald, John (2014), "Productivity and potential output before, during, and after the great recession," *NBER Macroeconomics Annual*, **29**(1), 1–51.

Feyrer, James (2002), "Demographics and productivity," Dartmouth College Working Paper 02-10, Hanover, NH: Department of Economics, Dartmouth College, available at http://dx.doi.org/10.2139/ssrn.325365.

Feyrer, James (2008), "Aggregate evidence on the link between age structure and productivity," *Population and Development Review*, **34**, 78–99, available at www.jstor.org/stable/25434760.

Fujita, S. and I. Fujiwara (2016), "Declining trends in the real interest rate and inflation: the role of aging," Working Paper 2016 16–29, Philadelphia, PA: Federal Reserve Bank of Philadelphia.

Fullerton, Howard and John Tschetter (1983), "The 1995 labor force: a second look," *Monthly Labor Review*, **6**(11), 3–10, available at https://stats.bls.gov/opub/mlr/1983/11/art1full.pdf.

Gagnon, Etienne, Benjamin K. Johannsen and David Lopez-Salido (2016), "Understanding the new normal: the role of demographics," Finance and Economics Discussion Series 2016-080, Washington, DC: Board of Governors of the Federal Reserve System, available at http://dx.doi.org/10.17016/FEDS.2016.080.

Goss, Stephen (2014), "Strengthening Social Security to meet the needs of tomorrow's retirees," *Testimony before Subcommittee on Social Security, Pensions, and Family Policy of the Senate Committee on Finance*, May 21, available at www.ssa.gov/oact/testimony/SenateFinance_20140521.pdf.

Hamilton, James D., Ethan S. Harris, Jan Hatzius and Kenneth D. West (2015), "The equilibrium real funds rate: past present, and future," Working Paper 16, Washington, DC: Hutchins Center on Fiscal and Monetary Policy, Brookings Institution.

Ikeda, Daisuke and Masashi Saito (2012), "The effects of demographic changes on the real interest rate in Japan," Working Paper 12-E-3, Tokyo: Bank of Japan, available at www.boj.or.jp/en/research/wps_rev/wps_2012/data/wp12e03.pdf.

Lee, Jin Young (2014), "The Plateau in US women's labor force participation: a cohort analysis," *Industrial Relations*, **53**(1), 46–71, available at https://ssrn.com/abstract=2369596.

Liu, Yihan and Niklas Westelius (2016), "The impact of demographics on productivity and inflation in Japan," Working Paper 16/237, Washington, DC: International Monetary Fund.

Maestas, Nicole, Kathleen Mullen and David Powell (2016), "The effect of population aging on economic growth, the labor force and productivity," NBER Working Paper 22452, Cambridge, MA: National Bureau of Economic Research.

Migration Policy Institute (2017), *Age-Sex Pyramics of Top Immigrant Origin Groups in US 2015*, Washington, DC: Migration Policy Institute, accessed September 17 at www.migrationpolicy.org/programs/data-hub/charts/age-sex-pyramids-top-immigrant-origin-groups.

National Academy of Sciences (2015), *The Growing Gap of Life Expectancy by Income: Implications for Federal Programs and Policy Responses*, Washington, DC: National Academies Press.

National Research Council of the National Academies (2012), *Aging and the Macroeconomy: Long-Term Implications of an Older Population*, Washington, DC: National Academies Press.

Reznik, Gayle L., David A. Weaver and Andrew G. Biggs (2009), "Social Security and marginal returns to work near retirement," Issue Paper 2009-02, Washington, DC: Social Security Office of Retirement and Disability Policy, available at www.ssa.gov/policy/docs/issuepapers/ip2009-02.html.

Sheiner, Louise (2018), "Effects of low productivity growth on fiscal sustainability in the United States," Working Paper 18-9, Washington, DC: Peterson Institute for International Economics.

Toossi, Mitra (2015), "Labor force projections to 2024: the labor force is growing, but slowly," *Monthly Labor Review* (December), Washington, DC: US Bureau of Labor Statistics, available at https://doi.org/10.21916/mlr.2015.48.

6. Improving fiscal accountability of tax expenditure: the case of the Earned Income Tax Credit in Korea

YoungWook Lee*

INTRODUCTION

Public policy programs in Korea are expanding in the form of tax expenditure, such as tax deductions and credits, separately from direct expenditure. For example, income support programs for low-income households have been introduced in the form of refundable tax credits, and various tax credits are implemented to raise employment and investment incentives. Accordingly, tax expenditure has increased steadily and accounted for 13.8 percent of total government tax revenue in 2016.

Unlike direct expenditure, however, tax expenditure is classified as a loss in tax revenue rather than an outlay with respect to the budget and is considered a "hidden expenditure." In this sense, policies carried out by means of tax expenditure are less likely to be examined in the budgetary review process. Furthermore, tightly restricted access to tax-related information makes assessment and management of tax expenditure even more difficult.

Also, policies that seek identical goals are sometimes implemented not only through tax expenditure but also through direct expenditure. Comprehensive monitoring of both tax and direct expenditure programs may be difficult because each expenditure program is managed independently by a different ministry. Policies targeting the same group and field need to be interconnected and evaluated against each other, but programs through tax and direct expenditures are likely to be monitored and analyzed as separate entities by the respective ministries.

In this sense, the fiscal accountability of tax expenditure could be weak without a thorough review system based on relevant information. This chapter addresses these concerns about tax expenditure by studying the Earned Income Tax Credit (EITC), a refundable tax credit in Korea. The above concerns about tax expenditure could be applied to the EITC case in that EITC benefits are provided in the form of tax expenditure. First, the EITC has been continually expanded, but there have not been any evaluations of its effectiveness. In Korea, the EITC was introduced in 2008 and has been expanding to support low-income working households and encourage their labor supply. In particular, against the recent social problem of the increasing working poor, the EITC coverage as well as its benefits have been expanded. However, the effectiveness of the EITC remains unchecked, and tax information on the EITC is hardly accessible even for evaluation purposes. Second, the EITC is one of the nation's welfare programs, but is managed by the Ministry of Finance separately from other welfare programs which, through direct expenditure, are mainly handled by the Ministry of Welfare. Thus, the EITC has not been reviewed from the perspective of the integrated welfare system.

This chapter examines the interconnections between the EITC and other welfare programs through direct expenditure, by studying the after-tax and after-transfer income and marginal tax rates of low-income households that receive EITC and cash transfer benefits. It finds that the interconnections between welfare programs through tax and direct expenditures create income reversals, in which more work results in less after-tax and after-transfer income, with marginal tax rates reaching up to 125 percent in some income ranges, contrary to the intended policy goals. Also, the total income with transfer benefits is higher at this stage than when the household subsequently gains enough earned income to exceed the income threshold of the transfer programs, at which point the household becomes ineligible for the transfer benefits. These results imply that the policy goals, such as encouraging recipients' employment and self-reliance, may not be fully reflected in the current welfare system. The conclusion is that interconnections between the EITC and other transfer programs, unless they are comprehensively monitored, may undermine the policy goals and the overall welfare system.

This chapter focuses on tax and direct expenditure programs in the welfare system, although in other sectors a comprehensive review of tax and direct expenditures could be much more important. Especially in sectors such as industry, small and medium-sized enterprises (SMEs), healthcare and agriculture, the relative scope of policies through tax expenditure is large compared with direct expenditure policies. However, as in the case of the EITC, information that encompasses both tax and direct expenditure programs in these sectors is not available, and the two expenditure modes have not been comprehensively reviewed in any sector. As long as tax and direct expenditure programs are introduced and expanded without any comprehensive monitoring, the policy goals pursued by both programs may be weakened.

The following section overviews tax expenditures in Korea. The third section studies the case of the EITC in terms of fiscal accountability. The final section draws policy implications from the EITC case and provides conclusions.

OVERVIEW OF TAX EXPENDITURE IN KOREA

Tax expenditure is financial support through the tax code, such as tax reduction or exemption, non-taxation, deduction, tax credit, application of favorable tax rates or deferral of tax. It reduces personal and corporate tax liabilities for various policy goals such as income support, increased employment and investment, SME support, and so on.

Tax expenditure increased by more than three-quarters from 2000 to 2016, when it reached 36 trillion Korean won (approximately $31 billion at the exchange rate of 1160 won per dollar; see Figure 6.1). The scale of tax expenditure has risen consistently, and the rate of tax reduction (that is, the proportion of revenue loss through tax expenditure among total tax

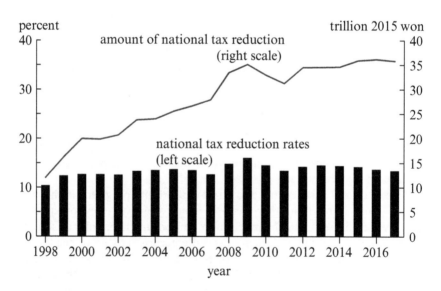

Note: The reduction rate is the reduction amount divided by the sum of the reduction amount and total revenue = (reduction amount)/(reduction amount + total revenue). Figures for 2016 and 2017 are estimates.

Sources: National Assembly Budget Office (2017), Korea Statistical Information Service and National Tax Service data.

Figure 6.1   Tax reduction rates and amounts in Korea, 1998–2017

Table 6.1   Tax and direct expenditures in 2017 by budget classification in Korea

	Tax expenditure		Direct expenditure		Tax expenditure in proportion to direct expenditure (%)
	trillion won	%	trillion won	%	
Total expenditure	37.0	100.0	400.5	100.0	9.2
Social welfare	10.3	27.9	119.1	29.7	8.6
Industry, SMEs and energy	10.6	28.8	16.0	4.0	66.3
Agriculture and fisheries	4.9	13.4	19.6	4.9	25.0
Health care	4.3	11.7	10.4	2.6	41.3

Note: Tax expenditures are based on estimates and direct expenditures are based on the budget.

Source: Government of the Republic of Korea (2016); Ministry of Strategy and Finance, open fiscal data.

revenue) remained at around 13 percent. In 2008 and 2009, support policies through tax expenditure increased in response to the 2008 economic crisis. In 2009, the tax reduction rate increased up to 15.9 percent and in 2017 stood at around 14 percent.

Table 6.1 compares tax and direct expenditures by budget classification. The amount of total tax expenditure is equal to 9.2 percent in proportion to total direct expenditure. The relative scale of tax expenditure, compared with direct expenditure, is large in sectors such as industry, SMEs, energy, healthcare, agriculture and fisheries. In particular, tax expenditure for industry, SMEs and the energy sector is equal to as much as 66 percent in proportion to direct expenditure.

In the social welfare sector, the scale of tax expenditure is relatively small compared to welfare spending through direct expenditure. Tax expenditure for social welfare is equivalent to 8.6 percent of total direct expenditure. However, the annual average growth of tax expenditure in the social welfare sector remained at 8.7 percent from 2014 to 2017, pointing to a rapid increase in social welfare spending in the form of tax expenditure. The expansion of the EITC and the introduction of the Child Tax Credit (CTC) in particular led to the rapid increase in tax expenditure for social welfare.

Tax expenditure can be more efficient in terms of administration than direct expenditure, because its operation depends on the existing tax system (OECD 2010). Using the information submitted at the time of tax filing, the government can implement tax expenditure without additional

Table 6.2   Sunset provisions from 2016

Sunset date	2016	2017	2018	2019 and beyond	No sunset provisions	Total
Number of tax expenditures	25	49	75	1	80	230
Tax expenditure (trillion won)	2.8	4.8	3.8	0.4	22.5	34.3
Share of tax expenditure (%)	8.2	14.0	11.1	1.2	65.5	100.0

Source: Ministry of Strategy and Finance (2016).

procedures that would include applications and supporting documentation. Also, as the benefits are given in the form of tax reductions, provisions can be made without another payment system.

There are also concerns, however, that public policies through tax expenditure may weaken fiscal accountability without a thorough review system for the hidden tax expenditure. In contrast to the primary function of the tax system, which is to raise revenue, the policy goal of tax expenditures is to provide financial support to various groups and fields. The Korean government adopted an in-depth performance evaluation system for tax expenditure to review its effectiveness in line with its policy goals. The evaluation is mandatory, however, only for those with sunset provisions near their sunset dates. As shown in Table 6.2, 65.5 percent of tax expenditure is not subject to sunset provisions and evaluation. A voluntary evaluation can be conducted on tax expenditures not subject to the sunset provisions, but this is only an arbitrary protocol, which lacks regular and systemic management procedures.

Also, policies targeting the same group and field are implemented through both tax and direct expenditures. Thus, to examine whether policies are effective vis-à-vis the respective target groups, those implemented through tax and direct expenditures should be examined together. An important aspect of this comprehensive review process is to check the possibility of similar or overlapping support programs and to determine which provides more effective support. Yet, each expenditure program is handled separately and by a different ministry. Also, there are not enough data that can help to discern the integrated support provided to the same group and field through tax and direct expenditures. For instance, the size of SME support programs through tax expenditure is substantial even compared to those through direct expenditure, but the current management system tracks support only from direct expenditures.

CONCERNS IN PURSUING POLICY GOALS THROUGH TAX EXPENDITURE: THE CASE OF THE EITC

This chapter addresses the concerns of fiscal accountability in pursuing policy goals through tax expenditure by studying the case of the EITC. The EITC is a welfare program through tax expenditure, which constitutes a welfare system in conjunction with transfer programs through direct expenditure. However, since the EITC, unlike other welfare spending programs, is provided through the tax code, it has not yet been reviewed together with other transfer programs within the overall welfare system of Korea. This chapter therefore examines the EITC from the perspective of its role in the integrated welfare system.

Overview of the EITC

The EITC is a refundable tax expenditure to support low-income working households. To be eligible for EITC benefits, a household must have earned income, which is a main difference from traditional transfer programs. In this sense, the EITC aims to encourage the labor supply of low-income families and support their income. An EITC was first introduced in the United States (US) in 1975 and, through several expansions, is now the largest cash transfer program for low-income households in that country. The large body of literature concerning the labor supply effect of the EITC finds a significant increase in US labor force participation, which is an EITC policy goal, especially for single women who are the main recipients of the EITC (Eissa and Liebman 1996; Meyer and Rosenbaum 2001; Meyer 2002; Hotz and Scholz 2006).

In Korea, the EITC was first introduced in 2008 to support the working poor and to encourage the contribution of low-income households to the labor supply. At the beginning, only families with children were eligible for EITC benefits, but the EITC has subsequently been expanded to cover families without children. In particular, poverty among the elderly has been a serious issue in Korea, and so the EITC coverage was extended in 2012 to single-person households without children or spouses for people aged 60 or older. The minimum age for such households was subsequently lowered, with a plan to extend EITC coverage by 2018 to those over the age of 30.

EITC benefits are calculated based on the amount of earned income, and can be represented graphically as shown in Figure 6.2 in terms of three phases: phase-in, flat and phase-out. As earned income increases, the EITC benefits increase in proportion in the phase-in. The benefits remain at the

earned income tax credit (10 000 won)

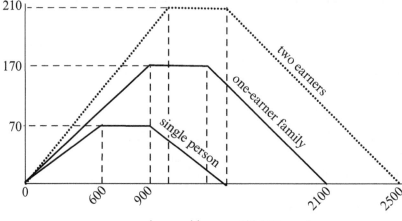

annual earned income (10 000 won)

Sources: Ministry of Health and Welfare (2015), Ministry of Land, Infrastructure and Transportation (2016), and National Tax Service (2016).

Figure 6.2   EITC schedule for a single-person, one-earner and two-earner families

maximum in the flat phase, and in the phase-out they decline gradually to zero as earned income increases. In the current EITC schedule, the benefits differ by type of household: single person without children or a spouse, one-earner family (with children and/or a spouse) and two-earner family (with children and a spouse). The maximum annual EITC benefits for the three categories respectively in 2016 were 0.7 million won ($600), 1.7 million won ($1500) and 2.1 million won ($1800). In the case of the CTC, the maximum annual benefit was 0.5 million won ($430) per child, and therefore total benefits increase with the number of children as shown in Figure 6.3.

Figure 6.4 shows the trend in tax expenditures for the EITC and the CTC. By 2017 the expenditure for the EITC had increased by more than 2.75 times since its introduction. In addition, the CTC was introduced in 2015, and the expenditure for the EITC and the CTC together hit 1.7 trillion won ($1.85 billion) in 2017.

Concerns of Fiscal Accountability: The Case of the EITC

The EITC has been gradually expanding since its introduction and has become one of Korea's major welfare programs. It has not, however,

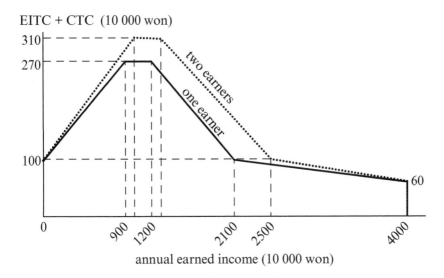

Sources: Ministry of Health and Welfare (2015), Ministry of Land, Infrastructure and Transportation (2016) and National Tax Service (2016).

Figure 6.3   EITC and CTC schedule for a family with two children

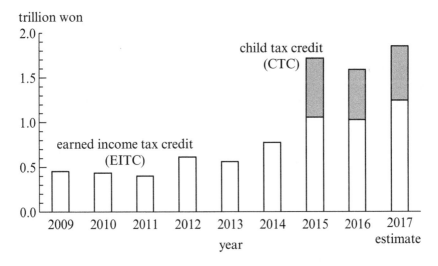

Note: Figures for 2017 are estimates.

Source: National Tax Service (2016).

Figure 6.4   Expenditure for the EITC and the CTC in Korea, 2009–17

been subject to appropriate review to determine its effectiveness. This is because the EITC is not subject to the sunset provisions and hence is not subject to a mandatory evaluation. Also, information needed to evaluate the EITC is not available, because access to the tax administration data on the EITC is highly restricted by the National Tax Service for privacy purposes. There are several publicly available survey datasets including questions about EITC benefits, but they are likewise limited, in that the low-income samples are so small that at most 100 individuals are identified as EITC recipients. Despite the data limitations, several studies have tried to examine the effectiveness of the EITC using the survey datasets. They show that the current EITC system has failed to achieve intended goals, such as poverty reduction and income redistribution, because the take-up rate of targeted groups has been low and the subsidy itself has been small (Lim 2012; Yun 2012; Jeong and Kim 2015; Kang et al. 2015).

This chapter focuses on the EITC as a welfare program that constitutes a welfare system for low-income households. It examines the interconnections between welfare programs through tax and direct expenditures in terms of an integrated welfare system. Specifically, it analyzes the EITC in connection to cash benefits provided by the National Basic Livelihood Security (NBLS) system, a traditional transfer program through direct expenditure.

The NBLS is a key public assistance program that provides cash and in-kind benefits to cover low-income households' livelihood, housing, healthcare and education according to income thresholds. Cash benefits of the NBLS include livelihood benefits for households with income below 29 percent of the median income, and housing benefits for those with income below 43 percent. The policy goal of the NBLS is to guarantee a minimum living standard to low-income families and to encourage their independence, which is consistent with the policy goal of the EITC.

The interconnections between tax and direct expenditure programs within the welfare system gained more significance as recipients of the NBLS's livelihood and housing benefits became eligible for the EITC in 2015. Previously, if a household received the NBLS's cash benefits, it did not receive EITC benefits. But from 2015, low-income working families were made eligible for both. At the same time, the government eliminated earned income exclusions, whereby a certain percentage of earned income is excluded from the calculations for NBLS benefits, because the EITC serves as a subsidy for earned incomes and replaces the exclusions.

Under the current welfare system, I examine the after-tax and after-transfer income and marginal tax rates across earned incomes, taking into account both tax and direct expenditure programs. The marginal tax rate is defined as the decrement in benefits or increment in taxes per additional

total annual income (10 000 won)

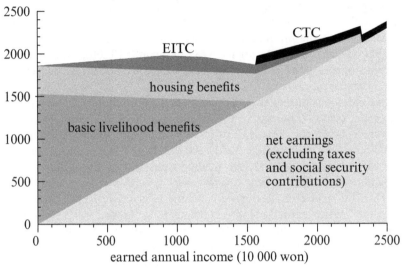

Source: National Tax Service (2016).

Figure 6.5 Income of four-member household (couple, one earner with two children)

1 won in earned income. The marginal tax rate is important because it is directly linked to labor supply incentives. If a rise in earned income leads to a significant increase in tax or decrease in existing benefits, there will be less incentive to increase the labor supply and income. Specifically, the nearer the marginal tax rate is to 100 percent, the closer the income from additional work is to zero, and when the marginal tax rate exceeds 100 percent, there may even be a loss in total income.

For the analysis, I make a tax and welfare benefit calculator for households. The calculator reflects information on household composition, the number of earners in a household, and the number of children. It calculates the amounts of income tax, social security contributions, and EITC and CTC benefits based on the current tax system. Also, cash benefits of the NBLS (livelihood and housing benefits) are calculated based on household composition and earned incomes. Then, after-tax and after-transfer incomes and marginal tax rates are calculated across earned incomes as final outputs of the calculator.

Figure 6.5 shows the after-tax and after-transfer income of single-earner households with four members including two children. First, households are entitled to livelihood benefits if monthly earned income is below the income threshold for livelihood benefits; that is, 29 percent of the median income of a four-member household or 1 273 516 won ($1100). If a household is eligible for livelihood benefits, 29 percent of the median income is guaranteed to the minimum living standard. The maximum amount of livelihood benefits for a year is 15 282 200 won ($13 200),[1] and as earned income increases, the livelihood benefits are reduced by the earned amount from the maximum benefits.

Second, housing benefits are provided to households whose monthly income is below 43 percent of the median income. If a household's earned income is below the income threshold of livelihood benefits, it can receive maximum housing benefits of 3 312 000 won ($2900) for a year. Then, after the earned income exceeds the income threshold of livelihood benefits, housing benefits are reduced at a flat rate.

Third, if a household's earned income is positive, EITC benefits are provided. When earned income increases to an annual 9–12 million won ($7760–10 340), which is the flat region of the EITC, the household receives the maximum EITC benefits of 1.7 million won ($1500). Beyond the flat region, the EITC benefits decline as earned income increases.

Fourth, CTC benefits are available for households with children if their annual earned incomes are below 40 million won ($34 500) and they do not receive livelihood benefits. Thus, after the households' earned incomes exceed the income threshold of livelihood benefits, CTC benefits are assumed to be provided instead of livelihood benefits. The maximum annual CTC benefits is 0.5 million won ($430) per child, and the benefits are reduced after the earned income exceeds the income threshold of the EITC.

With these welfare benefits, income taxes and social security contributions are also considered to calculate households' total incomes across earned incomes. When all these benefits and taxes are taken into consideration, households that earn an annual 9 million won are guaranteed to have a total income of a maximum of 19 742 200 won ($17 000). On the earned income of 9 million won, households receive livelihood and housing benefits and the maximum EITC benefits. Once earned income exceeds 12 million won, the household enters the phase-out stage of the EITC, wherein the EITC benefits are gradually reduced in line with the amount of earned income. Then, both EITC and NBLS livelihood benefits decrease as the household earns more, and the reduction in welfare benefits is greater than the increase in earned income. When the earned income nears the income threshold for livelihood benefits, total income is reduced further to 18 648 900 won ($16 100), which is lower than the total income for the households on an annual earned income of 9 million won. As such, the interconnections between the EITC and the NBLS's cash benefit

total annual income (10 000 won)

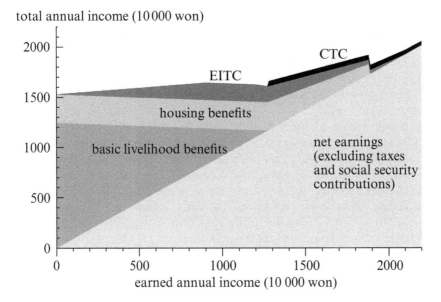

Figure 6.6   Income of three-member household (couple, one earner with one child)

create income reversals in which more work leads to less after-tax and after-transfer income.

Additionally, there are even cases wherein the total income is higher when the household is receiving both livelihood and EITC benefits than when the household becomes ineligible for livelihood benefits with increasing earned income. When earned income exceeds the income threshold for livelihood benefits, households receive CTC benefits instead of livelihood benefits, which leads to a jump in their total income. In such cases, however, the total income is 19 648 900 won ($16 900), which is lower than the maximum total income for the households on an annual earned income of 9 million won. Even if earned income increases by 6.7 million won ($5800), the total income is still lower. Considering additional benefits such as in-kind and deductions given to livelihood benefit recipients, it can naturally be expected that low-income households will have little incentive to work more and seek self-reliance.

The income reversals are also created for households with three members by the interconnections between EITC and NBLS cash benefits. Figure 6.6 shows after-tax and after-transfer income of a single-earner household with three members including a child. The maximum livelihood benefits for a three-member household are 12 455 000 won ($10 700), and the maximum housing benefits are 2 832 000 won ($2400) for a year. Households with positive earned incomes can get EITC benefits up to a maximum of 1.7 million won. Then, when earned incomes exceed the income threshold of livelihood benefits, households are assumed to receive CTC benefits of 0.5 million won for one child.

Similarly with the case of households with four members, when earned incomes are 9 million won, the total income of three-member households receiving livelihood benefits of the NBLS is highest at 16 434 960 won ($14 200). If the earned income exceeds 9 million won, the total income decreases as earned incomes increase, especially in the phase-out of the EITC, which starts from earned income of 12 million won.[2] When the household becomes ineligible for livelihood benefits with earned income exceeding the income threshold, the total income is 16 565 400 won ($14 300) with CTC benefits. Compared with a household on an earned income of 9 million won, the household earns 3.7 million won ($3200) more, but the total income increases by only 0.1 million won ($90). This structure could diminish low-income households' incentives to work and become independent of welfare.

It is evident in Figure 6.7, showing the marginal tax rate; it is difficult to expect an induced labor supply within the current welfare system. Having an earned income means a loss of that much in livelihood benefits, which means that the marginal tax rate of livelihood benefits is 100 percent. This

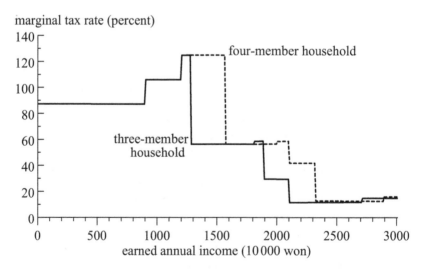

Figure 6.7   Marginal tax rates: three-member household (couple with one child) and four-member household (couple with two children)

structure severely weakens the incentive to work. When social security contributions are taken into consideration, the marginal tax rate increases to 106.1 percent.[3] Households with livelihood benefits do not have any tax liabilities because of low income, but still pay social security contributions on earned income.

To increase work incentives of welfare benefit recipients, earned income exclusions for livelihood benefits were applied, and therefore a certain percentage of earned income was not counted in the calculation of the benefits. With the exclusions, the marginal tax rate of NBLS livelihood benefits was reduced below 100 percent. However, as recipients of the NBLS's livelihood benefits became eligible for EITC benefits in 2015, the earned income exclusions were eliminated. Since the EITC likewise provides a subsidy for earned incomes, the government replaced the exclusions with the EITC. As a result, for households in the phase-in phase, where EITC benefits increase with earned incomes, the EITC lowers the marginal tax rate to 87.2 percent.

However, for those whose EITC benefits are in the phase-out region, the marginal tax rate reaches 125 percent, as more earned income entails a more substantial decrease in both livelihood and EITC benefits. In other words, such households will experience a $1.25 reduction in benefits for every additional $1 earned, leading to a decrease of $0.25 in the total income. This study provides illustrations for four-member and three-member households, but the income reversals happens in the case of households with two members as well.

Both the EITC and the NBLS are designed to support the incomes and self-reliance of low-income households, and hence to influence the income and labor supply incentives of such households. Despite the intention to provide low-income households with more incentives to work and become self-reliant, it is highly likely that these incentives will be minimal and even undermined for some income earners. These concerns have arisen over a weakening of policy goals as the policy programs remain unchecked within the overall social safety net.

The results suggest that the current welfare system, including tax and direct expenditure programs, is not consistent with common policy goals to promote recipients' employment and self-reliance. It should also be tested whether this theoretical concern is empirically happening. However, as mentioned above, data suitable for the study are not currently available, because tax information on the EITC is highly restricted. Also, even if the EITC information were accessible, the administrative data on the EITC and the NBLS are independently managed by different ministries, so the information on the recipients of these two programs is not linked. Several publicly available survey datasets include questions about both EITC and NBLS benefits received by households, but they are still limited for the study because of the small sample size for benefit recipients.

I briefly examine the distribution of earned incomes of households receiving both EITC and NBLS benefits using data from the Survey of Household Finances and Living Conditions. Interestingly, the frequency of households with earned incomes is higher in the flat phase of the EITC than in other income ranges. In this income range, the households get the maximum EITC benefit and the highest total income with EITC and other transfer benefits. This result does not directly suggest that households change their labor supply and income in response to the welfare incentives, but supports the concern that the current welfare system can make welfare recipients remain in welfare benefits and fail to encourage recipients' labor supply and independence.

CONCLUSIONS AND POLICY SUGGESTIONS

This chapter examines the EITC through tax expenditure in connection with transfer programs through direct expenditure. The interconnections between the EITC and other transfer programs cause income reversals in which after-tax and after-transfer income decreases the more the recipients work, in some income ranges. In such cases, the marginal tax rate exceeds 100 percent, and as earned income increases, the reduction in benefits is greater than the increase in additional earnings. Also, when households exit the transfer program, their total income becomes lower than when they were still receiving livelihood and EITC benefits. These results suggest that the interconnections between the EITC and transfer programs may undermine the policy goals and the welfare system as long as they are not comprehensively reviewed within the overall welfare system.

It is highly likely that comprehensive reviews, covering both tax and direct expenditure programs, are absent from other fields, as they are from welfare. For example, government support for individuals and companies is offered by both means of expenditure. While tax expenditure programs are handled by the Ministry of Finance, direct spending programs are managed by the spending department of each sector. Thus, each tax or direct expenditure program is likely to be independently monitored by a respective ministry. Also, tightly restricted tax information on tax expenditure is difficult to obtain, even for evaluation purposes, and is more difficult to combine with information on other spending programs through direct expenditure handled by different ministries. This lack of systematic review, covering both tax and direct expenditure programs for the same field and group, could be distorting the entire support system and weakening the policy goals that both expenditure programs seek.

To improve the fiscal accountability of overall tax expenditure, the structure of policy evaluation needs to be strengthened. First, information on tax expenditure must be made available for review and evaluation. Providing tax data carries the risk of confidentiality breaches, but a safeguard can be put into place to minimize the concern about personal information leaks. For this, as has been suggested by numerous researchers, it is worth considering circulating the needed information by providing samples of micro data on individual tax payments (Park 2006; Moon 2007). Moreover, the information must be provided in a timely manner in order to facilitate the appropriate review and evaluation.

To comprehensively manage tax and direct expenditures with identical policy goals, a database that covers both types of expenditure must be constructed. In the welfare sector, for example, various expenditure programs are implemented to support the income and self-reliance of the low-income households. If the respective data on welfare receipts were regularly entered into a database, along with information on income and job characteristics, this would enable a comprehensive evaluation through which relevant policies can be systematically developed and monitored.

Based on the constructed data, the comprehensive review covering both tax and direct expenditures should be strengthened along with an effectiveness check on respective tax expenditures. First, tax expenditure programs must be regularly evaluated and supervised. At present, only tax expenditures with sunset provisions are subject to the mandatory in-depth evaluation. This in-depth evaluation should be systemized further so that other programs not covered by the evaluation are also reviewed on a regular basis.

Also, in order to examine the overall effectiveness of tax and direct expenditures with identical policy goals, it is essential to check the integration and interconnection of pertinent policies within an overall system. To do so, a spending review at a sector level may be useful. The current sectoral review system is applicable only to direct expenditure programs. Comprehensive reviews need to be conducted on both direct and tax expenditure programs implemented in the same sector.

NOTES

* This chapter is a revised and translated version of Lee (2016).
1. Housing benefits are offered in the form of rent allowance, assuming that the residence is located in Gyeonggi Province.

2. Even in the flat region of the EITC, where the maximum EITC benefits are provided, the total income decreases as earned income increases, because social security contributions are imposed on the earned income.
3. The total social security contribution rate, including national pension, employment insurance, national health insurance and long-term care insurance, is 8.38 percent. But in the calculation of livelihood benefits, half of the national pension contribution is deducted. Thus, the social security contribution rate for livelihood benefits recipients is 6.1 percent.

REFERENCES

Eissa, Nada and Jeffrey B. Liebman (1996), "Labor supply response to the Earned Income Tax Credit," *Quarterly Journal of Economics*, **111**(2), 605–37.

Government of the Republic of Korea (2016), *2017 Tax Expenditure Statement*, Seoul: Government of the Republic of Korea (in Korean).

Hotz, V. Joseph and John Karl Scholz (2006), "Examining the effect of the Earned Income Tax Credit on the labor market participation of families on welfare," NBER Working Paper 11968, Cambridge, MA: National Bureau of Economic Research.

Jeong, Chan Mi and Jae-Jin Kim (2015), "The redistributive effects of the Earned Income Tax Credit and of the Child Tax Credit on one-earner and dual-earner households," *Korean Social Security Studies*, **31**(1), 233–53 (in Korean).

Kang, Shin-Wook, DaeMyung No, Hyon-Joo Lee, Wan-Sub Lim, Mun-Il Kwon, et al. (2015), "Evaluating the efficacy of main income security programs in Korea," Research Paper 2015-08, Sejong: Korea Institute for Health and Social Affairs (in Korean).

Korea Statistical Information Service (KOSIS) (n.d.), Online data, accessed September 12, 2017 at http://kosis.kr (in Korean).

Lee, YoungWook (2016), "Improving fiscal accountability of tax expenditures: focusing on income tax expenditure," in Heesuk Yun (ed.), *Enhancing Fiscal Sustainability through Strengthening Fiscal Account Ability*, Research Monograph 2016-06, Seoul: Korea Development Institute (in Korean), pp. 15–59.

Lim, Byung In (2012), "Income redistributive effect of a new Korean EITC system," *Journal of Korean National Economy*, **30**(2), 147–69 (in Korean).

Meyer, Bruce D. (2002), "Labor supply at the extensive and intensive margins: the EITC, welfare, and hours worked," *American Economic Review*, **82**(2), 373–79.

Meyer, Bruce D. and Dan T. Rosenbaum (2001), "Welfare, the Earned Income Tax Credit, and the labor supply of single mothers," *Quarterly Journal of Economics*, **116**(3), 1063–1114.

Ministry of Health and Welfare (2015), *Guidelines for 2016 National Basic Livelihood Support*, Seoul: Ministry of Health and Welfare.

Ministry of Land, Infrastructure and Transportation (2016), *Guidelines for 2016 Housing Benefits*, Seoul: Ministry of Land, Infrastructure and Transportation (in Korean).

Ministry of Strategy and Finance (2016), "Open Fiscal Data, National Budget," available online at www.openfiscaldata.go.kr/portal/service/openInfPage.do (in Korean).

Moon, Seong Hwan (2007), "Improving the system for taxation information disclosure: focusing on information disclosure at the National Assembly," Economic Issue Brief 19, Seoul: National Assembly Budget Office (in Korean).

National Assembly Budget Office (2017), "NABO Fiscal Trends and Issues Vol. 1," Seoul: National Assembly Budget Office (in Korean).

National Tax Service (2016), "2,540 Thousand Households Guided to Claim the EITC and CTC," press release, May 4 (in Korean).

Organisation for Economic Co-operation and Development (OECD) (2010), *Tax Expenditures in OECD Countries*, Paris: Organisation for Economic Co-operation and Development.

Park, Myung Ho (2006), "How to provide more information on national taxes," Public Finance Brief 06-05, Seoul: Korea Institute of Public Finance (in Korean).

Yun, Heesuk (2012), "Problems in the decision-making process for welfare policies: focusing on the EITC," KDI FOCUS 24, Seoul: Korea Development Institute (in Korean).

PART III

Fiscal soundness and accountability

7. The future of public employee pensions in the United States

Andrew G. Biggs

INTRODUCTION

By far the most common form of pension for United States (US) state and local government employees is the traditional "final salary" defined benefit (DB) plan, in which retirement benefits are calculated as a given percentage of final earnings multiplied by the employee's number of years of job tenure. For instance, a final salary plan might offer a benefit equal to 1.6 percent of the average of the final three years of pay, multiplied by years of service. Thus, a full-career employee with 35 years of service would retire with a benefit equal to 56 percent of their final salary. In addition, most public employees participate in the Social Security program administered by the federal government, which requires contributions from both employers and employees. For an employee whose final salary was $75 000, which is reasonably typical for state and local government employees, Social Security would provide a benefit equal to about 37 percent of final pay. Together, the employee would receive a total retirement benefit equal to about 93 percent of their final pay. Financial advisors tend to recommend a "replacement rate" of about 70 percent of final salary in order to maintain one's pre-retirement standard of living. These basic illustrations indicate that most full-career public employees would likely be well prepared for retirement.

In the US private sector, coverage by defined benefit pensions has declined significantly. In 1979, 28 percent of private sector employees had only a DB pension and an additional 10 percent had both a DB and a defined contribution (DC) plan. Ten percent of private sector workers had only a DC plan. By 2014, only 2 percent of private sector workers had only a DB plan, while an additional 11 percent had both DB and DC pensions. Thirty-four percent of employees had only a DC retirement plan (EBRI 2015). In the public sector, however, DB coverage remains strong. All federal government employees are automatically enrolled in a final-salary DB plan. Likewise, in state and local government 93 percent of full-time employees continue to be offered a defined benefit pension (BLS 2016).

As the following section describes, the costs and financial risks of defined benefit plans have increased. Many plans have become more generous over time, with "benefit enhancements" enacted during the late 1990s that are difficult or impossible to repeal. Lower interest rates have reduced pension investment yields, while pensions' search for investment returns have caused plan managers to take on additional investment risk. Pension contribution costs have competed with other government spending priorities. In some cases, pension contributions have lost that competition, such that many state and local governments fail to make the full contribution calculated by the plan's actuaries. In other cases, however, rising pension costs have reduced resources available for education, law enforcement, healthcare and other priorities of state and local governments.

For these reasons, many policymakers in the US are rethinking pension plan design and considering reforms that would reduce and stabilize the costs of providing retirement benefits to public employees. However, pension reforms are fraught with legal and political difficulty. It is legally almost impossible for state and local governments to renege on pension benefits that already have been earned, and it is legally difficult for governments even to alter the rate at which current employees earn future benefits (Monahan 2012). Likewise, public employees remain a powerful interest group in many state and local governments. The same political influence that caused pension benefits to be increased is brought to bear to prevent or reduce the impact of pension reforms. In coming years, however, pensions are likely to remain an important and controversial topic for state and local government lawmakers.

THE INCREASING RISKS OF PENSIONS TO STATE AND LOCAL GOVERNMENT BUDGETS

The principal characteristic of a DB pension is that the plan sponsor – the government in the case of public employee plans – bears most or all of the investment risk. When a DB pension plan runs a shortfall, the sponsoring government is responsible for increasing pension contributions so as to return the plan to full funding over some specified period of time, usually ranging from 20 to 30 years. While public sector pensions are subject to a number of risks, including changes to longevity, to the incidence of disability and to other factors, the largest risk facing government budgets is investment risk. When a government pension fund loses money or even simply produces returns below the assumed rate, which currently is on average about 7.6 percent, the plan sponsor must increase future contributions to make up the difference. The extent to which any required increase in pension contributions impacts the sponsoring government's budget depends upon how large the pension fund is relative to the government budget and how large the investment loss was.

Thus, what I term "pension budgetary risk" is a function of two simple factors: the size of the pension fund relative to the government budget and the risk of the fund's investments (Biggs 2013). These two factors have a multiplicative effect: *pension budgetary risk* = *pension assets* (as a percent of budget) × *pension investment risk* (expressed, for instance, as the standard deviation of annual investment returns).

A given percentage loss to a pension fund will put a greater burden on the sponsoring government's budget if the pension fund is large relative to the overall government budget. Likewise, the probability of a large annual investment loss will rise as the risk of the pension's portfolio increases. Both of these contributing factors have increased significantly over the past several decades. Importantly, the size and investment risk of a pension fund interact on a multiplicative basis, allowing for a substantially increased impact on a sponsoring government's budget as these two factors increase.

In 1975, for instance, state and local pension assets were equal to only 49 percent of annual government expenditures, according to data from the Federal Reserve's Flow of Funds and the Census Bureau's Survey of State and Local Government Finances (see Figure 7.1). By 2012, pension assets had nearly tripled to 143 percent of government outlays. By itself, the increasing size of pensions relative to their sponsors' budgets implies that the budgetary cost of addressing a given percentage loss in pension assets would have nearly tripled.

As a result of rising pension assets relative to budgets, a given percentage loss in pension investments today would have nearly three times the impact on state and local budgets as in 1975. For instance, imagine that a pension plan's assets declined by 10 percent. In 1975, this loss would have been equal to 4.9 percent of state and local budgets; a similar 10 percent loss in 2012 would be equal to 14.3 percent of state and local budgets. As a result, the plan's amortization payments would be nearly three times larger relative to the sponsoring government's budget, simply by virtue of the growing relative size of pension plans. Thus, even if the volatility of public pension assets remains the same, pensions' year-to-year impacts on state and local budgets have roughly tripled.

Larger pension assets relative to their sponsor's budgets might be a healthy sign, if rising assets were the result of the plans becoming better funded and thus better able to pay the benefits they have promised.

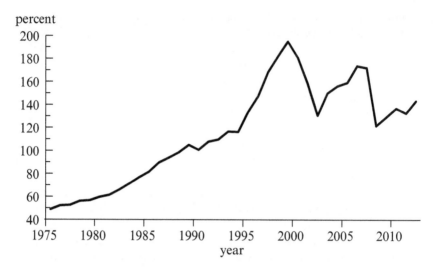

Sources: Federal Reserve Flow of Funds and US Census Bureau data.

Figure 7.1   US state and local pension assets as a share of state and local government budgets, 1975–2012

However, according to the Federal Reserve, which utilizes pension liabilities as calculated for the National Income and Product Accounts, state and local plans today are no better funded than they were in 1980 in terms of the ratio of assets to liabilities.

In addition to greater size, state and local government pensions have increasingly taken on additional investment risk in hopes of improving future investment returns. Riskier investments offer higher returns, which plan sponsors hope will help offset the falling yields on fixed income investments. But increased risk also brings with it the chance of a significant loss. Public plans historically have assumed investment returns of around 8 percent, although in recent years the average plan's assumed return has declined slightly to around 7.5 percent. The expected investment return may be thought of as the combination of the return on safe assets plus a premium for taking investment risk. Because of falling yields on safe assets, pensions must take more risk to have the expectation of receiving high returns.

In the 1970s, most state and local pension investments were in bonds and other fixed return assets. Through the 1980s and 1990s, pensions began to invest more heavily in stocks. And beginning in the late 1990s and accelerating through the present, state and local pensions shifted to so-called "alternative investments," which include hedge funds, private equity, real estate and other non-standard categories. These alternatives carry even greater risk than stocks, along with substantially higher investment fees.

In 2015 the typical state and local plan held about half of its assets in stocks and an additional one-quarter in alternatives. Bonds, the asset class whose risk characteristics most closely match the benefit liabilities of public plans, fell to only about one-quarter of total pension investments (Pew Charitable Trusts 2017). This shift to alternative investments has led to higher administrative fees paid by public pensions, which have been a matter of some public controversy. State and local pensions are not very transparent in disclosing their outside fees, but one of the more transparent plans – the Missouri State Employees Retirement System – reports that it spends about 1.5 percent of assets under management on outside investment fees. A number of public pensions are reconsidering alternative investments due to disappointing returns and high fees. However, without access to alternatives public plans would have difficulty in maintaining their assumed investment returns, given low expected returns on stocks and bonds (see Aubry et al. 2017a).

Table 7.1 details the evolution of state and local pension investments since 2001. From 2001 through 2016, the share of pension investments in risky assets – here defined as equities, alternative investments and real estate – rises from 64 to 72 percent. This is an effort to maintain assumed investment returns in the face of significantly lower yields on low-risk investments. Over the 2001 to 2016 period, state and local pensions lowered their average assumed return by 0.5 percentage points, despite a 2.9 percentage point decline in the riskless yield on one-year US Treasury securities. This implies that in 2016, public pensions assumed they will earn a risk premium of 7.5 percentage points over the riskless yield, up from 4.6 percentage points in 2001.[1]

Whether public pensions will in fact earn such a premium is debatable. Aubry et al. (2017b) survey a number of independent investment advisors and conclude that an annual return of 5.5 percent is "consistent with the forecasts of many investment firms." Similarly, Biggs (2015), using a survey of investment advisors conducted by the Pension Consulting Alliance, finds that for a 70:30 stock–bond portfolio the advisors on average project an annual return of 5.9 percent over the next decade. While future returns are not known, what is clear today is that state and local pensions are taking greater risks in hopes of achieving higher future returns.

Biggs (2014a) uses a simulation model to demonstrate how rising pension investment risk leads to greater volatility of required pension contributions by governments. At times these contributions rise to levels that governments cannot or will not make, which leads to skipped contributions and increases in unfunded pension liabilities. Figure 7.2

Table 7.1   *US state and local pension investment practices and changing riskless yields, 2001–16*

Year	Share of portfolio held in risky assets (%)	Assumed investment return (%)	One-year US Treasury yield (%)	Assumed risk premium (%)
2001	64.1	8.0	3.5	4.6
2002	62.6	8.0	2.0	6.0
2003	64.5	8.0	1.2	6.7
2004	67.5	8.0	1.9	6.1
2005	68.7	8.0	3.6	4.3
2006	69.5	7.9	4.9	3.0
2007	70.4	7.9	4.5	3.4
2008	68.2	7.9	1.8	6.1
2009	67.4	7.9	0.5	7.4
2010	67.7	7.8	0.3	7.5
2011	69.8	7.8	0.2	7.6
2012	71.1	7.7	0.2	7.5
2013	72.7	7.7	0.1	7.5
2014	73.1	7.6	0.1	7.5
2015	72.7	7.6	0.3	7.3
2016	72.4	7.5	0.6	6.9

Sources: Public Plans Database and Federal Reserve data.

simulates a stylized pension plan for which the sponsor invests with a target annual return of 8 percent. Assuming an 8 percent annual return can be produced consistently, the total cost for the system is 11 percent of employee payroll. Employees pay a fixed contribution of 6 percent of their wages. The government has an expected contribution of 5 percent of payroll, shown as a horizontal line in Figure 7.2. The 5 percent expected employer contribution is based on the assumed 8 percent annual return, but the actual contribution can rise above 5 percent if returns have been below expectations, or can fall as low as zero if returns are high and the plan becomes overfunded.

However, once investment returns are allowed to vary from year-to-year in a realistic fashion, employer pension contribution can vary considerably relative to rates that are assumed in the absence of investment risk. Figure 7.3 shows ten sample government contribution paths from selected Organisation for Economic Co-operation and Development (OECD) countries for a stylized pension system that, in the absence of investment

employer contribution as a percent of payroll

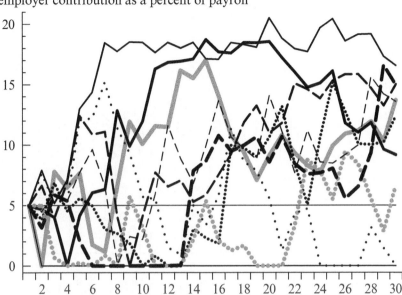

Figure 7.2   Sample employer contribution rates for a plan of 30 years with a static employer rate of 5 percent of payroll

risk, has an annual government contribution equal to 5 percent of employee payroll. As Figure 7.2 demonstrates, however, in many years investment returns above the assumed rate mean that no government contribution was needed. In other years, however, low investment returns would require government contributions three to four times the level that would be expected absent investment risk. Those are rates that budget-makers rarely plan for, and as required contribution rates rise, it becomes more common for a state or local government to short-change the contribution.

Importantly, the transition from low to high required contributions can occur quickly. This demonstrates that public pensions' current approach to investment return sensitivity analysis, in which the plan actuary feeds in steady annual returns that are higher or lower than the assumed rate, is inadequate. The investment risk to sponsors of public sector pensions is not merely that average returns will be lower than the assumed rate, though surveys of pension investment advisors indicate that such risk is considerable. Rather, the risk is that even if a pension accurately predicts investment returns over the very long term, the pension cannot wait forever for such returns to materialize. Public pensions in the United States

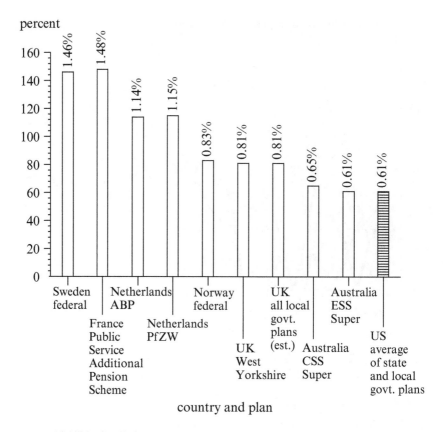

Note: Liabilities for all plans are valued using a 4.5 percent nominal discount rate.

Source: Ponds et al. (2011).

Figure 7.3   *Funded ratios of public employee plans in selected OECD countries, using a consistent liability discount rate, 2008*

generally amortize unfunded pension liabilities over a period of 20 to 30 years. Though this is considerably longer than the seven-year amortization period which is mandated for private sector defined benefit pensions, even a period of three decades does not guarantee that an assumed long-run return will be realized.

To manage a pension plan that takes a great deal of investment risk requires that the pension sponsor have considerable space within its budget to increase annual pension contributions as needed. This fiscal space has shrunk considerably as pensions have tripled in size relative to their sponsors' budgets. Moreover, other costs – including healthcare costs both for public employees and for health programs aimed at the public – have increased dramatically over the past several decades.

VALUING PUBLIC PENSION LIABILITIES

The foregoing discussion is relevant to how public employee pensions value their benefit liabilities. Liability valuation is not a mere accounting exercise. Rather, the value of the pension's current and accruing liabilities determines how much the sponsoring government must contribute each year to fund those benefit liabilities. Secondarily, the value of new benefits accruing to public employees in a given year – the so-called "normal" or "service" cost – allows for comparisons of the generosity of public sector pensions to retirement plans offered in the private sector.

While pension benefits are earned in the present, most benefits are paid out years into the future. The average duration of a public pension plan's total liabilities is generally about 15 years. For new benefits earned by employees in the current year, the duration is typically about ten years longer. Over long periods, simply adding up the nominal values of future retirement benefits will provide a distorted view of the pension's liabilities. Since a given dollar of contributions made today can earn interest over time, future benefit liabilities should be discounted to the present at an appropriate interest rate. The present value of plan liabilities can then be used to calculate how much the government must contribute each year to assure the appropriate funding of those future benefits.

The policy question is what interest rate is appropriate to use in discounting future benefit liabilities. In this area US state and local pensions are outliers relative to the rest of the pension world. In general, both public and private sector pensions consider their liabilities to be bond-like, in the sense of providing fixed, guaranteed benefits due to take place at specified points in time. Public sector employers intend the benefits they offer to be guaranteed; they describe the benefits to their employees in those terms, and in the United States most benefit obligations are considered to be contractual obligations that can be altered only under the most extreme of financial circumstances.

For these reasons, most pensions value their liabilities using a discount rate derived from bond yields. In the United States, for instance, corporate pensions are required under federal law to discount their liabilities using a corporate bond yield. Likewise, Table 7.2 draws upon Van der Wal (2014), a Dutch central bank study of the value of pension benefit liabilities. It shows that in 2012, US state and local pension plans were utilizing

Table 7.2   Discount rates used by public sector pensions in different countries

Country	Rate in 2012 (%)	Reference rate
Australia	6.0	Expected return on government bonds over long term
Canada	5.0–6.5	Expected return on government bonds over long term, plus mark-up for risk premium
Switzerland	3.5	Expected return on portfolio of two-thirds stocks, one-third government bonds, minus 0.5%
Netherlands	2.4	Public pension assets are managed under private sector rules; riskless return plus ultimate forward rate for very long-term liabilities
United Kingdom	6.4	Expected return on investments, calculated as inflation rate plus approximately 3% real return
United States	8.0	Expected return on risky assets

Source: Van der Wal (2014).

discount rates that were substantially greater than the rates that overseas plans applied to qualitatively similar liabilities.

Differences in the discount rates used to value liabilities can generate dramatic differences in the amount of funding performed for each unit of future promised benefits. Ponds et al. (2011), in a study conducted by the OECD, compare liability valuation and funding for public employee systems in the United States, Canada, the Netherlands, Sweden, the United Kingdom (UK), Australia, Norway and France. Each system uses different accounting standards, importantly including different discount rates to value pension liabilities. At the time, the United States and Australia used the highest discount rates to value their pension liabilities, averaging 8 percent. Since that time Australia has lowered the discount rate for its funds to about 6 percent, leaving today's average US public pension discount rate of about 7.6 percent the highest in the group. Pensions in the Netherlands, which are among the best-funded in the world, used a discount rate of just 3.5 percent. The UK and Canada valued liabilities using interest rates of between 4 and 6 percent. As Dutch economist Theo Kocken stated, "We had lengthy discussions about this in the Netherlands. But all economists now agree. The expected-return approach is a huge economic offense, hurting younger generations" (Walsh 2014).

In addition to merely listing the differences in accounting assumptions used by different countries' public pensions, the OECD authors revalued each pension using consistent standards, so their funding levels could be compared on an apples-to-apples basis. Ponds et al. valued different countries' pension liabilities using a consistent 4.5 percent interest rate. Using this discount rate, US state and local plans would be around 61 percent funded. The closest plans to the US level would be Australia's pensions for federal government employees and public safety workers, which are between 61 and 65 percent funded. But other countries' public employee plans are far better funded than US state and local government plans. The UK's local government employee pensions would be around 81 percent funded. Canada's two main pensions – the Public Service plan and the Ontario Teachers plan – would be 81 percent and 108 percent funded, respectively. The two Dutch plans examined by the OECD would be 114 percent funded with liabilities valued using a 4.5 percent discount rate, and Sweden and France's plans would be nearly 150 percent funded. These figures imply that nearly all of the developed countries analyzed by the OECD contribute a great deal more to funding public pension liabilities than do US state and local plans. The Dutch, Swedish and French plans have set aside roughly twice as much money per dollar of promised retirement benefits than US state and local pensions have done.

In 2014, the Society of Actuaries' Blue Ribbon Panel on Public Pension Funding, of which the author of this chapter was a member, recommended that state and local pensions report both plan liabilities and the normal cost of accruing benefits as valued using the yield on riskless securities such as US Treasury bonds. Similarly, in 2016 the Actuarial Standards Board's Pensions Task Force concluded that "a market-based alternative liability measurement should be calculated and disclosed for all valuations of pension plans for funding purposes."

If state and local pension liabilities were valued using a 3 percent nominal interest rate,[2] total liabilities for the plans would rise from the plans' own reported value of $4.8 trillion calculated under a 7.6 percent average discount rate to $8.3 trillion. Unfunded liabilities would rise from $1.4 trillion to $4.8 trillion, and the plans' overall funding ratio would fall from 72 percent to 42 percent. A US corporate plan that was so poorly funded would be required under federal law to take prompt action to improve its funding status. However, state and local government pensions are not subject to federal regulation regarding accounting, disclosure or funding. Unless a sponsoring government decides to enact reforms on its own, there is no outside regulator to require such changes.

COULD THE FEDERAL GOVERNMENT SERVE AS A MODEL?

A reader will note that attention so far has been paid exclusively to pensions provided for state and local government employees. This focus may be merited, in that state and local governments form the great majority of public sector employment in the United States, their pensions are the most grievously underfunded, and state and local governments lack the federal government's broad fiscal capacity, making the burden of pension costs on state and local government services more potent.

However, it is worth briefly reviewing two options for state and local pension reform that would involve the federal government. The first is to fund state and local plans using the accounting standards that are required by the federal government for corporate defined benefit pensions. The second would transform state and local plans to a mixed defined benefit and defined contribution system resembling that which the federal government offers to most current employees.

As discussed above, state and local pensions in the United States operate under laxer accounting and funding standards than do corporate defined benefit pensions or public employee pensions in a number of other developed countries. One option would be for state and local pensions – either voluntarily or via federal mandate – to operate under the same standards that the federal government requires for pensions operated by private sector employers. As noted above, this would involve measuring plan liabilities using a substantially lower discount rate. US corporate pensions must value their liabilities using a corporate bond yield. Currently, the Mercer Pension Discount Yield Curve generates average discount rates between 3.3 and 3.9 percent, depending upon the average duration of a plan's liabilities. Using 3.6 percent as a proxy, public plans' total liabilities would be about $3 trillion higher when measured using a corporate bond yield than the 7.6 percent assumed return on a risky portfolio of assets: a 62 percent increase.

In addition, however, corporate pensions must address unfunded liabilities more quickly than state and local plans. Typically, state and local pensions take between 20 and 30 years to pay off their unfunded liabilities. By contrast, corporate pensions generally must pay off their unfunded liabilities within a period of seven years.[3] Roughly speaking, this will imply amortization payments that are four times larger than a state and local plan would pay, but the corporate plan returns to full funding four times more quickly.

If lower discount rates and shorter amortization periods were combined, total required contributions for state and local plans could increase substantially. While the totals would differ plan by plan, the use of a lower discount rate would by itself raise annual contributions substantially, as noted above. In addition, however, a shorter amortization period would dramatically increase annual amortization payments. Biggs (2016) finds that applying corporate pension discount rates and amortization periods to state and local pensions would increase the average total employer contribution in 2015 from 24 percent of employee wages to 105 percent of wages.

Even a decade past the Great Recession of 2008, a large number of state and local governments were failing to make their full contributions, even using accounting standards that require substantially lower contributions than do federal regulations for corporate pensions. Applying private sector standards that would roughly quadruple annual contributions would only worsen that problem. Thus, pension reforms may focus more on reducing pension costs than on better funding of existing benefit levels.

In this context, the retirement plans made available for federal employees could potentially serve as a model. However, several important caveats need to be borne in mind. Up through the mid-1980s, the federal government offered its employees only a defined benefit pension. These employees were not covered by Social Security, nor did they participate in a defined contribution, 401(k)-style retirement plan. This is similar to how some state and local governments provide retirement benefits today; most provide only a defined benefit pension and Social Security, and a substantial number of state and local government employees are not even covered by Social Security.

However, beginning in 1987, all newly hired federal employees were covered under a new system which provided the combination of Social Security coverage, a scaled-down defined benefit pension called the Federal Employees Retirement System and a defined contribution plan known as the Thrift Savings Plan. Relative to the previous defined benefit plan, which offered a benefit equal to approximately 2 percent of final earnings multiplied by years of service, the Federal Employees Retirement System offers a benefit multiplier of only 1 percent of final pay. For this, most current federal employees pay 0.8 percent of annual wages. In addition, federal employees may receive an employer match to contributions they make to the defined contribution Thrift Savings Plans. The federal government contributes 1 percent of pay to the Thrift Savings Plan regardless of the employee's own contributions; then matches the next 3 percent of pay dollar-for-dollar; then offers a 50 percent match on the next 2 percent of pay contributed to the plan.

Recently, at least one state has moved to a mixed DB–DC model that is similar to that the one offered to federal government employees. In 2017

Pennsylvania enacted legislation that would offer newly hired employees a choice of several pension options (Independent Fiscal Office 2017). One would be purely defined contribution, with employees contributing 7.5 percent of pay and receiving a 3.5 percent employer contribution. Employees also could choose from one of two hybrid plans. In the first, employees would contribute 5.5 percent of salary to the DB plan while receiving a benefit equal to 1.25 percent of final salary, multiplied by years of service. In addition, the employee would contribute 2.75 percent of salary to the defined contribution plan, without an employer match. Alternately, the employee could contribute 5.0 percent of salary to a DB plan with a 1.0 percent multiplier, plus 3.0 percent of salary to the DC plan. In addition, the employee contribution rate to the defined benefit plans could be altered up or down by up to 3 percentage points if the investment return on the DB plan over the most recent ten years was greater than 1 percentage point below or above the assumed rate of 7.5 percent. This risk-sharing provision reduces the sensitivity of employer contributions to changes in the long-term investment return by about one-half.

Nevertheless, the overall cost of Pennsylvania's reformed pension system remains high when employer costs are valued using a discount rate appropriate to the risk of the benefits being offered. Assuming a 3 percent discount rate, the normal cost of the reformed system, including employer matching contributions to the defined contribution accounts, would rise to about 14 percent of payroll. That amount is nearly five times the median private sector employer contribution to employees' 401(k)-style retirement plans (BLS 2014). Thus, even when traditional pension benefits are trimmed and risk is shared between government and employees, public sector retirement plans remain expensive relative to their private sector counterparts.

This should not be surprising, since even the reformed federal retirement system is not inexpensive. The Congressional Budget Office (Falk 2012) found that the federal government's costs of maintaining the two-tier federal employee retirement system totaled 20.7 percent of employee wages, with 16.2 percent funding the defined benefit Federal Employees Retirement System plan and 4.5 percent of wages contributed to the defined contribution Thrift Savings Plan. According to the Congressional Budget Office, this cost is nearly three times the 7.8 percent of pay that similarly qualified employees in large private sector businesses receive from their employers. Relative to the median employer DC plan contribution of 3 percent of pay found by the Bureau of Labor Statistics, the relative cost difference for the federal government is even larger.

DEFINED CONTRIBUTION MODELS

A more radical change would be for public employees to follow private sector workers in transitioning from defined benefit to defined contribution retirement plans. Even assuming an employer contribution substantially higher than the 3 percent of wages rate that is common in the private sector, total government pension contributions could fall substantially compared with current levels. However, the timing of that decline depends upon a number of factors. The first is how quickly employees are shifted to DC plans. A "hard freeze," in which both current and future employees are enrolled in a DC retirement plan, would freeze accrued benefit liabilities in place and lead to a relatively rapid reduction in pension costs. A "soft freeze," in which current employees continue to accrue benefits in the existing DB plan, while only new hires are enrolled in DC plans, would eventually reach the same level of annual cost savings but would take a substantially greater period of time to reach that point.

The second factor is the level of unfunded liabilities under the government's current DB plan. Shifting employees to a new DC plan reduces or eliminates the accrual of future DB plan liabilities, but does not directly reduce liabilities that already have been accrued. Thus, the DB plan sponsor would still need to pay off the DB plan's remaining unfunded liabilities. The principle advantage of a DC retirement plan is to reduce the ongoing costs of providing retirement benefits to employees, not to eliminate unfunded liabilities that already have accrued.

One concern regarding a shift from DB to DC pensions is that such a change would endanger the retirement security of public employees. To be sure, any reform that reduced government pension costs would either reduce employees' future retirement benefits or demand that employees contribute more toward their pensions. However, many public employees currently receive pension benefits that, in combination with Social Security, are well in excess of levels generally regarded as necessary to maintain those individuals' pre-retirement standard of living (Biggs 2014b).

Moreover, it does not appear that the economy-wide shift from DB to DC retirement plans has reduced savings in the United States. Figure 7.4 uses Federal Reserve Board data to represent combined employer pension and household retirement savings as a percentage of personal incomes. From 1945 through 1975 – the year in which employee participation in defined benefit plans peaked as a percentage of the workforce – total retirement savings rose from 31 to 70 percent of personal incomes. The most prominent DC plan, the 401(k), was formally introduced in 1979 and gained market share through the 1980s and 1990s. From 1975 to 2015, total retirement savings further increased from 70 to 189 percent of personal

percent

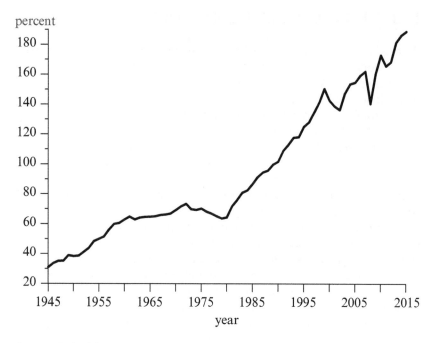

Source: Federal Reserve Board data.

*Figure 7.4   US employer pension assets and household retirement saving,
as a percentage of personal income, 1945–2015*

incomes. While it is impossible say what is the optimal level of savings relative to the incomes that such savings must eventually replace in retirement,
it seems clear that the shift from DB to DC pensions has not slowed down,
and may have accelerated, the rate of increase in retirement savings. In
most cases, both employers and employees contribute to 401(k)-type plans,
whereas employees did not contribute to private sector defined benefit
plans. This could account for some of the increase in retirement savings in
recent decades.

CONCLUSIONS

State and local governments face increasing pressures from the rising
and increasingly volatile costs of public employee pensions. Lawmakers
increased pension benefits during the strong economy of the late 1990s,
but face legal restrictions on clawing back those benefit enhancements as

the economy has slowed and investment returns have fallen below assumed levels. Governments have increased contributions, which places pressure on other budget priorities, but often have not made the full contributions required to return their plans to full funding. To reduce contribution costs, state and local pensions have increased investment risk-taking, relying upon unusual accounting rules that allow US state and local plans, unlike most other pensions, to calculate the liability value of guaranteed benefits using the assumed return on a risky portfolio of assets. The result of greater risk-taking, however, is increased volatility of required employer contributions.

Some policymakers have considered reforms that would reduce the costs and risks of public employee pensions. Incremental reforms could include: more conservative funding standards similar to those required for US corporate pensions, although these would require dramatic near-term contribution increases; a shift to a two-tier system of a scaled-back defined benefit plan and a supplemental defined contribution plan, similar to the system offered to federal government employees; or a full shift to defined contribution pensions, with the time path of savings based upon whether the change was limited to newly hired employees or applied to current employees.

NOTES

1. The 7.5 percent average assumed return in Table 7.1 is calculated on a plan-weighted basis. On an asset-weighted basis, the average assumed return would be slightly higher.
2. Equal to the current 2.5 percent yield on 20-year US Treasury securities, plus a 50 basis point increase to account for the liquidity premium paid on Treasuries that is not applicable to non-tradable public pension liabilities.
3. In Canada, unfunded pension liabilities for public plans are amortized over 15 years. In the Netherlands, a pension that falls below 105 percent funding must produce a plan to return to 120 percent funding within ten years.

REFERENCES

Actuarial Standards Board (2016), *Report of the Pension Task Force of the Actuarial Standards Board*, Washington, DC: Actuarial Standards Board, available at www.actuarialstandardsboard.org.

Aubry, Jean-Pierre, Anqi Chen and Alicia H. Munnell (2017a), "A first look at alternative investments and public pensions," State and Local Pension Plans 55, Boston, MA: Center for Retirement Research at Boston College, available at https://crr.bc.edu.

Aubry, Jean-Pierre, Caroline V. Crawford and Alicia H. Munnell (2017b), "State and local pension plan funding sputters in FY 2016," State and Local Pension

Plans 56, Boston, MA: Center for Retirement Research, available at https://crr.bc.edu.

Biggs, Andrew G. (2013), "The multiplying risks of public employee pensions to state and local government budgets," *AEI Economic Perspectives*, December, available at https://www.aei.org/research-products/report/the-multiplying-risks-of-public-employee-pensions-to-state-and-local-government-budgets.

Biggs, Andrew G. (2014a), "The public pension quadrilemma: the intersection of investment risk and contribution risk," *Journal of Retirement*, **2**(1), 115–27.

Biggs, Andrew G. (2014b), "Not so modest: pension benefits for full-career state government employees," *AEI Economic Perspectives* (March), Washington, DC: American Enterprise Institute, available at www.aei.org.

Biggs, Andrew G. (2015), "The public pension funding trap," *Wall Street Journal* (May 31).

Biggs, Andrew G. (2016), "How much would it cost for state and local governments to actually fully fund their pensions?" *Forbes* (April 1), available at www.forbes.com.

Bureau of Labor Statistics (BLS) (2014), National Compensation Survey, Table 52, "Savings and thrift plans: maximum potential employer contribution, private industry workers," update available at www.bls.gov.

Bureau of Labor Statistics (BLS) (2016), National Compensation Survey, Table 2, "Retirement benefits: access, participation, and take-up rates; state and local government workers" (March 2016), update available at www.bls.gov.

Employee Benefit Research Institute (EBRI) (2015), "FAQs about benefits – retirement issues. What are the trends in US retirement plans?," Washington, DC: Employee Benefit Research Institute, available at www.ebri.org.

Falk, Justin (2012), "Comparing benefits and total compensation in the federal government and the private sector," CBO Working Paper 2012-04, Washington, DC: Congressional Budget Office.

Independent Fiscal Office, State of Pennsylvania (2017), "Actuarial Note Transmittal, Amendments 01354 and 01558 to Senate Bill 1," Harrisburg, PA: Pennsylvania Independent Fiscal Office, available at www.senatorbaker.com/wpcontent/uploads/sites/28/2017/06/SB-1-Actuarial-Note-Transmittal.pdf.

Monahan, Amy B. (2012), "Statutes as contracts? The 'California Rule' and its impact on public pension reform," *Iowa Law Review*, **97**(4), 1029–83.

Pew Charitable Trusts (2017), *State Public Pension Funds Increase Use of Complex Investments*, Washington, DC: Pew Charitable Trusts, available at www.pewtrusts.org.

Ponds, Eduard, Clara Severinson and Juan Yermo (2011), "Funding in public sector pension plans: international evidence," OECD Working Papers on Finance, Insurance and Private Pensions 8, Paris: Organisation for Economic Co-operation and Development.

Society of Actuaries (2014), *Report of the Blue Ribbon Panel on Public Pension Plan Funding*, Schaumburg, IL: Society of Actuaries, available at www.soa.org.

Van der Wal, Dirk (2014), "The measurement of international pension obligations: have we harmonised enough?", DNB Working Papers 424, The Hague: Netherlands Central Bank, Research Department, available at https://ideas.repec.org/p/dnb/dnbwpp/424.html.

Walsh, Mary (2014), "No smoke, no mirrors: the Dutch pension plan," *New York Times* (October 11).

8. Fiscal implications of the 2015 government employees pension reform in Korea

Dohyung Kim, Taesuk Lee and Yongok Choi

INTRODUCTION

The 2015 reform of the Government Employees Pension System (GEPS) has been acclaimed as one of the major achievements of the incumbent government at the time. In 2016, a year after the reform, the Ministry of Personnel Management took the unusual step of publishing a white paper assessing the 2015 reform, which was described as the most consequential measure among all rounds of GEPS reform. The white paper pointed out that the reform package reduced the projected cumulative deficits of the GEPS over the next 70 years by about 497 trillion won, an achievement truly greater than any in the previous rounds of GEPS reform in 1995, 2000 and 2009 (Ministry of Personnel Management 2016).

Detailed information on the financial consequences of the 2015 GEPS reform, however, is surprisingly difficult to obtain from publicly available sources. For example, the white paper, the only source publicly available on the actuarial projections on post-reform development of the GEPS, contains just one appendix table documenting the reduction in the projected deficits (Ministry of Personnel Management 2016: 309). An official report on the financial status of the GEPS does contain another table on the changes in the projected overall government burden of the GEPS, but the report has not been publicly disclosed (Government Employees Pension Service 2015b).

This opacity is a major obstacle for understanding the nature of the GEPS reform and hence for careful assessment of the reform. We find only a handful of research attempts to evaluate the pension reform, and these qualitative studies had to keep the discussion on the financial impact of the reform minimal, as they were able to obtain information solely from the two tables mentioned above (Lee and Kim 2015; Jung and Kim 2015).

Using the actuarial model developed in Lee et al. (2016), this chapter presents the actuarial projections on the post-reform developments of the GEPS, focusing on the total government expenditure of the GEPS as a measure for the overall fiscal burden of the GEPS. Furthermore, we quantify the consequences of each reform measure included in the comprehensive reform package to better understand the projected fiscal outcomes.

We confirm the official projections that the 2015 reform will substantially decrease the deficits (40.5 percent) over the next 70 years, but also note that the overall fiscal burden due to the GEPS, which includes subsidies for closing the deficits, retirement allowances and the government's matching contributions, will remain substantial over the same projection period. Our analysis on the marginal impact of individual measures in the reform package reveals that about a third of the reduced pre-reform deficits (hence government subsidies) are simply replaced by the increased post-reform government matching contributions, leaving the annual fiscal burden sizeable even after the reform, which amounts to 0.85 percent of gross domestic product (GDP) over the next 70 years.

The next section briefly describes the structure and the evolution of the GEPS. The third section explains the background of the 2015 reform and describe the reform measures. The fourth section presents the 70-year projections on several outcomes of the GEPS to assess the financial and fiscal impact of the reform, followed by conclusions.

THE GOVERNMENT EMPLOYEES PENSION SYSTEM IN KOREA

On January 1, 1960, the GEPS was introduced as the first public pension in Korea by amendment of a set of clauses in the Government Employees Act, which governs both the government employees and soldiers. Two years later, a separate pension system for government employees was established based on the 1962 Government Employees Pension System Act.

Although ancillary, the clauses in the 1960 Act are notable because they included many anticipatory design features, which were repealed or changed subsequently but eventually reinstated in the later reforms. First, the 1960 Act specified the pensionable age of 60, which was abolished in the 1962 Act. This removal generated early retirement of government employees who enjoyed the full benefits without any adjustment until the pensionable age of 60 was reintroduced in the 1995 reform for those newly employed. Second, in the 1960 Act, the benefits were calculated based on the average lifetime earnings, which was changed into a final-salary benefit calculation in the 1962 Act. More than 40 years passed before the benefit

percent of taxable income

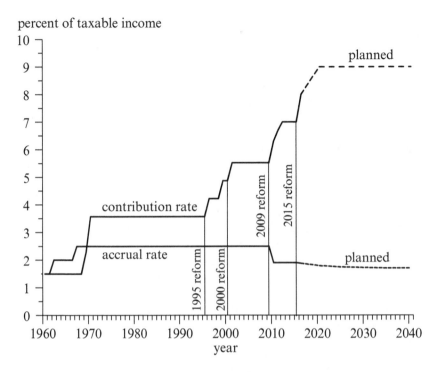

Source: GEPS (2015a) and 2015 Government Employees Pension Act data.

Figure 8.1   *Contribution and accrual rates of the government employees*
             pension in Korea, 1960–2040

calculation based on average lifetime earnings was reintroduced in the
2009 reform. Lastly, the government's contributions needed to just match
the employees' contributions in the 1960 Act, whereas the government
contributions were calculated as a share of the budget after the 1962 Act.
This change lead to government contributions consistently higher than
employee contributions, which has never been rectified.

The period between the 1962 Act and the 1995 pension reform can be
characterized by benefit expansion as can be seen in Figure 8.1, showing
the evolution of the contribution rate and the accrual rate as percentages
of taxable income during 1960–2040. The 1962 and 1966 Acts raised the
accrual rate from 1.5 percent in 1960 to 2 percent and then 2.5 percent,
respectively, which remained unchanged for more than four decades up
to the 2009 reform. There were two rounds of increase in the contribution
rate in 1969 and 1970 to finance the increased accrual rate in the 1960s
and the introduction of the option for a lump-sum claim of benefits in

1970. In 1980, the GEPS also expanded its coverage by making temporary government workers eligible.

At the beginning, the GEPS was designed as a fully funded defined benefit system to which the government and the employees contributed in equal proportions of the salary. Due to generous benefits and low contributions before 1995, the pension system began operating at a deficit in 1993. With the depletion of the pension fund in 2000, the system permanently transited to a pay-as-you-go system. Among the several causes behind the depletion of the pension fund, this unsustainable cost–benefit structure explains more than 60 percent of the unfunded debt of the GEPS (Yoo et al. 2014).

The deficits of the GEPS in 1993 led to the 1995 pension reform, which raised the contribution rate, and reintroduced the pensionable age of 60 as well as an early retirement pension. Even with these reform measures, the financial status of the GEPS did not improve but worsened quickly with the massive forced retirement of government employees in the aftermath of the 1997 Asian crisis. In the face of imminent pension deficits that were not covered by the existing fund, the 2000 reform provided an explicit guarantee that any deficit in the GEPS would be financed from general taxes.

The 2000 reform did include some modest measures that can improve the financial status of the system, such as raising the contribution rate and benefit indexation to inflation instead of wage growth. However, the latter was effectively nullified by a measure in 2003 (Choi 2010). Not surprisingly, the government subsidies grew fast to close mounting pension deficits. According to the projections before the 2009 reform, the subsidies would have amounted to 2 percent of GDP in 2050 and 2.57 percent in 2070, severely threatening the fiscal soundness of the government (Kim and Moon 2011). In consequence, the 2009 pension reform raised the contribution rate further and decreased the accrual rate for the first time in the history of the GEPS. The government was able to cut the accrual rate from 2.5 percent to 1.9 percent largely because the disparity in benefits between the GEPS and the National Pension[1] became much more pronounced by the 2007 reform of the National Pension, which allowed a gradual decrease in the accrual rate to 1 percent by 2028.

THE 2015 REFORM

Background

There are two major concerns behind the 2015 reform. First, the deteriorating financial status generated by past promises was not corrected by the reform measures in 2009, which just modified promises for the future. Moreover, the system dependency ratio, shown in Table 8.1, kept rising through 2015 as life expectancy improved. In consequence, the pension deficits grew fast again, as can be seen in Figure 8.2. The government subsidies closing the financial gap was projected to exceed 17 trillion won in 2039, which would have amounted to 0.71 percent of GDP in 2039 or 4 percent of the actual 2015 government budget.

Second, the disparity in benefits between the GEPS and the National Pension remained substantial even after the 2009 GEPS reform. The statutory accrual rate of the GEPS in 2015 was about twice as large as that of the National Pension, and the replacement rate of the GEPS was 50 percent higher than the National Pension's. Table 8.2 shows that the accrual rate for government employees is higher than that of the private employees for the average worker (monthly taxable income of 2.0 million won), and the disparity is even larger when the income level is higher. The disparity cannot be fully explained by either the higher contribution rate of the GEPS or the absence of the retirement pension for the government employees (Lee and Kim 2015).

Reform Measures

The concern for the sustainability of the GEPS and the disparity between the GEPS and the National Pension led to several measures implemented in the 2015 reform. The major measures and their expected effects on the revenues and the expenditure of the GEPS are listed in Table 8.3. Revenue-increasing measures include the gradual increase in the contribution rate from 7 percent of the taxable income in 2015 to 9 percent in 2020 (R1) and extending the maximum years of contribution from 30–33 years to 36 years (R7), although the latter will also increase the pension cost in the long run.

Most of the other measures are cost-saving. The accrual rate for retirement benefits decreases gradually from 1.9 percent in 2015 to 1.7 percent in 2035 (R2). Survivors' benefits are cut from 70 percent of the retirement benefits to 60 percent for all the new recipients (R3). The pensionable age of those who were employed before 2009 increases gradually from 60 in 2015 to 65 in 2033 (R4). Lastly, the inflation indexing is suspended temporarily for the succeeding five years (R5).

Other measures exist that are intended to address equity concerns rather than sustainability concerns. For instance, the eligibility condition for a retirement pension was relaxed by reducing the minimum service years immediately from 20 years' contribution to ten years' contribution (R6). Also, redistribution was introduced for part of the accrual rate. As

Table 8.1 Demographic and financial status of the Government Employees Pension System in Korea, 1990–2015

Year	Number of contributors	Number of pensioners	Dependency ratio (%)	Revenue (billion won)	Expenditure (billion won)	Balance (billion won)	Subsidies (billion won)	Subsidies (% share of expenditure)
Prereform								
1990	843262	25396	3.0	790	724	66	—	—
1991	884648	29719	3.4	981	918	63	—	—
1992	922098	34333	3.7	1277	1210	67	—	—
1993	939674	40849	4.3	1608	1615	−7	—	—
1994	948151	48016	5.1	1752	1935	−183	—	—
1995	957882	56343	5.9	1999	2637	−639	—	—
1995 reform								
1996	971303	63693	6.6	2476	2432	44	—	—
1997	981759	72889	7.4	2731	2808	−76	—	—
1998	952154	89322	9.4	3316	5070	−1753	—	—
1999	913891	128940	14.1	4563	7315	−2752	—	—
2000	909155	150463	16.5	3437	4383	−946	—	—
2000 reform								
2001	913192	160721	17.6	3459	3519	−60	60	1.7
2002	930835	169915	18.3	3951	3574	378	0	0.0
2003	947616	181726	19.2	4359	4414	−55	55	1.2
2004	964593	195310	20.2	4752	4926	−174	174	3.5
2005	986339	218006	22.1	5290	5899	−610	610	10.3
2006	1009145	236274	23.4	5530	6178	−648	648	10.5
2007	1021771	255565	25.0	5816	6805	−989	989	14.5
2008	1030256	279766	27.2	6400	7829	−1429	1429	18.3
2009	1047897	293096	28.0	5728	7631	−1903	1903	24.9

2009 reform								
2010	1 052 407	311 429	29.6	7116	8423	−1307	1307	15.5
2011	1 057 958	326 509	30.9	7581	8939	−1358	1358	15.2
2012	1 064 472	348 493	32.7	8656	10 352	−1696	1696	16.4
2013	1 072 610	366 482	34.2	8764	10 762	−1998	1998	18.6
2014	1 081 147	395 630	36.6	9987	12 542	−2555	2555	20.4
2015	1 093 038	426 068	39.0	10 604	13 677	−3073	3073	22.5

Source: GEPS (2015a).

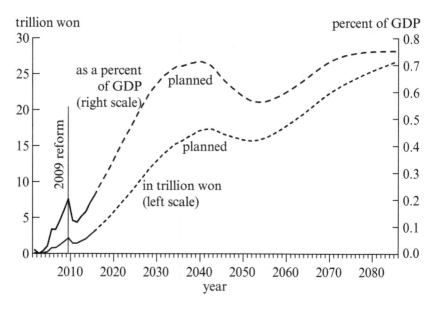

Figure 8.2   *Government subsidies for the government employees pension*
                before the 2015 reform, 2001–85

Table 8.2   *Accrual rates for private employees and government employees*
               by income level in Korea

Monthly taxable income	Private sector			Government employees		
	National pension	Retirement pension	Total	Retirement benefits	Retirement allowances	Total
2.0 million won	1.00	0.50	1.50	1.90	0.20	2.10
3.0 million won	0.83	0.50	1.33	1.90	0.20	2.10
4.5 million won	0.67	0.50	1.17	1.90	0.20	2.10
6.0 million won	0.50	0.50	1.00	1.90	0.20	2.10

Note: The contribution rates are 4.5% for private employees and 7% for government employees. It is assumed that employees contribute for 30 years.

Source: Lee and Kim (2015: 833, Table 2.4).

can be seen in Table 8.4, these changes made the structure of the GEPS more like that of the National Pension, except that there is no explicit government guarantee for the National Pension. This post-reform parallel structure opens a possibility to integrate the GEPS in the future

Table 8.3 Reform measures in Korea and expected effects, pre- and post-2015

Reform measures	Pre-2015	Post-2015	Expected financial impact
Raising contribution rate (R1)	7%	9%	higher revenue
Reducing the accrual rate for retirement benefits (R2)	1.9%	1.7%	lower expenditure
Reducing survivors' benefits (R3)	60–70%	60%	lower expenditure
Raising pensionable age (R4)	60 years	65 years	lower expenditure
Suspending inflation indexing for five years (R5)	CPI	2016–20	lower expenditure
Reducing minimum service year (R6)	20 years	10 years	–
Raising maximum years of contribution (R7)	30–33 years	36 years	higher revenue and expenditure
Lowering the ceiling for taxable income (R8)	180%	160%	lower revenue and expenditure

Source: Data from the 2015 Government Employees Pension Act.

Table 8.4 Comparison between the GEPS and the national pension

Pension rules	Pre-reform GEPS	Post-reform GEPS	National Pension
Minimum service years for pension entitlement	20	10	10
Maximum service years for contribution	33	36	42
Pensionable age	60/65	65	65
Accrual rate for retirement benefits	1.9	1.7	1.0
Survivors' benefits	70%	60%	60%
Redistribution	no	yes	yes
Explicit government guarantee	yes	yes	no

Source: Data from the 2009 and 2015 Government Employees Pension Acts and the 2007 National Pension Act.

into the multi-tiered retirement income system which consists of the Basic Pension,[2] the National Pension, retirement pensions and individual savings accounts, as has been recently done in Japan (Sakamoto 2011).

EVALUATING THE 2015 GEPS PENSION REFORM

In this section, we evaluate the fiscal consequences of the 2015 reform by focusing on the developments of the government subsidies and overall fiscal burden from the GEPS. Before examining the fiscal implications of the pension reform, we first evaluate the financial impact of the 2015 reform. Then, we document the developments of the subsidies and overall fiscal burden between 2016 and 2085. In particular, we explain the divergent developments of the subsidies and overall fiscal burden by decomposing the aggregate fiscal impact into the marginal impacts of individual measures included in the 2015 reform package. For a decomposition analysis, we consider the changes in the projections of the matching contributions, deficits (subsidies) and the overall fiscal burden as measures for fiscal outcomes. For simplicity, we do not consider the changes in the retirement allowances separately, as they are barely affected by the reform measures (Figure 8.3), which do not generally alter the number of participants.

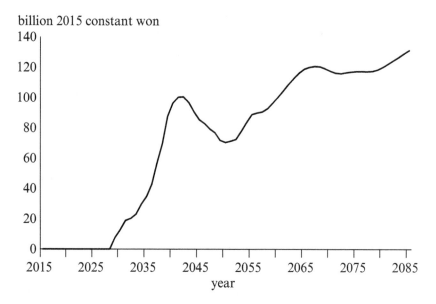

*Figure 8.3   Projected government employee retirement allowance in Korea
            at the maximum service year, following the 2015 reform,
            2015–85*

Table 8.5   Assumptions for projections

Key assumptions	Source
Demographic:	
Number of government employees	Estimates from historical records
Death rate	National life table
Retirement rate	Estimates from historical records
Economic:	
Wage growth	Ministry of Finance
Inflation	Ministry of Finance
Rate of return	Ministry of Finance
Program-specific	2013 historical data

Note: Baseline projections used in the analysis rely on the standard median assumptions that have been adopted by the official government projections. The full range of sensitivity analysis can be found in Lee et al. (2016). The projected deficits and total government expenditure can be substantially larger than the baseline projections, given the well-known fact that death rates are much lower among government employees than among the general population.

Source: Lee et al. (2016).

Financial Impact of the 2015 Reform

We first evaluate the financial prospects of the GEPS after the 2015 reform using several standard financial measures such as income rate (r^I), cost rate (r^C) and deficit rate (r^D), which are defined as $r_t^D = \frac{REV_t}{GS_t}$, $r_t^C = \frac{EXP_t}{GS_t}$ and $r_t^D = \frac{DEF_t}{GS_t}$, where GS_t denotes the gross salary at year t, REV_t the pension revenue at year t (participant's contributions and government's matching contributions excluding the government's subsidies), EXP_t the pension expenditure at year t, DEF_t and the pension deficits at year t defined as $(REV_t - EXP_t)$. For assumptions, see Table 8.5.

Table 8.6 shows that the projected level of the income rate, expenditure rate and deficit rate for the years 2016 to 2085 before and after the 2015 pension reform, as well as its changes (the delta Δ columns). For brevity, the projections in Table 8.6 are presented at five-year intervals after 2030. Columns 1, 5 and 9 show that, before the 2015 reform, the projected income rate was quite low compared with the cost rate, resulting in a high deficit rate throughout the projection period. The post-reform income rate in column 2 is about 30 percent higher than the pre-reform level, with the change gradually phasing in until around 2030 due to the gradual increase in the contribution rate as well as the maximum service year. In contrast, columns 4 and 8 show that, before and after the reform, the projected cost

Table 8.6 Projected financial status of the GEPS before and after the 2015 reform, 2016–85

Year	Income rate (%)				Cost rate (%)				Deficit rate (%)			
	Pre (1)	Post (2)	Δ (3)	%Δ (4)	Pre (5)	Post (6)	Δ (7)	%Δ (8)	Pre (9)	Post (10)	Δ (11)	%Δ (12)
2016	14.6	16.7	2.1	14.3	21.1	20.6	−0.5	−2.4	6.5	3.9	−2.6	−40.0
2017	14.6	17.2	2.6	17.9	22.0	21.0	−1.0	−4.6	7.3	3.7	−3.6	−49.1
2018	14.6	17.7	3.1	21.4	22.9	21.4	−1.5	−6.6	8.3	3.7	−4.6	−55.8
2019	14.6	18.3	3.7	25.0	23.9	21.9	−2.0	−8.4	9.3	3.6	−5.7	−61.0
2020	14.6	18.7	4.2	28.6	25.0	22.5	−2.5	−10.2	10.5	3.7	−6.7	−64.2
2021	14.4	18.6	4.1	28.6	26.0	23.4	−2.6	−9.9	11.5	4.9	−6.7	−57.9
2022	14.3	18.4	4.1	28.6	27.0	24.3	−2.6	−9.8	12.7	5.9	−6.7	−53.1
2023	14.1	18.2	4.0	28.6	27.9	25.2	−2.7	−9.6	13.7	7.0	−6.7	−48.9
2024	14.1	18.1	4.0	28.6	28.9	26.1	−2.8	−9.6	14.8	8.0	−6.8	−46.0
2025	14.1	18.1	4.0	28.6	30.2	27.3	−2.9	−9.6	16.1	9.1	−6.9	−43.2
2026	14.2	18.2	4.0	28.6	31.4	28.3	−3.0	−9.7	17.2	10.1	−7.1	−41.1
2027	14.3	18.4	4.1	28.6	32.6	29.3	−3.4	−10.3	18.3	10.9	−7.5	−40.7
2028	14.5	18.6	4.1	28.6	34.0	30.2	−3.8	−11.3	19.5	11.6	−8.0	−40.8
2029	14.6	19.2	4.6	31.3	35.1	30.9	−4.2	−12.1	20.4	11.6	−8.8	−43.1
2030	14.8	19.4	4.6	30.9	36.1	31.3	−4.8	−13.2	21.3	11.9	−9.3	−43.9
2035	15.2	20.1	4.9	32.1	39.0	31.3	−7.7	−19.6	23.8	11.2	−12.5	−52.8

Year												
2040	15.2	20.3	5.1	33.6	39.6	32.3	−7.2	−18.3	24.4	12.1	−12.3	−50.6
2045	15.6	20.4	4.9	31.4	37.2	33.2	−4.0	−10.7	21.6	12.7	−8.9	−41.1
2050	15.6	20.6	5.0	31.8	34.7	32.8	−1.9	−5.5	19.0	12.2	−6.9	−36.1
2055	15.5	20.6	5.0	32.2	33.9	32.0	−1.9	−5.6	18.4	11.5	−6.9	−37.6
2060	15.4	20.5	5.1	32.8	34.9	32.6	−2.2	−6.4	19.4	12.1	−7.3	−37.6
2065	15.4	20.4	5.0	32.8	36.2	33.6	−2.6	−7.2	20.8	13.1	−7.6	−36.8
2070	15.5	20.5	5.0	32.3	37.3	34.4	−2.9	−7.9	21.9	13.9	−7.9	−36.3
2075	15.5	20.5	5.0	32.3	37.5	34.4	−3.1	−8.3	22.0	13.9	−8.1	−36.8
2080	15.5	20.5	5.0	32.1	37.2	34.1	−3.1	−8.3	21.7	13.6	−8.1	−37.2
2085	15.5	20.5	5.0	32.1	36.8	33.8	−3.0	−8.2	21.3	13.3	−8.0	−37.7

Note: Income, cost and deficit rates are defined as revenue, expenditure and deficit as percentages of the gross payroll. Delta (Δ) denotes the difference between the post- and pre-reform rates, and %Δ the percentage change from the pre-reform rate.

rate does not change as much in proportion as did the projected income rate, except for the period around 2035, where the effect of an increase in pensionable age kicks in. Although these features seen in columns 4 and 8 lead some authors to conclude that the 2015 reform was "predominantly revenue-increasing rather than cost-saving" (Lee and Kim 2016), a careful comparison between the level changes in income and cost (columns 3 and 7) shows that the magnitudes of the changes in the level of revenue and cost are quite similar to each other, contributing in comparable proportions to the reduced deficit by around 40 percent over the projected years.

Post-reform Fiscal Burden of the GEPS

In this section, we evaluate the fiscal impact of the 2015 reform by examining the development of the government subsidies for the GEPS as well as the overall fiscal burden from the GEPS. The overall fiscal burden from the GEPS consists of three components. The matching contributions of the government and the retirement allowances are the responsibilities of the government as the employer of civil servants. In contrast, the government subsidies for closing the deficits in the GEPS are an ad hoc guarantee that is provided by the 2000 GEPS Act, which mandates that all the deficits of the GEPS since 2001 are to be financed by government subsidies. Hence, the projected deficits and subsidies are identical in magnitude with opposite signs.

Table 8.7 presents the projected subsidies and overall fiscal burden over the same 70-year projection period before and after the 2015 reform. Columns 1–6 show that, following the 2015 reform, the cumulative annual subsidies over 2016–85 will decrease from 1193.2 trillion won to 710 trillion won; a 40.5 percent cut from the pre-reform level or about 18 percentage points of real GDP. Notice, however, that the cumulative savings in overall fiscal burden following the reform are smaller in size than those in subsidies over the same period. Columns 7–12 show, that following the 2015 reform, the cumulative annual fiscal burden over 2016–85 will decrease from 1942.2 trillion won to 1620 trillion won; a 16.6 percent cut from the pre-reform level or about 12.2 percentage points of real GDP. Although the expected savings in subsidies by the pension reform were substantial, the projections suggest that about a third of the cumulative savings in subsidies during 2016–85 will be achieved by shifting the burden from subsidies to government's contributions.

To see this more clearly, we graphically present the contributions to the projected outcome measure of the individual measures included in the 2015 reform package. For each reform measure R1 to R8, the contribution is calculated by the changes in outcomes when a reform measure was

Table 8.7 Projected subsidies and overall fiscal burden before and after the 2015 reform in Korea

Year	Subsidies						Overall fiscal burden					
	Pre-reform		Post-reform		Differences		Pre-reform		Post-reform		Differences	
	tr. won (1)	%GDP (2)	tr. won (3)	%GDP (4)	tr. won (5)	%GDP (6)	tr. won (7)	%GDP (8)	tr. won (9)	%GDP (10)	tr. won (11)	%GDP (12)
2016	3.7	0.25	2.2	0.15	-1.46	-0.10	10.16	0.68	9.34	0.63	-0.82	-0.05
2017	4.2	0.27	2.1	0.14	-2.06	-0.13	10.86	0.71	9.61	0.62	-1.25	-0.08
2018	4.8	0.30	2.1	0.13	-2.67	-0.17	11.57	0.73	9.88	0.62	-1.69	-0.11
2019	5.4	0.33	2.1	0.13	-3.30	-0.20	12.39	0.76	10.25	0.63	-2.14	-0.13
2020	6.1	0.37	2.2	0.13	-3.94	-0.23	13.21	0.79	10.60	0.63	-2.60	-0.16
2021	6.8	0.40	2.9	0.17	-3.96	-0.23	13.90	0.81	11.28	0.65	-2.62	-0.15
2022	7.6	0.43	3.5	0.20	-4.01	-0.23	14.62	0.83	11.95	0.68	-2.68	-0.15
2023	8.2	0.46	4.2	0.23	-4.02	-0.22	15.26	0.85	12.56	0.70	-2.70	-0.15
2024	9.0	0.49	4.8	0.26	-4.12	-0.22	16.21	0.88	13.42	0.73	-2.79	-0.15
2025	9.7	0.52	5.5	0.29	-4.21	-0.22	17.27	0.92	14.39	0.77	-2.87	-0.15
2030	13.2	0.64	7.4	0.36	-5.79	-0.28	21.24	1.03	17.01	0.82	-4.22	-0.20
2035	15.6	0.69	7.4	0.33	-8.23	-0.37	23.70	1.06	17.26	0.77	-6.44	-0.29
2040	17.2	0.71	8.5	0.35	-8.71	-0.36	26.20	1.08	19.55	0.81	-6.65	-0.27
2045	16.6	0.64	9.8	0.38	-6.8	-0.26	26.0	1.01	21.3	0.83	-4.7	-0.18
2050	15.8	0.58	10.1	0.37	-5.7	-0.21	26.3	0.96	22.9	0.84	-3.4	-0.12

Table 8.7 (continued)

Year	Subsidies						Overall fiscal burden					
	Pre-reform		Post-reform		Differences		Pre-reform		Post-reform		Differences	
	tr. won (1)	%GDP (2)	tr. won (3)	%GDP (4)	tr. won (5)	%GDP (6)	tr. won (7)	%GDP (8)	tr. won (9)	%GDP (10)	tr. won (11)	%GDP (12)
2055	16.2	0.57	10.1	0.35	−6.1	−0.21	27.6	0.97	24.1	0.84	−3.6	−0.13
2060	18.0	0.61	11.2	0.38	−6.8	−0.23	30.2	1.02	26.1	0.88	−4.1	−0.14
2065	20.3	0.66	12.8	0.42	−7.5	−0.24	32.9	1.07	28.2	0.92	−4.7	−0.15
2070	22.6	0.72	14.4	0.46	−8.2	−0.26	35.7	1.13	30.5	0.97	−5.3	−0.17
2075	24.2	0.74	15.3	0.47	−8.9	−0.27	38.1	1.16	32.3	0.99	−5.8	−0.18
2080	25.6	0.75	16.0	0.47	−9.5	−0.28	40.5	1.19	34.3	1.00	−6.2	−0.18
2085	26.7	0.75	16.7	0.47	−10.1	−0.28	42.9	1.21	36.4	1.02	−6.5	−0.18
Sum	1193.2	43.73	710.0	25.59	−483.2	−18.14	1942.2	71.89	1619.9	59.68	−322.4	−12.21

Note: The overall fiscal burden includes government's matching contributions, retirement allowances, and subsidies. The projected amount is expressed in 2015-constant trillion won and relative to real GDP. The "sum" denotes the cumulative sum over the all years between 2016 and 2085. tr. won = trillion won. %GDP = percentage of GDP.

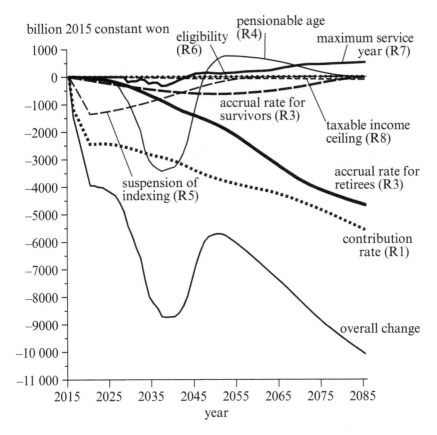

Figure 8.4   Projected subsidies following the 2015 reform, 2015–85

introduced, with all the other measures held constant at the pre-reform level. This can be thought of as a marginal effect of a reform measure, and for a given year, the total sum of the individual effects of R1–R8 years roughly equals the overall change when all the measures were introduced. The sum of marginal effects, however, does not add up exactly to the aggregate effect of the reform package because of the interactive effect among reform measures, though its size is limited.

Figure 8.4 shows the contributions of individual reform measures to the savings in government subsidies. The saving from the increased contribution (R1) stands out, while the saving from the reduced accrual rate for retirees (R3) is also substantial. The rise in pensionable age (R4) contributes to reduced subsidies only in the medium run as the rise is not uniform across cohorts. It is interesting to note that, although the

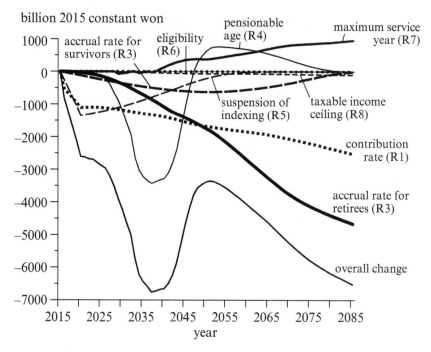

Figure 8.5　Projected overall fiscal burden following the 2015 reform, 2015–85

temporary suspension of indexing for five years (R5) is an emergency measure for containing the rising fiscal cost in the short run, it does have a persistent financial impact in the long run as it permanently lowers the base (primary benefit amount) of all the existing pensioners, based on which the subsequent benefits will be calculated.

Similarly, Figure 8.5 shows the contributions of individual reform measures to the savings in the total government expenditures. A comparison between Figures 8.2 and 8.4 shows that the difference comes from the higher contribution rate (R1) and maximum service years (R7), the only measures that affect the revenue among the reform measures. Indeed, the differences between subsidies and total government expenditures are entirely explained by these two measures that affect the government's matching contributions, as can be seen in Figure 8.6. These findings suggest that, when evaluating the fiscal impact of reforming a public pension with an explicit guarantee such as the GEPS, focusing on expected deficits can underestimate the changes in the overall fiscal burden.

To get an idea of the size of the projected fiscal burden after the 2015

billion 2015 constant won

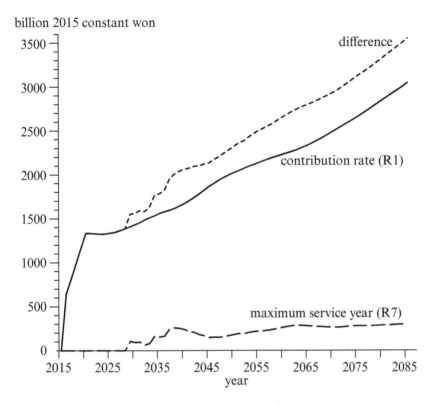

Figure 8.6   Projected matching contributions following the 2015 reform, 2015–85

reform, we present the projected subsidies and the total government expenditure for the GEPS in terms of a share of the projected government tax revenues along with those for the Basic Pension. Columns 1 and 3 in Table 8.8 show that the government subsidies for the GEPS amounts to around 4 percent of the tax revenue over 2016–60, and the total government expenditure for the GEPS to around 5 percent of the tax revenue. For comparison, we present the projected government expenditure for the Basic Pension, which provides a basic safety net for the bottom 70 percent of all the elderly in Korea. Columns 3 and 5 show that the magnitude of the fiscal burden of the GEPS is about half or a third of the fiscal burden of the Basic Pension. In terms of per pensioner expenditures presented in columns 2 and 6, the per pensioner subsidies for the retired government employees will be greater than those for the disadvantaged elderly, and the disparity will grow even larger over time.

Table 8.8 Post-reform fiscal burden of the GEPS in Korea, 2016–60

| Year | GEPS | | | | | | Basic pension | | | |
| | Subsidies | | Total fiscal expenditures | | | | Total fiscal expenditures | | | |
	Tax revenue share (%) (1)	Per capita (million won) (2)	Tax revenue share (%) (3)	Per pensioner (million won) (4)			Tax revenue share (%) (5)	Per pensioner (million won) (6)		
2016	1.6	8.5	4.0	21.7	3.4	6.5
2017	1.7	9.2	4.0	21.2	3.4	6.2
2018	1.9	10.1	3.9	20.7	3.3	6.1
2019	2.1	10.8	3.9	20.5	5.5	9.8
2020	2.3	11.7	3.9	20.2	5.7	9.6
2021	2.5	12.5	4.0	20.6	5.8	9.6
2022	2.6	13.3	4.2	21.0	5.9	9.5
2023	2.8	13.9	4.3	21.3	6.1	9.4
2024	3.0	14.6	4.4	21.9	7.4	11.0
2025	3.1	15.3	4.6	22.6	7.6	10.7
2026	3.3	15.9	4.8	23.0	7.7	10.4
2027	3.4	16.3	4.9	23.2	7.9	10.2
2028	3.6	16.8	5.0	23.4	8.0	10.0
2029	3.7	17.1	5.0	22.8	9.6	11.4
2030	3.8	17.4	4.9	22.4	9.7	11.0
2031	3.9	17.7	4.9	22.1	9.8	10.6
2032	4.0	17.8	4.8	21.5	9.9	10.1
2033	4.1	18.0	4.7	20.9	10.0	9.7
2034	4.1	18.2	4.6	20.5	11.7	10.8
2035	4.1	18.3	4.5	20.2	11.8	10.3

Year						
2036	4.1	18.4	4.6	20.3	11.9	9.9
2037	4.2	18.6	4.6	20.5	11.9	9.5
2038	4.2	18.8	4.6	20.9	11.9	9.1
2039	4.2	18.9	4.7	21.4	13.5	9.9
2040	4.2	19.0	4.7	21.5	13.4	9.5
2041	4.1	18.9	4.7	21.7	13.3	9.1
2042	4.1	18.9	4.7	21.9	13.2	8.7
2043	4.0	18.7	4.7	22.2	13.0	8.4
2044	3.9	18.5	4.7	22.7	14.6	9.2
2045	3.8	18.2	4.8	23.4	14.5	8.9
2046	3.7	18.1	4.9	24.1	14.3	8.6
2047	3.6	18.0	4.9	24.7	14.2	8.3
2048	3.5	17.8	4.9	25.1	14.0	8.0
2049	3.4	17.7	4.9	25.4	15.7	8.8
2050	3.3	17.7	4.9	25.6	15.4	8.6
2051	3.3	17.6	4.8	25.9	15.1	8.3
2052	3.3	17.7	4.8	26.1	14.8	8.1
2053	3.2	17.8	4.8	26.4	14.4	7.9
2054	3.2	18.0	4.8	26.7	16.0	8.7
2055	3.2	18.2	4.8	27.0	15.7	8.5
2056	3.3	18.4	4.8	27.3	15.4	8.3
2057	3.3	18.7	4.9	27.6	15.1	8.2
2058	3.4	19.0	4.9	27.9	14.9	8.0
2059	3.4	19.4	5.0	28.3	16.6	8.9
2060	3.5	19.7	5.0	28.6	16.4	8.8

Sources: NABO (2016) for the projections of the national tax revenue and the fiscal expenditures for the Basic Pension. Authors' projections for the GEPS.

percent of government revenue

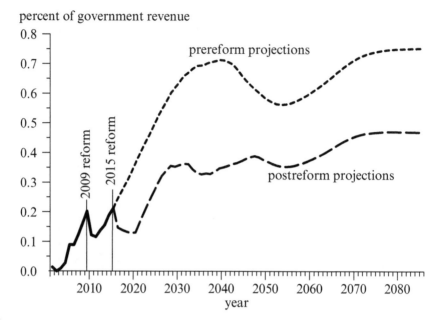

Figure 8.7   Government subsidies for the government employees pension system after the 2015 reform, 2001–85

We have seen that the GEPS will continue to impose substantial pressure on the government budget in the medium run even after the 2015 reform. As can be seen in Figure 8.7, it is interesting to note that both the 2009 and 2015 GEPS reforms coincided with subsidies, a highly visible indicator of fiscal pressure, exceeding 0.2 percent of GDP. Although the GDP share of subsidies will reach its pre-reform level as late as 2023, as some of the pre-reform subsidies are replaced by increased government matching contributions following the reform, a demand for reforming the GEPS may arise again in near future. With the mounting fiscal pressure over time, the substantial subsidies for the retired government employees will be increasingly difficult to justify politically, as shown by the comparison of the per pensioner subsidies between the GEPS and the Basic Pension.

Alternative Scenarios

Our baseline projections rely on the same assumptions as those used for the government's 2015 official projections. However, the projection assumptions are often subject to optimism bias, which may understate the actual fiscal burden. The evident optimism bias in the official projections on the GEPS can be found in the use of the demographic assumption that the life expectancy of the civil servants is not different from that of the general population, while there is ample evidence that the age-specific mortality rate of the government employees is much lower. In recent years, for instance, the age-specific death rate of the male pensioners of the GEPS was about half of that of the male population in Korea across the ages over 60 (Lee et al. 2016). Furthermore, the 2015 official projection assumptions do not reflect recent changes in the personnel management plan: specifically, that the new government would hire 134 000 additional government employees over a five-year period on top of the previous schedule of 40 000 new hires. In either case, the actual fiscal burden from the GEPS would exceed the baseline projections. Therefore, we present the projected fiscal burden based on alternative scenarios.

For the scenario analysis, we consider two alternative demographic assumptions: (1) the mortality rate of the government employees is lower than that of the general population; (2) the number of government employees increases faster than the previous schedule for the five years 2018–22. For an alternative scenario on the mortality rate, we employ the age-specific mortality rate forecasts created using the historical records on the mortality of the government employees, instead of using the life table of the general population (Choi et al. 2017). For an alternative scenario on the number of government employees, we employ the announced schedule of new hires between 2018 and 2022 (174 000 in total).

Table 8.9 shows changes in the projected overall fiscal burden (differences from the baseline post-reform projections) when an alternative demographic assumption is used. Columns 1 to 4 show that, when the government-employee–specific mortality rate is used, the projected overall fiscal burden increases substantially. The cumulative increase in the fiscal burden over the next 70 years amounts to 236 trillion won or 8.25 percentage points of real GDP, which is comparable to the savings in the fiscal burden through the 2015 reform (322 trillion won). Columns 5 to 8 show that, when the announced schedule of new hiring of government employees is fully realized, the overall fiscal burden actually decreases until 2050, as the new hires contribute to the GEPS. But eventually the burden rapidly mounts after 2050, and the cumulative increase in the overall fiscal burden will amount to 94 billion won or 2.73 percentage points of real GDP.

CONCLUDING REMARKS

It appears that the 2015 GEPS reform will entail greater financial improvements in pension finance than any previous reform was able to achieve.

Table 8.9 Projected fiscal burden based on alternative demographic assumptions in Korea, 2016–85

Year	Alternative death rate				Alternative personnel policy			
	Δ (1)	CumΔ (2)	% GDP (3)	Cum% (4)	Δ (5)	CumΔ (6)	%GDP (7)	Cum% (8)
2016	128	185	0.01	0.01	0	0	0.00	0.00
2017	199	384	0.01	0.03	0	0	0.00	0.00
2018	273	657	0.02	0.04	−38	−38	0.00	0.00
2019	347	1004	0.02	0.06	−116	−154	−0.01	−0.01
2020	419	1423	0.02	0.09	−199	−353	−0.01	−0.02
2021	504	1928	0.03	0.12	−278	−630	−0.02	−0.04
2022	596	2524	0.03	0.15	−359	−989	−0.02	−0.06
2023	690	3214	0.04	0.19	−399	−1388	−0.02	−0.08
2024	789	4003	0.04	0.23	−404	−1792	−0.02	−0.10
2025	891	4894	0.05	0.28	−415	−2208	−0.02	−0.12
2026	997	5890	0.05	0.33	−433	−2641	−0.02	−0.15
2027	1106	6997	0.06	0.39	−454	−3094	−0.02	−0.17
2028	1217	8213	0.06	0.45	−481	−3575	−0.02	−0.19
2029	1308	9521	0.06	0.51	−505	−4080	−0.02	−0.22
2030	1420	10942	0.07	0.58	−529	−4609	−0.03	−0.24
2035	1981	19722	0.09	0.99	−608	−7511	−0.03	−0.38

2040	2584	31417	0.11	1.48	−686	−10731	−0.03	−0.51
2045	3245	46292	0.13	2.07	−620	−14190	−0.02	−0.65
2050	3909	64537	0.14	2.76	114	−15439	0.00	−0.70
2055	4547	86064	0.16	3.52	1101	−11584	0.04	−0.56
2060	4860	109948	0.16	4.34	2966	−1190	0.10	−0.21
2065	4951	134519	0.16	5.15	3730	16723	0.12	0.38
2070	5013	159568	0.16	5.96	3805	35667	0.12	0.99
2075	5025	184594	0.15	6.73	3821	54715	0.12	1.58
2080	5076	209886	0.15	7.49	3918	74088	0.11	2.16
2085	5586	236435	0.16	8.25	4064	94110	0.11	2.73

Note: Δ is defined as a change from the 2015 baseline projections and expressed as 2015-constant billion won. CumΔ is a cumulative change from 2016. %GDP denotes Δ as a percentage share of real GDP and Cum% a cumulative change in the real-GDP share from 2016.

However, the reform is insufficient to contain the rising pension deficits of the GEPS in the long run. Although the reform significantly reduced pension deficits, part of the saving in subsidies is simply replaced by increased government matching contributions, which will exert pressure on the government budget just as subsidies do. Furthermore, we have seen that the baseline projections are quite sensitive to the demographic assumptions, especially the mortality rate of the government employees. Therefore, the actual fiscal burden from the GEPS may exceed the projected fiscal burden whenever the assumptions used for projection turn out to be too optimistic.

To minimize optimism bias often seen in the official projections, the government should be prepared to disclose information by allowing access to detailed information for researchers. Also, to enhance fiscal sustainability of the GEPS and hence that of the government, structural-reform proposals need to be considered in the future as a serious alternative to a piecemeal parametric reform, as was the case in the United States and Japan. These proposals may include integrating the GEPS into the National Pension as proposed by Yoo et al. (2014), with or without the individual savings accounts proposed by Moon et al. (2007).

NOTES

1. The mandatory public pension scheme for the general population, the National Pension, began in 1988 with coverage for workers of urban private sector companies with ten or more employees. It was gradually expanded during the next decade to cover smaller companies and then rural employees (farmers, fishermen and the self-employed). Finally in 1999, self-employed urban workers were included.
2. For the elderly population, the National Pension scheme was introduced too late in their lives for them to participate, and so a non-contributory pension called the Basic Old-Age Pension scheme was introduced in 2008. The bottom 70 percent (in terms of income and wealth) among people aged 65 or older were eligible for monthly benefits financed from general revenues. The scheme was turned into the Basic Pension in 2014 to increase the benefits in response to rapidly rising poverty and suicide among the elderly.

REFERENCES

Choi, Jaesik (2010), *Explaining the Government Employees Pension System*, Seoul: Government Employees Pension Service (in Korean).
Choi, Yongok, Taesuk Lee, Dohyung Kim and Shinyoung Kim (2017), *A Study on Input Premises for the GEPS Projection*, Sejong: Korea Development Institute.
Government Employees Pension Service (GEPS) (2015a), *The GEPS Statistical Yearbook*, Seoul: Government Employees Pension Service.
Government Employees Pension Service (GEPS) (2015b), *Long-term Projections*

on the *Government Employees Pension System*, Seoul: Ministry of Personnel Management (in Korean).

Jung, Changlyul and Jinsoo Kim (2015), "An evaluation of the Korean civil-service pension reform and its development plan," *Studies in Social Security*, **31**(4), 227–52 (in Korean).

Kim, Jae-Kyeong and Hyung-Pyo Moon (2011), "Pension systems for public sector employees in the Republic of Korea," PIE/CIS Discussion Paper 499, Center for Intergenerational Studies, Institute of Economic Research, Hitotsubashi University, Tokyo.

Lee, Taesuk Yongok Choi and Dohyung Kim (2016), "Actuarial modelling of public pension schemes: focusing on projection models for the government employees pension system in Korea," KDI Research Paper 2016-04, Sejing: Korea Development Institute (in Korean).

Lee, Yong Ha and Won Sup Kim (2015), "Evaluating the reform in 2015 and the new reform plan of the Government Employees Pension Scheme," *Korean Journal of Applied Statistics*, **28**(4), 827–45 (in Korean).

Ministry of Personnel Management (2016), *The White Paper on the 2015 Government Employees Pension Reform*, Seoul: Ministry of Personnel Management (in Korean).

Moon, Hyung-Pyo, Hangyong Lee, Yongha Kim, Geonsik Ryu, Jaesik Choi, et al. (2007), *Retirement Pension and Individual Savings Account for Government Employees*, Seoul: Korea Development Institute (in Korean).

National Assembly Budget Office (NABO) (2016), *Long-Term Fiscal Projections in Korea: 2015–2060*, Seoul: National Assembly Budget Office (in Korean).

Sakamoto, Junichi (2011), "Civil service pension arrangements in Japan," PIE/CIS Discussion Paper 500, Center for Intergenerational Studies, Institute of Economic Research, Hitotsubashi University, Tokyo.

Yoo, Gyungjoon, Jaesik Choi, Yongha Kim, Moonil Kwon and Sanghoon Ahn (2014), *Reform Proposals for the Government Employees Pension System*, Seoul: Korea Development Institute (in Korean).

PART IV

Fiscal accountability sector

9.   Medicare financing and affordability
Marilyn Moon

Much of the debate about Medicare's future in the United States centers on the question of whether we as a society can "afford" this program. Affordability is a concept that requires an examination of a number of measurable facts and analyses, but also slips quickly into issues of value judgments that go beyond strict economic analysis. While many analysts are uncomfortable in dealing with value judgments and thus avoid the topic altogether, an examination of at least some of the assumptions contained within that debate can be helpful in informing how an answer to the issue of affordability can be reached. Thus, this chapter examines objective measures that can assess the burdens of financing healthcare for the Medicare population. It also suggests how to put the issues in an appropriate context for discussing affordability.

BASIC PRINCIPLES

Medicare is a social insurance program established to assure that all eligible individuals (mainly people aged 65 and above) have access to acute healthcare services. Encompassed in this description are a number of elements that are essential for framing questions of affordability.

First, healthcare is viewed as an insurable event. This means that whether we are dealing with private or social insurance, there are benefits to be gained from pooling risks and smoothing the financial shocks that arise from expensive illnesses. While this would seem like a standard, non-controversial assumption, recent debates over changes to the Affordable Care Act indicate that this is not a universally accepted or understood concept (Rovner 2017). If people believe that individuals can be held accountable for a substantial share of the variation in healthcare spending, then pooling of risk becomes less acceptable. Some of the claims that "people should be able to buy only the coverage they need" comes perilously close to arguing that we can all control our healthcare spending, either by making specific choices (such as not having children or avoiding risky behaviors) or by engaging in healthy life styles that can predictably hold down a large portion of healthcare spending. Analysis in this area does not support such a conclusion, however, as only a small share of high healthcare spending can be avoided by eliminating coverage for services such as maternity care. Most of the high costs represent unpredictable events or care for chronic conditions over which individuals have little control (Cutler 2017). The value of insurance is to protect against catastrophic losses by pooling risk.

In addition, social insurance differs from private insurance in important ways: principally, by assuming that access is determined not on the basis of ability to pay but on membership in a particular defined group. That is, purchase of private insurance is limited to those who can pay the premiums; no allowances are made for differences in income or special needs. The expectation is that individuals pay for the average costs of care for the group to which they belong. Social insurance explicitly assumes that some groups – usually those with low incomes or with special needs such as healthcare conditions – will receive subsidies that give them access to the benefits. Indeed, that is one of the specific goals of social insurance. In the case of Medicare, for example, individuals pay into the system through taxation reflecting their wages and incomes, and receive benefits (when eligible) based on their need for care. Thus, some people receive Medicare even when their contributions would never be sufficient to cover the average costs of their benefits (and some pay substantially more than those average costs).

Second, Medicare was explicitly created as a "pay-as-you-go" system in which younger individuals pay taxes (both payroll taxes and general revenues) that fund the current needs of beneficiaries; primarily those aged 65 and over. While there are trust funds, they were established to help ensure stable funding with enough of a cushion to assure that revenues would be sufficient to meet needs over time. They were never intended to be accounts tied to individual contributions that would later be drawn down in benefits (Myers 1970). While Medicare (and Social Security) both benefitted from a growing population that made financing more affordable, with a large number of younger taxpayers supporting a smaller cohort of beneficiaries, there has never been a sense that each generation must be accountable for fully funding its own benefits over time. Implicitly, the system allows for some intergenerational redistribution.

Together these concepts help to clarify what types of measures are more or less valid in understanding the debate about Medicare's affordability, and they call into question some popular measures used to criticize Medicare. It is also important to note that the debate about Medicare's future is also part of a larger debate about the size and scope of the federal budget. While this can also be applied to discussions about Social Security, to a large extent, much of the debate about funding entitlements for seniors has shifted to Medicare, making it the more likely battleground for future budget cuts. That adds an additional dimension to any discussion about Medicare and cannot be readily ignored.

MEASURING MEDICARE'S FINANCIAL STATUS

How then should questions about the affordability of Medicare be framed? First, we know that Medicare is a large program that has grown rapidly since its inception in 1966, rising from 0.71 percent of gross domestic product (GDP) in 1970 to 3.63 percent in 2016 (Boards of Trustees 2017a). Medicare's growth reflects both expansion in the number of beneficiaries as older Americans have grown as a share of the population (and with the addition of the disabled in 1972), and that healthcare spending per capita has risen rapidly. This latter phenomenon is not confined to Medicare. In fact, Medicare's per capita growth has often been at a slower rate than that for private insurance for younger populations (Boccuti and Moon 2003; MedPAC 2013). Further, the rapid increase in the number of beneficiaries has been predicted since Medicare's earliest days. The baby boom generation and expanded life expectancies were both trends that were well known in 1965. And discussions about the need for increasing tax rates over time were part of the legislative debate and early planning for Medicare's needs (Myers 1970).

Often, however, the discussion about affordability centers on the fact that revenues are not growing as fast as outlays. For many policymakers, revenues are taken as fixed, and thus the predicted imbalances in funding (often centered on the Part A trust fund) are used as "proof" that benefits must be reduced. These arguments ignore or reject the possibility of greater funding for the program. While the cap on wages subject to tax has been eliminated, the actual Federal Insurance Contributions Act (FICA) tax rate has been unchanged since 1987 despite substantial growth in Medicare spending (Boards of Trustees 2017a). Rejecting any revenue enhancements makes the lack of affordability of Medicare a self-fulfilling prophesy and implicitly answers the question of who should pay as "not taxpayers." With no new revenues, the trust fund that has been established to protect Part A will be depleted without cuts in benefits. In reality, the changes necessary for Medicare over time likely require either cuts in benefits or new revenues (or both); a debate that is fraught with value judgments and political sensitivities. Advancing the debate requires a candid discussion of who should pay for healthcare – taxpayers or beneficiaries – and that is where this discussion of affordability begins.

Two different concepts are often used in describing Medicare's financial status. One is based on whether taxpayers now bear an inordinate burden of costs and how that will grow over time. Another common way that Medicare is currently judged is through estimates of the lifetime contributions made into the program compared with the lifetime benefits expected by various groups of beneficiaries. That second indicator is actually at odds with the basic principles of Medicare, that explicitly rejected a sense of one generation fully paying for itself with no intergenerational redistribution. Nonetheless, it has gained considerable currency in the current debate and is often used to justify cuts in Medicare.[1] A better use of this measure is to indicate whether it is meeting the principle of social insurance by subsidizing low-income groups.

Neither of these approaches actually answers the question about affordability. Each measure raises issues about burdens, but affordability needs also to consider burdens relative to available resources. Further, it is also important to consider whether taxpayers or beneficiaries are in a better position to absorb greater burdens.[2] Only then will policymakers have the information necessary to make reasonable choices about the future.

THE BURDEN OF MEDICARE COSTS ON TAXPAYERS

One popular way that people highlight the issue of burden is to point to the share of taxpayers relative to beneficiaries. This ratio has been declining over time and that decline is accelerating as the baby boom generation has begun to pass the age of 65. For example, it was 3.1 in 2016 but will be just 2.4 in 2030 (Boards of Trustees 2017a). But this measure is inadequate, since it is limited to the demographic balance between old and young in the United States. It does not take into account other important aspects of the financing abilities, including the resources available to taxpayers to pay that burden. And perhaps even more significantly, it implies that only younger taxpayers are bearing the burdens of Medicare and that shifting burdens onto beneficiaries does not impose its own hardships. Images of seniors as "takers" of resources is a common characterization in playing out this scenario. Over time, all three of these key variables have changed, making it important to take a more inclusive look at the issue of annual burdens on both taxpayers and beneficiaries from Medicare.

Results for 2016

The first step in this analysis is to examine how much these two groups currently pay on an annual basis. With several colleagues, I have examined this issue at several points in time and found that beneficiaries pay much more on an annual basis than many analysts have assumed (Moon and Storeygard 2002; Moon et al. 2016). Beneficiaries pay premiums and cost-sharing for their benefits each year, but in addition, they also pay both income and payroll taxes toward the costs of their care. Over time, their contributions into these tax bases have expanded substantially as the age of retirement has risen and more beneficiaries remain in the labor force for longer. Thus, their share of taxes has also gone up.

And, Medicare has changed as well. While Part D (a voluntary drug benefit) was added in 2006, increasing Medicare's costs, beneficiaries have also been asked to pay more through income-related premiums, higher copays, taxation of Social Security benefits and a new added tax on those with high incomes. Thus, over time, taxpayers' share of the costs of Medicare has actually declined and will continue to decline as older Americans remain longer in the labor force and as income-related elements in the law that raise premiums over time for higher-income beneficiaries become even more important.

To calculate respective burdens, I estimate the share of total income and payroll taxes paid by seniors, and assume the remainder is the responsibility of taxpayers aged 20 to 64.[3] First, I subtract the aggregate amounts of income taxes that represent the portion of the taxation of Social Security benefits that is allocated to Part A of Medicare. Then, after netting out those amounts, I calculate the share of payroll and income taxes that seniors pay on average. The amount remaining is the portion attributable to taxpayers.

The second major contribution by beneficiaries comes from premiums paid for Parts B and D. One simplifying adjustment necessary for this analysis attributes the costs of the premiums on a per beneficiary basis, but attributes the share of taxes across all persons aged 65 and over. A full calculation of tax contributions limited to Medicare beneficiaries would require omitting contributions from the approximately 2 percent of people aged 65 and above who do not participate in Medicare, and adding contributions from the disabled population (who constitute about 11 percent of all beneficiaries). Since the focus here is on the elderly, this simplifying assumption only modestly affects the results, likely underestimating what beneficiaries contribute, since payroll and income tax contributions from disabled beneficiaries are not included.

Finally, I add cost sharing for Medicare covered services to the estimate, since these payments are a required contribution from beneficiaries.[4] Not included, however, are estimates of services such as vision and dental services and long-term care services that are not covered by Medicare. Estimates of those costs would increase even further the share that beneficiaries pay toward the costs of their own care. Although these are substantial, they do not fall within the usual discussion of Medicare spending. Thus the resulting beneficiary and taxpayer shares are for only a portion of all healthcare spending by the elderly, and are likely a slightly conservative estimate of the beneficiary share.

The resulting measure for 2016 indicates what share of Medicare costs for covered services are the responsibility of taxpayers under the age of 65 compared with older beneficiaries. Since much of the discussion about reducing Medicare is to ease burdens on younger taxpayers, it is important to be clear that the burden is shared between the two groups; and to an extent not often appreciated by casual observers of the program. In 2016, taxpayers were responsible for 58.9 percent of the costs of Medicare services, while beneficiaries or their families or former employers were responsible for 41.1 percent (Figure 9.1). It is important to note, however, that the dollar amounts shown in Figure 9.1 indicate the per capita amount of health spending per Medicare beneficiary. And since there were on average more than three young taxpayers per beneficiary in 2016, the amount that each taxpayer would pay on average is less: actually $2429 in 2016. This estimate includes the copayments required of beneficiaries in addition to the share they pay toward the federal costs of the program. If

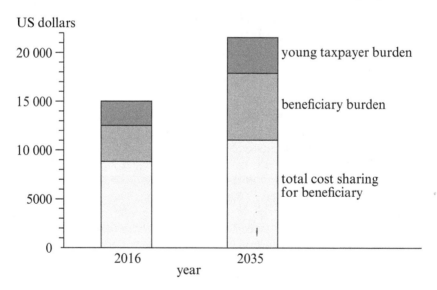

Source: Derived from data from Boards of Trustees (2017a, 2017b).

Figure 9.1   *Share of Medicare benefits borne by taxpayers and beneficiaries with cost sharing, 2016 and 2035*

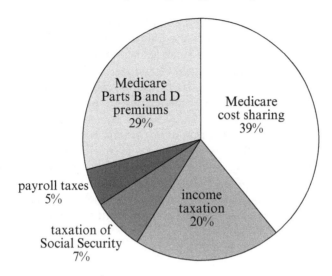

Source: Derived from data from Boards of Trustees (2017a, 2017b).

Figure 9.2   Components of beneficiary share of Medicare

these copayments were excluded from the estimates, the shares would be 70.5 percent and 29.5 percent, respectively, for taxpayers and beneficiaries.

Figure 9.2 indicates the various components of the burdens on beneficiaries from taxes, premiums and cost sharing. The largest shares are for cost sharing, premiums and income taxes, in that order. Payroll taxes and taxation of Social Security remain small, but will increase over time.

Results for 2035

This measure can also be projected forward in time. I focus on 2035 since the baby boom will be fully absorbed into Medicare by that point. Again, relying on the Medicare trustees' projections, it is possible to project the shares to both taxpayers and beneficiaries. The burden on beneficiaries will rise over time, for several reasons. Beneficiaries will pay a larger share of payroll and income taxes, both because they will represent a larger share of the population and because they are more likely to remain in the workforce compared with today's seniors.

To examine future burdens, some further simplifying assumptions are needed. First, I assume that payroll taxes will be increased one way or another to cover the costs of future benefits, even though the payroll tax rate currently is set too low to fund the program beyond 2030. Second, although elderly contributions to payroll and income taxes will likely keep rising relative to younger taxpayers, continuing the trends described above, I use projections available from the Labor Department through 2020 to increase these shares and then assume an increase that reflects only the rise in the share of the population aged 65 and above after 2020. This yields a conservative estimate of the growth in seniors' contributions to Medicare.

By 2035, the shares paid by beneficiaries are projected to rise to 48.8 percent and the taxpayer share to fall to 51.2 percent even with no change in public policy. Future generations of beneficiaries will bear a greater share of the costs of their care than today even without cuts in coverage. As mentioned above, this is in part because of the growth in taxes paid by seniors as a share of the population, but also because Parts B and D of Medicare are projected to grow faster over time, and beneficiaries pay premiums and higher cost sharing for these portions of the program.

Burdens Relative to Resources

For 2016, the per beneficiary burden totals $6172, or approximately 16.6 percent of the average incomes of persons aged 65 and above (Table 9.1). The per taxpayer share was $2429 and represented 5.3 percent of the per capita incomes of people aged 20 to 64.[5]

Over time, burdens will rise on both taxpayers and beneficiaries even with no policy changes. To put this into context and pose the question of whether the burdens will be untenable, it is useful to look at how burdens will change in terms of per capita gross domestic product (GDP); a figure that is used in making projections of future taxes and benefits. The way to think about this is what will happen to the rate of growth of real GDP – which is a command on resources available to be distributed as income – after accounting for the costs of Medicare. How much will Medicare costs depress the real growth on a per capita basis? Thus, I use a measure of real per capita GDP for persons aged 20 and above as the measure against which to assess the burdens of Medicare.

This measure looks at how much the taxpayer burden will grow relative

Table 9.1   Medicare burdens as shares of income, 2016

Source	Per capita burden (US$)	Average income (US$)	Burden as a share of income (%)
Elderly beneficiaries	6172	37189	16.6
Taxpayers	2429	46142	5.3

Source: Derived from Boards of Trustees (2017a, 2017b).

to GDP on a per capita basis. Between 2016 and 2035, GDP per adult is expected to rise by 55.3 percent in real (inflation-adjusted) terms (Figure 9.1). That means a substantial increase in the potential standard of living for young taxpayers. If the burden of Medicare on taxpayers' resources is subtracted from this measure, the rate of growth in real GDP falls, but only to 54.6 percent. The burden from Medicare rises, but not enough to substantially dampen the outlook for increasing economic well-being over time for younger taxpayers. Again, a careful look at the numbers suggests that critics of Medicare often overstate the financing challenges that will face this program in the future.

Another issue related to whether taxpayers should pay less over time for Medicare is the issue of how this would be accomplished. Unless the view is that we should spend less on healthcare for seniors, the argument for lower burdens on taxpayers is essentially one of shifting costs onto beneficiaries. This is where the issue of affordability arises. Which group – taxpayers or beneficiaries – is in a better position to pay more over time? It is difficult to look at this in terms of changing relative burdens, because of the difficulty in projecting incomes for specific groups of the population. Will incomes for workers or retirees grow faster over time? Historically, workers' incomes have risen faster, but with some of the periods of stagnation in wages – and in particular the wage declines associated with the severe recession of 2008 to 2010 – seniors' incomes were somewhat more protected because of their heavy reliance on Social Security (Moon 2015). Any assumptions made about who will be relatively better off over time will essentially determine the results. If the gap between seniors' incomes and those of taxpayers remained the same, the burdens on seniors would rise relative to taxpayers, as indicated by the growth in the share paid by beneficiaries in Figure 9.1. This is where individual judgments about equity and fairness must take over.

LIFETIME CONTRIBUTIONS AND BENEFITS

In the last few years, the most popular measure regarding Medicare's burdens on the young has centered on what various cohorts of Americans will have paid into the Medicare program over their working lives, and comparing those amounts to what these cohorts can expect to draw out of the program. The general approach is to choose a particular year in which beneficiaries reach age 65 (when they become eligible for Medicare) and estimate what people at varying levels of wages will have paid into the system in payroll taxes (which fund Part A of the program). Since the tax rate is fixed (and since 1987 there is no upper bound limit on wages subject to tax), contributions rise steadily with wages. But these revenue estimates are reflective of only one segment of the Medicare program, and ignore income tax and premium contributions that fund Parts B and D.[6]

The more controversial part of the measure is how to deal with benefits. Two sets of assumptions are critical in terms of what the results look like and what they "show" about contributions versus benefits. First, it has become rather standard to include all Medicare benefits in the estimates (Steurele and Quackenbush 2015; National Bipartisan Commission on Future of Medicare 1999), even though payroll taxes fund only Part A of the program. And since Part A now represents just 40 percent of all Medicare's benefits, this offers a biased view that exaggerates benefits relative to contributions. Parts B and D of Medicare are funded by general revenue (mostly income tax) contributions and premiums from beneficiaries. Findings that use the full Medicare beneficiaries are essentially guaranteed to show that beneficiaries have not "fully paid" for their benefits. And since Parts B and D are growing as a share of total Medicare, this bias gets worse over time. This analysis is based on work done with a colleague (Guo and Moon 2018), and in this paper we estimate benefits only for Part A.

The second assumption is more subtle, and controversial. To generate estimates in "real" (inflation adjusted) dollars, people traditionally use the consumer price index for both wages and health benefits. But since healthcare prices have risen much faster than other prices, this makes it appear that benefits are going up over time when in fact they have been quite stable. The Part D drug benefit added in 2006 has been the main expansion of the program in terms of benefits; other changes over the years have modestly added benefits (the addition of hospice care, for example) or cut benefits (through increased copays such as the Part B deductible). The effect of using the standard consumer price index (CPI) measure is to make it appear that future cohorts of beneficiaries are drawing greater benefits relative to those reaching 65 at earlier dates, when in fact future cohorts have to pay more out-of-pocket to receive the same level of care over time. For our estimates, we use the CPI to adjust wages, but the CPI for medical care to adjust benefits. This also has a large impact on the findings, particularly in comparing earlier to later cohorts of individuals. It is controversial because it can be argued that we are comparing apples and oranges, and that is a valid argument if the principal goal is to look only at absolute resources paid into the program. But we argue that the validity of this measure largely centers on comparing different cohort groups, so that using the basic CPI for health care is misleading in another way.

Our estimated benefit for a male turning 65 in 2030 is $82 000 in 2015 dollars (see Table 9.2). The amount would be slightly higher for women ($87 000), who have longer life expectancies. Since wage contributions

Table 9.2   Net Medicare lifetime benefits by assumptions for single male 2030 cohort (US$)

Assumptions	Net Medicare benefits (benefits minus taxes) by wage level				
	Benefits	Low	Average	High	Maximum taxable
CPI medical and Part A only	82 000	31 000	6000	(23 000)	(105 000)
CPI overall and Part A only	120 000	70 000	44 000	17 000	(66 000)
CPI overall and Parts A, B and D	300 000	250 000	224 000	197 000	115 000

Source: Guo and Moon (2018).

expressed in 2015 dollars ranged from $51 000 for low-wage workers to $186 000 for those at the Social Security taxable maximum, the net impact would be split with low-wage workers receiving positive net benefits relative to wage contributions, and the net impacts falling as wages rise. The findings for these younger persons are similar to those for people first drawing Medicare in 2015.

If instead we used the assumptions that others have used (which we believe are faulty), our estimates of benefits would be nearly three times higher. That is, instead of $82 000 in benefits, the amount would be $300 000 (Table 9.3). Taking out benefits from B and D drops the estimated level to $120 000. At the very least, this is the standard that should be used. The different inflation adjuster accounts for much of the rest of the difference.

Our findings indicate that many beneficiaries will have contributed

Table 9.3   Net Medicare lifetime benefits by assumptions for single male 2030 cohort (US$)

Assumptions	Net Medicare benefits (benefits minus taxes) by wage level				
	Benefits	Low	Average	High	Maximum taxable
CPI medical and Part A only	82 000	31 000	6000	(23 000)	(105 000)
CPI overall and Part A only	120 000	70 000	44 000	17 000	(66 000)
CPI overall and Parts A, B and D	300 000	250 000	224 000	197 000	115 000

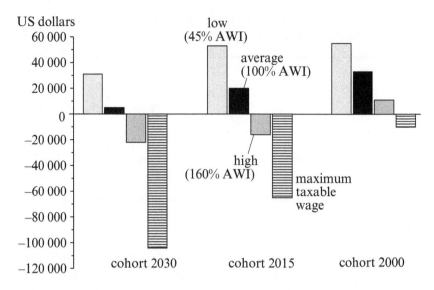

Source: Guo and Moon (2018).

Figure 9.3   *Net lifetime Medicare benefits for a single male, by cohort 2000, 2015 and 2030 by taxable wage level as compared to Average Wage Index (AWI)*

substantially toward their benefits and that the Medicare program is much more in balance than the claims made about the program (for example, NICHM 2015; Moffit 2015). As shown in Figure 9.3, the present value of expected benefits is less than the estimated contributions for those turning age 65 in 2015 in the top two wage categories. And since Medicare was intended to be a progressive program, offering greater protections to those with average or lower incomes, this is actually what one would expect from a well-functioning Medicare program. Indeed, many people who have focused on the average workers and whether they are contributing sufficiently are distorting how not only the Medicare program is supposed to work but also how our tax system is designed. Average taxpayers do not fully pay for the government benefits they receive. The nature of our public programs of all types is to ask higher-income taxpayers to pay more, assuring that the "average" taxpayer pays less than the cost of "average" benefits received.

Another faulty assumption made by people who use this measure to "prove" we cannot afford Medicare is that these calculations represent the overall average contributions versus benefit drawdowns. But even for the "average" individual, these are hypothetical examples and cannot be totaled up in any aggregate sense. To do so, we would have to know how to weight the various examples, and would need many more examples to fill in the distribution. This is a much more complicated analysis and has not yet been undertaken by any of those making these lifetime estimates.

Finally, this measure takes a lifetime perspective, when the program was actually established as a pay-as-you-go system with current taxpayers paying for current beneficiaries. It is not a "funded" system that implies a lifetime balance approach. It is useful only if we make the assumption that we expect each generation to pay for itself; a consideration explicitly rejected at Medicare's passage. The major way in which it is useful is if we believe as a society that each succeeding generation of Americans will not be better off – contrary to what has generally been the case. But then the solution almost becomes a self-fulfilling prophecy: to protect younger generations, we must cut their expected benefits.

CONCLUSION

Affordability is often cast in terms of what the federal budget can sustain without crowding out other resources. In that sense, the question often becomes: how much should we ask taxpayers to pay? Are the burdens of future Medicare benefits too much to ask of taxpayers when examined on a current accounts basis? This claim – that reforms are necessary because Medicare is simply unaffordable – is essentially predicated on arguing that burdens on future taxpayers will become untenable. That argument is overstated. Changes that shift costs even more to beneficiaries could make the program unaffordable to a different group.

Just as I have criticized others for overstating the financing challenges facing Medicare, certainly one should not argue that there is no problem, or that no changes should be made to the program to seek to reduce its costs over time. Indeed, it is in the interest of all Americans, young and old, to find ways to reduce the costs of healthcare. And a legitimate argument can be made that without those changes, burdens on future taxpayers and beneficiaries will rise. What I do question here is the magnitude of those burdens, and the impression that beneficiaries themselves are not paying much toward the costs of their own care.

NOTES

1. For example, policymakers such as Senators Rob Portman and Bob Corker. Multiple editorials and blogs have picked up on the issue of whether or not individuals have paid

2. as much in taxes as they will draw in Medicare benefits in the future. See also the commentary by Steurele (2011).
2. Yet another issue that might be tackled is whether the level of Medicare spending is appropriate: are we spending too much on healthcare for this population? If so, then burdens could be reduced on both taxpayers and beneficiaries. Given the level of additional resources devoted to healthcare by beneficiaries out-of-pocket, and the relatively modest benefit package under Medicare compared with employer coverage, for example, this seems not to be the case. Certainly efforts to hold the line on "costs" of care can and will be important policy issues to tackle as well.
3. The Medicare and Social Security Trustees Reports for 2017 (Boards of Trustees 2017a, 2017b) constitute the principal source of data, supplemented with projections from other sources, including Internal Revenue Service information on income taxation and data from the Labor Department on labor force projections for older workers.
4. Estimates for Part A cost sharing are derived from the trustees report that indicates the number of deductibles and copayments estimated for 2016. For Part B, I assume the 20 percent copayment applies to reported reimbursements and add 80 percent of the deductible (assuming not all beneficiaries hit the deductible each year). Part D copayments were estimated from calculations of the Medicare Current Beneficiaries Survey provided in private correspondence from estimates by the Kaiser Family Foundation.
5. The per taxpayer amount is lower in dollars than the taxpayer share might seem to imply because there are more taxpayers than beneficiaries, by a ratio of 3.03 to 1. Also, published data on incomes from the Current Population Survey are used for individuals aged 18 to 64 and aged 65 and above.
6. In practice, generating those estimates is much harder overall, and it is not clear what share of income taxes to allocate to Medicare. As dedicated taxes into the system, payroll taxes are an easier measure to use.

REFERENCES

Boards of Trustees (2017a), *The 2017 Annual Report of the Boards of Trustees of the Federal Hospital Insurance and Federal Supplementary Medical Insurance Trust Funds*, Washington, DC: Boards of Trustees of the Federal Hospital Insurance and Federal Supplementary Medical Insurance Trust Funds.

Boards of Trustees (2017b), *The 2017 Annual report of the Boards of Trustees of the Social Security Trust Funds*, Washington, DC: Boards of Trustees of the Social Security Trust Funds.

Boccuti, Cristina and Marilyn Moon (2003), "Comparing Medicare and private insurance: growth rates in spending over three decades," *Health Affairs*, **22**, 230–37.

Cutler, David (2017), "Should healthy people have to pay for chronic illnesses?", *Washington Post* (March 17), available at www.washingtonpost.com.

Guo, Jing and Marilyn Moon (2018), "Lifetime taxpayer contributions and benefits of Medicare and Social Security," *Contemporary Economic Policy*, **36**(3), 483–92.

Medicare Payment Advisory Commission (MedPac) (2013), *A Data Book: Health Care Spending and the Medicare Program*, Washington, DC: Medicare Payment Advisory Commission.

Moffit, Robert (2015), "Most senior citizens haven't paid for their Medicare and Social Security benefits," *Daily Signal* (December 22), Washington, DC: Heritage Foundation, available at www.dailysignal.com.

Moon, Marilyn (2015), "Improving Medicare financing: are we up to the challenge?", *Generations*, **39**(Summer), 164–71.

Moon, Marilyn, Jing Guo and Yan Wang (2016), "Can we afford Medicare?", Issue Brief May 2016, Washington, DC: Center on Aging, American Institutes for Research, available at www.air.org.

Moon, Marilyn and Matthew Storeygard (2002), *Solvency or Affordability? Ways to Measure Medicare's Financial Health*, San Francisco, CA: Henry J. Kaiser Family Foundation, available at http://webarchive.urban.org.

Myers, Robert (1970), *Medicare*, Homewood, IL: Richard D. Irwin.

National Bipartisan Commission on Future of Medicare (1999), "Medicare financing sources," Staff Memorandum (February 17), Washington, DC: National Bipartisan Commission on the Future of Medicare.

National Institute for Health Care Management (NICHM) Foundation (2015), *The Budget Deficit and Health Entitlements (May 2015)*, Washington, DC: National Institute for Health Care Management Foundation, available at www.nihcm.org.

Rovner, Julie (2017), "Conservatives' goal to relax mandatory health benefits unlikely to tame premiums," *Kaiser Health News* (April 24), San Francisco, CA: Kaiser Family Foundation, available at https://khn.org.

Steuerele, Eugene (2011), "How lifetime benefits and contributions point the way toward reforming our senior entitlement programs," *NIHCM Foundation Expert Voices in Health Care Policy, August 2011*, Washington, DC: National Institute for Health Care Management, available at www.urban.org.

Steuerele, Eugene and Caleb Quakenbush (2015), "Social Security and Medicare taxes and benefits over a lifetime: 2015 update," Research Report, Washington, DC: Urban Institute.

10. SME financial policy in Korea: evaluation and recommendations

Chang Gyun Park

INTRODUCTION

As the era of rapid growth led by large-scale conglomerates started to show signs of slowly coming to a halt in late 2000s, interest in small and medium-sized enterprises (SMEs) increased as an alternative engine for growth and employment in Korea. On the other hand, a lot of SMEs are confronting difficulties in securing credit that is essential to growth, due to various frictions in the financial market such as information asymmetry and institutional misalignment. Many countries have taken measures to help bridge the financing gap SMEs experience in the financial market. Korea also possesses a long history of policy efforts to support SMEs in the financial market since the 1960s, when its economy started to take off, and financial support is thought to have significantly contributed to the performance of the Korean economy.

However, many critics argue that financial support by the government resulted in major inefficiency in allocation of credit resources. It is not difficult to identify SMEs that benefited from credit guarantee programs for a very long period of time, sometimes longer than 20 years. Recently, the list of SMEs successful in obtaining multiple benefits, from government programs that were functionally equivalent but operated by different agencies, was announced to raise public concern. It is repeatedly pointed out that a considerable portion of policy support, direct or indirect, is directed toward the SMEs with the capacity to satisfy the need for external finance without government assistance. Responding to the criticism, policymakers have constantly adjusted the policy framework to eliminate the faulty incentive structure embedded in government programs, and to improve policy performance. Yet, several important problems still remain unsolved. For instance, the size of government programs to help SMEs is too large compared with other countries, without clear evidence of effectiveness and efficiency of the programs.

This chapter tries to find fundamental reasons for the poor performance of the government programs to assist SMEs in the financial market, and for the lack of an institutional scheme to secure the accountability of policymakers and their agencies, and suggests ways to improve effectiveness and efficiency of government policies to help narrow the financing gap in the SME sector by enhancing accountability. Originating in public administration literature, the concept of accountability has been extending its scope and coverage in diverse directions to share meanings with notions of good governance, transparency, democratic decision-making and implementation, efficiency, responsiveness and responsibility.

Bovens (2010) suggests that we understand diverse aspects of accountability from two different perspectives; accountability as a virtue, and accountability as a mechanism. Accountability is conceived as a normative concept in the former case, in that it is a set of standards for the evaluation of the behavior of public actors, or as a desirable state of affairs in public organization, including government pursuits. In the latter case, accountability is used in a narrower and descriptive sense. It is approached as an institutional arrangement or social relation that involves an obligation to explain and justify conduct. That is, accountability is a relation or mechanism between an actor (the accounter) and a forum (the accountholder). Explanation should not be limited to providing information on the performance of the actor, but extended to accept the possibility of debate, or of questions by the forum and answers by the actor. In addition, explanation sometimes involves the possibility of judgment of the actor by the forum, including imposition of sanctions, formal or informal, on the actor for poor performance, or of rewards for adequate performance.

Following Bovens (2010), accountability is defined here as the relation or mechanism between the actor and the forum. The actor can be either an individual involved in policies to assist SME financing, such as an official or civil servant, or an organization such as a public institution or an agency. The forum can be an individual such as a superior, a journalist or a member of the general public, or it could be an institution such as the parliament, the lawcourt, or the audit office. The relationship between the actor and the forum can be interpreted as an example of a principal–agent relation. The forum, being the principal, delegates authority or assigns tasks to the actor as an agent and holds the agent accountable for the performance.

Bovens (2010) argues that the relationship between the actor and the forum usually consists of at least three elements: informing, questioning and judgment. First, an accountable relation requires that the actor is obliged to inform the forum about their conduct by providing enough information about the performance of tasks, about outcomes of policy, or about procedure of policy as planned and executed. The second element, questioning, requires that the forum, if needed, should be able to interrogate the actor and raise issues on the adequacy of information or the legitimacy of the conduct. The third element means that the forum may pass judgment, positive or negative, on the conduct or performance of the actor. Judgment should also include the possibility of imposition of sanctions of some kind on the actor when the performance is poor, or illegitimate behavior was demonstrated by the actor.

To sum up the discussion, we can structure accountability as a mechanism with three questions: (1) Who is accountable? (2) To whom are they accountable? (3) What are the legal and institutional grounds for the relationship between the accounter and the account-holder? Table 10.1 illustrates the player in the accountability scheme of SME financial policy in Korea according to the three questions.

This chapter identifies the problems of SME financial policy in Korea in the context of lack of accountability as a mechanism, and suggests policy directions to improve the performance of SME financial policy by systemizing the accountability scheme. It argues that the lack of accountability in SME financial policy has resulted in various problems, such as the excessive magnitude of financial assistance by the government, competition among policy agencies with effectively the same economic function,

Table 10.1   Players in the accountability scheme in Korea

Questions	Players
Who is accountable?	Ministries of the central and local governments Bank of Korea Government Agencies: Small and Medium Business Corporation (SBC), Korea Credit Guarantee Fund (KODIT), Korea Technology Finance Corporation (KTFC), Regional Credit Guarantee Foundations (RCGFs), Korea Development Bank (KDB) and Korea Venture Investment Corporation (KVIC)
To whom are they accountable?	Ministries in charge of performance evaluation (Office of the Prime Minister and Ministry of Strategy and Finance) The Board of Audit and Inspection The National Assembly Members of the general public
What are the grounds?	Laws, rules and regulations related to financial assistance to SMEs The performance evaluation system

and inefficient distribution of financial resources inconsistent with market demand. To put it more in detail, I specify the hypothesis that the absence of clear policy objectives is the primary reason for the lack of an institutional scheme to ensure accountability, which led to criticism against the current state of SME financial policy in Korea. Finally, I offer policy tasks to improve efficiency and effectiveness of SME financial policy by strengthening institutional schemes for accountability.

TOPOGRAPHY OF SME FINANCING POLICY IN KOREA

Policy Programs to Overcome the Financing Gap in the SME Sector

For productive discussion, I start with the definition of SME financing policy. In this study, SME financing policy is defined as the policy that intervenes in the allocation of financial resources by the government, or more broadly by the public sector, to help narrow the financing gap in the SME sector. In Korea, the qualifications for beneficiaries of SME financing policy are described by law. Article 3 of the Framework Act on Small and Medium Enterprises and Annex 1 of the enforcement decree of the Act define SMEs as the firms that satisfy the quantitative qualifications on the number of employees and magnitude of equity or sales. However, firms that are affiliated with large companies in terms of ownership structure are not regarded as SMEs, even though they satisfy the quantitative qualifications.

Multiple government departments and agencies are involved in SME financing policy. The list includes central and local governments, the Small and Medium Business Corporation (SBC), Korea Credit Guarantee Fund (KODIT), Korea Technology Finance Corporation (KTFC), Regional Credit Guarantee Foundations (RCGFs), Korea Development Bank (KDB), Agricultural Policy Insurance and Finance Service (APIFS) and Korea Venture Investment Corporation (KVIC).[1]

Figure 10.1 illustrates the current institutional scheme of SME financing policy in Korea. The central government provides SMEs with loans financed by government revenue or public funds. The SBC, the agency of the Ministry of SMEs and Startups, administers the largest SME loan programs. The SBC selects qualified SMEs and provides credit either by direct lending or by indirect lending utilizing a commercial bank as agency. The SME loan programs by the SBC offer more favorable conditions to SMEs than those of commercial banks. Interest rates are lower and standards for loan approval are less stringent. In principle, all SMEs are eligible for

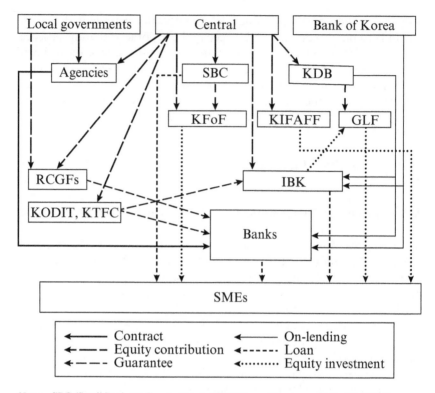

Note: SBC (Small Business Corporation), KDB (Korea Development Bank), KFoF (Korea Fund of Funds), KIFAFF FoF (Ministry of Food, Agriculture, Forestry and Fisheries Fund of Funds), GLF (Growth Ladder Fund), RCGFs (Regional Credit Guarantee Foundations), IBK (Industrial Bank of Korea), KODIT (Korea Credit Guarantee Fund), and KTFC (Korea Technology Finance Corporation).

Figure 10.1   Schematic illustration of SME financing policy in Korea

loan programs of the SBC as long as they meet qualification conditions of each program. Several ministries of the central government also offer loan programs to promote selected industries or policy agendas under their jurisdictions. For instance, the Ministry of Culture, Sports and Tourism offers a loan program catering for SMEs producing sports equipment, and the Ministry of Employment and Labor has a loan program for SMEs installing facilities to prevent accidents in the workplace.[2] In addition, local governments offer various loan programs to SMEs located within their own jurisdictions.

   Loan guarantees are provided by commercial banks to facilitate SME loans by protecting them from credit risk. KODIT, KTFC and RCGFs are three important public facilities that provide credit guarantees to SMEs. They provide SMEs with various types of guarantee products based on contributions from the government and banks, along with guarantee fees paid by SMEs. KDB supplies SMEs with credit though an on-lending facility. Under on-lending schemes, financial intermediaries such as banks and finance companies borrow funds from KDB and lend them to SMEs. KDB sets the upper limit on loan size and interest rate, under which financial intermediaries are free to choose loan conditions.

The Bank of Korea (BOK) also runs an on-lending program called Financial Intermediary Assistance Loans. The program is intended to facilitate SME loans by banks through providing discounted stand-by funds to them. A policy announcement by the BOK has made clear that the program targets five strategic areas: trade finance, long-term investment, micro-enterprises, technology-based start-ups and regional SMEs. The program is unique in that, unlike other central banks, the BOK makes use of preferential credit provisions to specific sectors as a part of monetary policy. Banks seem to prefer the BOK's on-lending program to KDB's, since the former allows more flexibility to banks in setting interest rates and loan conditions.

The Korean government also provides a financing facility to inject equity capital into SMEs particularly in the early stage of the business life cycle. KVIC is in charge of the Korea Fund of Funds (KFoF), established in 2005 to provide a stable capital source for venture investment. KFoF is not a venture capital fund, but a fund of funds that make investments in qualified venture capital funds as limited partners. Eight ministries and government agencies[3] contributed 3.4 trillion Korean won to the fund, which is scheduled to terminate its operations in 2035. The Ministry of Food, Agriculture, Forestry and Fisheries' fund of funds is an investment vehicle that provides ministry funds to venture capital funds, which in turn make equity investment in SMEs in agricultural, fisheries and food industries. APIFS makes investment decisions on behalf of the fund, which had an outstanding investment balance of 0.65 trillion Korean won at the end of 2015. Another fund of funds, the Growth Ladder Fund, was established in 2016 with 1.2 trillion Korean won committed to provide equity capital to SMEs, including start-ups based on funding from KDB, the Industrial Bank of Korea (IBK) and the Banks' Foundation for Young Entrepreneurs.[4]

The Magnitude of SME Financial Policy

According to Table 10.2, the outstanding balance of loans and equity investment by the public sector to help SMEs narrowing financing gap

Table 10.2 Policy financing to SMEs, 2015

Type and source	Amount (trillion won)	Share of total (%)
Loans		
SBC (loan)	3.9	2.8
Ministries (loan)	4.7	3.4
Local government (loan)	6.0	4.4
KODIT (guarantee)	49.2	35.7
KTFC (guarantee)	20.7	15.0
RCGFs (guarantee)	18.9	13.7
KDB (on-lending)	14.5	10.5
BOK (on-lending)	15.3	11.1
Subtotal loans	133.2	96.7
Equity investments		
KFoF	3.8	2.8
MIFAFF FoF	0.7	0.5
Subtotal equity investments	4.5	3.3
Total policy financing	137.7	100.0

Note: The figures are outstanding balances of programs.

Sources: Government of Korea budget report data for 2015 and annual reports of various institutions.

was estimated to be 137.7 trillion Korean won in 2015,[5] amounting to 8.9 percent of gross domestic product (GDP), which is considerably higher than in other countries.[6] On the other hand, Table 10.3 shows the trend in the ratio of policy SME loans to total SME loans during 2008–15. Approximately 20 percent of total SME loans by banks were supported, directly or indirectly, by the government. The statistic indicates that the government intervenes in the SME financial market to a significant degree and that most of uncollateralized SME loans by banks are backed by government support, given that the majority of them are collateralized.

Another noticeable feature of SME financial policy in Korea we can point out from Table 10.2 is that policy means are predominantly skewed toward loans: 96.7 percent of policy finance provided in 2015 was involved in debt capital; 64.4 percent were credit guarantee. Loans, on-lending and credit guarantees are different products in terms of contractual arrangement of legal duties and rights. All of them are financial vehicles through which firms finance debt capital, and they play the same economic function. Credit guarantee is particularly attractive to policymakers, since a large stock of bank loans amounting to five to ten times of the guarantee fund can be generated.

Table 10.3   SME policy loans in Korea, 2008–15 (trillion won)

Type	2008	2009	2010	2011	2012	2013	2014	2015
Credit guarantee	49.0	67.5	70.5	69.9	71.3	75.5	74.6	88.8
On-lending	8.1	10.7	10.9	15.1	20.2	28.4	25.2	30.3
Policy loans (A)	57.1	78.2	81.8	85.0	91.5	103.9	99.8	119.1
SME loans (B)	421.8	441.6	438.8	452.6	458.5	485.9	522.4	576.5
SME loans as a share of policy loans (A/B in %)	13.5	17.7	18.6	18.8	20.0	21.4	19.1	20.7

Note: The credit guarantee is the sum of the year-end outstanding balances of KODIT, KTFC and RCGFs. On-lending is the sum of the year-end outstanding balances of KDB and BOK.

Sources: Data from annual reports of various institutions and Financial Supervisory Services of Korea.

Theoretical Discussion on SME Financial Policy

Market failure results in inefficiency in resource allocation, which constitutes the theoretical basis of government intervention. Moreover, it is known that the market mechanism does not bring us good solutions to the equity problem. The major factor that causes market failure in the SME financial market is information asymmetry. Adverse selection and moral hazard in financial contracts limit the trading volume in the financial market to a lower than socially optimal level. On the other hand, some argue that considering the importance of SMEs in the national economy, especially in the labor market, a strong SME sector is important in maintaining the stability of the economy and is closely related to better income distribution. They argue that policy effort to promote the SMEs may produce beneficial effects due to improved equity.

A gap may exist in information on credit risk between borrower and lenders, and some of the borrowers will face difficulty in getting funds, even if they are willing to pay the market interest rate. Excess demand for funds should be resolved through interest rate adjustment under normal circumstances. In the presence of information asymmetry, the mechanism of interest rate adjustment may not work. When a lender raises the interest rate upon observing excess demand, two offsetting effects arise in the lender's profitability. The higher interest rate improves profitability, since successfully repaid loans bring more interest revenue to the lender. At the same time, the higher interest rate may cause negative impacts on the lender's profitability, due to lower loan quality and excessive risk-taking by the borrowers.[7] As the interest rate increases, lenders may soon reach the point where it is not profitable to raise the interest rate further in response to excessive demand for funds. As excess demand for funds persists, lenders select borrowers to whom funds are distributed. That brings inefficient resource allocation where equilibrium trading volume does not reach the socially optimal level. The government adopts various measures to correct this market failure in the SME financial market and to improve the efficiency of resource allocation. However, the existence of information asymmetry does not necessarily justify government intervention since it is not unusual for the market itself to come up with a solution to difficulties arising from asymmetric information. Both lenders and borrowers have incentives to bear the costs necessary to overcome information asymmetry. For instance, lenders may be willing to pay the price for establishing a credit scoring system to quantify the credit risk of borrowers. Borrowers also can take measures to outmaneuver the negative impact of information asymmetry, such as sending signals relevant to credit risk to lenders and offering collateral. In addition, financial information asymmetry can be eased as the SME financial market develops. The accuracy of credit evaluation improves as production and dissemination of information on SMEs accelerate and analytical skills advance.

Nevertheless, it is very difficult for SMEs to overcome information asymmetry. They possess only a short history of financial transactions and few assets for collateral, so that accurate assessment of the ability of SMEs to create future cash flow is not an easy task. In particular, start-ups and technology-intensive SMEs may confront much more serious challenges in getting funds. Given the fact that they produce a large spillover effect as engines of growth, policy efforts should be taken to address the difficulties they face in the financial market.

Some argue that the government should intervene in resource allocation in the SME financial market to raise equity. SMEs accounted for 87.9 percent of total employment in 2014. Large manufacturing companies used to be the major players in the labor market, but their ability to create new jobs has been constantly weakened. The process accelerated especially after the foreign exchange crisis in 1997. SMEs have been filling the gap left by them. In spite of the increased importance of SMEs in employment, the wage gap between large enterprises and SMEs has gradually widened, which implies that the economic status of SME employees, who are likely to belong to lower classes in the income distribution, may have been adversely affected. It is argued that the government should provide policy programs to help SMEs to get funds in the financial market, which is expected to lead to the facilitation of growth of SMEs and improvement of economic conditions of their employees.

The need to improve efficiency or equity should not be abused as a basis for unconditional financial support by the government for SMEs. The severity and extent of information asymmetry vary depending on when and where they happen and can sometimes be eased by voluntary market participants without government intervention. Therefore, information asymmetry alone cannot justify government intervention in the financial market for SMEs, and policy intervention should be targeted at limited areas where the problem is thought not to be resolved without external support. For example, for technology-based start-ups, the uncertainty surrounding future cash flows is high, and information on their ability to repay is very expensive to come by. However, the means to address the problems are not readily available, and policy intervention may be called for to improve allocative efficiency. The equity-based argument for government intervention in the SME financial market seems to be a good instrument to achieve policy goals, if the reference point is placed on large enterprises. Yet, equity is a relative concept, and heterogeneity among SMEs is widespread. We cannot exclude the possibility that the gap between small and large enterprises is bigger than that between SMEs themselves in different sectors, and therefore the logical foundation for SME support based on the equity argument is sometimes shaky. There are, however, some occasions when most people may agree on the necessity of financial support to SMEs. If SMEs are confronted with a threat to their survival stemming from large external shocks over which they have no control, such as natural disasters and sudden disruptions of financial markets, financial support by the government is needed to provide emergency assistance and maintain employment. The government is also asked to provide financial support to SMEs when it is necessary to mitigate shocks on employment arising from structural shifts in competitiveness, by inducing an orderly restructuring process.

PROBLEMS OF SME FINANCIAL POLICY AND POLICY DIRECTION

Evaluation of SME Financial Policy: Accountability Perspective

Adopting Bovens's (2010) approach, I understand accountability as the relationship between an actor and a forum and thus evaluate the accountability of SME financial policy in Korea from the viewpoint of core elements such as the duty to provide information by the actor, the right to raise questions and investigate by the forum, and the possibility of performance evaluation.

To begin, I consider public institutions providing financial support, directly and indirectly, to SMEs as the bearers of accountability, or the accountee. They include the central government, local governments and public agencies providing financial support to SMEs on behalf of the government, such as SBC, KODIT, KTFC, IBK, KDB and KVIC. In addition, the BOK also can be regarded as an accountee, since it has its own program to promote credit to SMEs. Next, the list of the accounters of SME financial policy includes five major players: the Office of the Prime Minister and the Ministry of Strategy and Finance (MOSF), which are jointly in charge of the performance evaluation system; the Board of Audit and Inspection, which has the authority to investigate the legality and appropriateness of measures and actions taken by accountees; the National Assembly; and the general public. Finally, the performance evaluation system, along with related laws and regulations, are examples of means to examine accountability.

First of all, I reach a negative conclusion as to whether or not the accountees provide relevant information in a transparent and objective manner. In most cases, a significant amount of information is provided to the public through annual reports or the internet. It is not difficult to find detailed information on the general features of most programs of SME financial policy such as the distribution of funds by target group and usage of funds. However, information on the decision-making process and the performance of policies is not systematically provided on a regular basis. More extensive and detailed information is provided to the ministries in charge of the performance management system, the auditors and the National Assembly, since it is mandated by law. However, only information explicitly requested by the accounter institutions is provided in most cases, and it is hard to find cases in which the accountees voluntarily disclose important information on SME financial policies. It is common that institutions demanding accountability do not possess the expertise to overcome information asymmetry between them and accountee institutions.

The biggest problem in information provision to secure accountability of SME financial policy is that the information on policy effects is rarely disclosed to outsiders. Policy effects can be assessed by policy objectives. It is not practically possible to examine policy effects, since policy objectives are not clearly defined. This is the main reason why several recent studies assessing effects of SME financial policy have employed various indicators to measure policy effects: growth rate, profitability, financial stability and employment. It is arguable whether these indicators are true measures of SME financial policy. In addition, it is very difficult to obtain an overall picture of the overall magnitude of financial support targeting SMEs, since most information is provided at the level of the agencies that administer the respective government programs. The absence of a comprehensive and systematic system to manage information on SME financial policy is one of the most important reasons why the magnitude of policy-aided SME financing is so large in Korea.

Relevant laws and the performance management system furnish the accounters such as the National Assembly, the Office of the Prime Minister and MOSF with the authority to raise issues on and investigate appropriateness of decisions by accountees and policy effects, which is applied to all government policies accompanying fiscal expenditure. In fact, SME financial policy has been subject to frequent investigation on efficacy and appropriateness by the accounters, particularly the National Assembly and the Board of Audit and Inspection. In addition, SME financial policy was selected twice, in 2011 and 2014, as the subject of in-depth studies administered by MOSF, which is significant in that an in-depth study is conducted annually for fewer than ten government policies.

The distorted incentive scheme made it difficult to maintain accountability of SME financial policy, and this may lead to a continuous increase in the magnitude of financial support to SMEs without confirming policy effects. It is clear that the beneficiaries of the policy, the SMEs, will oppose any attempts to reform the structure or reduce the size of the policy for reasons of efficacy or efficiency. Agencies administering the policy through delegation from the government will also be against altering the current scheme, out of concern for the possibility of reduction in their influence and scope of business. The ministries possessing legal jurisdiction over the policy, most notably the Ministry of SMEs and Startups and the Financial Services Commission, have little incentive to respond proactively to social demand for adjusting the size and structure of SME financial policy, as long as they are not forced to. The National Assembly is the core member of the accounters but does not possess a strong incentive to call for structural reform to reduce the size and improve efficacy of SME financial policy, since the members of the National Assembly perceive owners of SMEs as an important political base in their electoral districts. The social attitude toward SMEs is very favorable in Korea, and the demand for accountability by the general public is not strong. The general perception among the general public is that large enterprises were the primary beneficiaries of development strategy since the 1960s, and that SMEs should be compensated for past sacrifice. The Korean government had long given priority to large enterprises in access to credit resources provided by commercial banks, and SMEs were obliged to rely on more expansive sources of credit.

It is difficult to cast a favorable verdict on SME financial policy in terms of the quality of the performance evaluation system and feedback of evaluation results. Policy objectives, the starting point of evaluation, are not clearly defined, so it is very difficult to reach agreement on performance indicators that are the subjects of measurement in evaluation. As a result, it is very difficult to take measures to link evaluation results to the incentive scheme of the accountees. Without consensus on policy objectives and performance indicators, the accountees would not accept evaluation results, especially when they are unfavorable, and thus any attempt to link the magnitude of the policy budget or compensation scheme of the accountees would face strong resistance.

In sum, the overall verdict on the accountability of SME financial policy is not favorable, and the fundamental reason seems to lie in the lack of clearly delineated policy objectives, which makes it difficult for institutional arrangements to ensure accountability in order to function properly. Without rigorous verification of the efficacy of the policy, larger fiscal resources have been pumped into the policy, causing various problems such as oversized government intervention in the SME financial market, lack of policy efficacy and inefficient allocation of fiscal resources. The performance management system consists of four steps: setting up policy objectives, designing policy schemes, implementation, and performance measurement with feedback. Therefore, a clear description of policy objectives is both a basis for measuring policy effects and a starting point for ensuring accountability.

The Framework Act for Small and Medium Enterprises is the legal foundation for government assistance to SMEs. Article 1 of the Act provides rather abstract goals of SME policy, such as fostering SMEs, advances in corporate structure of SMEs and the balanced growth of the national economy. Four important agencies of SME financial policy – IBK, KDB, KODIT and KTFC – were all established by legislation through applicable Acts. However, the objectives of SME financial policy suggested by the various Acts[8] are too abstract to have practical implications. As discussed in the previous section, market failure should be the necessary condition for government intervention in markets in order to be justified from an economic point of view. Therefore, financial support for SMEs should be limited to cases where resource allocation for market equilibrium is different from socially optimal allocations in term of efficiency or equity. It seems, however, that various laws related to SME financial policy are intended to provide financial support to SMEs without further qualification, which is too broad a specification of the policy target. Since not all SMEs fail to obtain funds in the markets due to market failure, government support should be limited to SMEs that have difficulty in securing funds even if they have the ability to repay. In addition, in cases where SME financial policy is initiated to maintain stability in the labor market, the policy target should be limited to the SMEs that face difficulties in structural transition.

The current system offers financial support for practically all SMEs, even if they have the ability to obtain necessary financial resources without government help, as long as they satisfy qualification conditions specified mostly by size variables. That is the main reason why SME financial policy is being maintained on an excessively large scale and the allocation of funds is inefficient, which ultimately leads to lack of accountability.

Excessive Magnitude of Policy-Supported Funding

It is repeatedly pointed out that the magnitude of SME financial support in Korea is too great. We have no consensus on the optimal level of government intervention in the SME financial market, since we do not have a formal economic model. It is, however, a useful exercise of great practical value to check whether or not the magnitude of policy supported funding in Korea is too big by comparing it with other countries with similar economic environments.

Figures 10.2 and 10.3 report the magnitude of policy loan to SMEs relative to GDP and to total SME loans, respectively, in selected Organisation for Economic Co-operation and Development (OECD) countries. We can easily confirm that loans to SMEs supported by government policy play a much more significant role in Korea than in most of the OECD member countries. In 2014, policy loans to SMEs in Korea reached 4.28 percent of GDP and 12.18 percent of total SME loans by the banking sector. Korea belongs to the group where governments play the most significant roles in the SME financial market, including Greece, Mexico, Chile and Japan.

Table 10.3 also implies that the current level of SME policy loan in Korea is rather excessive compared with other OECD countries. Just before the global financial crisis in 2008, 13.5 percent of total SME loans by the banking sector were somehow involved with support from SME financial policy, including credit guarantee and on-lending facilities. The ratio surged to 17.7 percent in 2009 as the Korean government significantly increased credit guarantees through KODIT and KFFC to help SMEs in getting loans in the hostile environment caused by the crisis. Since then, the ratio increased steadily to exceed 20 percent in 2015. The Korean financial market recovered stability quickly after 2010, and funding conditions for SMEs steadily improved, as shown in Table 10.4. In spite of the improvement in funding conditions for SMEs, government involvement in SME policy loans has been increasing, and the current magnitude of SME policy loans cannot be justified by the traditional rationale for government intervention in markets.

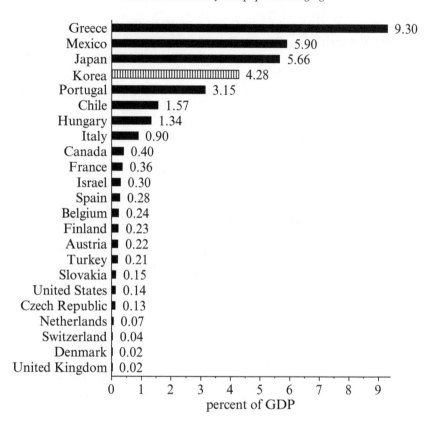

Source: OECD data.

Figure 10.2   SME policy loans as a share of GDP in selected countries, 2014

The current heavy level of government involvement in the SME financial market may hinder the development of private suppliers of funding and lead to a permanent and dominant presence of the government in the market. It also induces a moral hazard of financial institutions as well as SMEs. The conditions of policy loans in terms of interest rate, length of loan maturity and magnitude of loan are far more favorable to SMEs than commercial entities can provide, which attracts many firms that can obtain loans without government assistance. Since virtually all SMEs are qualified for SME policy loans, public agencies and financial institutions that select beneficiaries tend to favor SMEs with better financial prospects that may not need government support. On the other hand, it is hard to deny the possibility that at least some portion of the policy loans is utilized for the

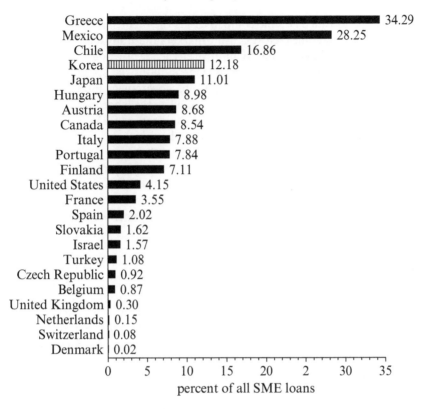

Source: OECD data.

Figure 10.3 *SME policy loans as a share of all SME loans in selected countries, 2014*

Table 10.4 *Funding conditions for SMEs, 2008–15 (%)*

	2008	2009	2010	2011	2012	2013	2014	2015
Funding condition index	65.9	85.2	89.3	84.6	81.7	85.5	82.9	82.9
Loan growth rate	13.9	4.7	−0.6	3.1	1.3	6.0	7.3	10.4
Average interest rate	7.31	5.65	5.68	6.00	5.66	4.92	4.60	3.87
Arrears rate	1.70	1.09	1.30	1.34	1.02	0.88	0.84	0.73

Sources: BOK, Financial Supervisory Services and Korea Association of SMEs data.

survival of so-called zombie companies. As the financial market develops, measures to overcome factors causing market failure advance, and the need for government intervention to improve efficiency of resource allocation is generally lessened. Meanwhile, as change in industrial structure becomes much faster than in the past, demand for government intervention may increase to facilitate restructuring and stabilize the labor market. If this is the case, the portion of SME policy loans directed to SMEs in declining industries under the restructuring process should increase. But there is no clear evidence for that.

Unless we can find evidence that the degree of market failure in the Korean SME financial market is exceptionally serious compared with other countries with a similar economic environment, and that the problems have become more serious in recent years, we may reach the conclusion that the magnitude of SME policy loans presented in Table 10.2 or Figure 10.2 is disproportionately large.

A shown in Figure 10.1, the structure of SME financial policy in Korea is extremely complex. The complicated structure of the policy scheme has made it almost impossible to accurately grasp the current state, let alone to control the scale of SME financial policy through coordination across various agencies in charge of different programs. Both the central and local governments are carrying out large-scale SME financial policies directly or through various agencies. The central bank, the BOK, is also involved in the provision of SME credit, utilizing its own on-lending facility. It seems that they are competing against each other rather than cooperating in extending scarce financial resources efficiently.

All programs in Table 10.5 share the common policy objectives of

Table 10.5   SME financial policy in Korea

Funding	All SMEs			Targeted SMEs	
	FSC	MSS	BOK	Central government	Local government
Debt					
Guarantee	KODIT KTFC	–	–	–	RCGFs
Lending	–	SBC	–	various loan programs	various loan programs
On-lending	KDB	–	FIAL	–	–
Equity	GLF	KFoF	–	MIFAFF FoF	–

Note: FSC = Financial Services Commission. MSS = Ministry of SMEs and Startups. BOK = Bank of Korea.

helping SMEs secure funds. The difference lies in the financial facility or instruments through which financial resources are provided. A large body of theoretical discussion indicates that firms possess separate demands for debt and equity (Harris and Raviv 1991). Except for three facilities to provide equity capital, no differences exist among programs in Table 10.5 from the SMEs' point of view, since all of them are facilities established to provide debt capital.

Various public entities are competing against each other to offer financial instruments with little functional distinction, so that the size of SME financial policy has been increasing with little control or coordination. In spite of continuous criticism by the National Assembly and the Board of Audit and Inspection as well as academics, the fundamental problem of lack of accountability has not yet been properly addressed.

Weak Evidence for Policy Effectiveness

The effectiveness of SME financial policy has been constantly the subject of heated debate among academics. Although conflicting evidence has been reported, the overall conclusion is that we cannot clearly identify the effects of the policy.

Kim (2005) is the first rigorous empirical assessment on the effectiveness of SME financial policy in Korea. Borrowing the empirical framework from Ashenfelter (1978) to account for selection bias, Kim (2005) conducts an analysis comparing profit margins between beneficiaries and non-beneficiaries of policy loans provided by SBC, and finds no evidence for policy effectiveness. Criticizing insufficient control for selection bias in Kim (2005), Kim et al. (2008) construct the comparison group with more sophistication and conclude that policy loans by SBC contributed to higher profit margins of the beneficiaries. Even with more careful treatment on selection bias, Kim et al. (2008) are still not free from it, nor from other econometric problems such as heterogeneity across firms.

More recently, a group of researchers have utilized the propensity score matching estimator to eliminate selection bias. Two interesting examples are Park et al. (2011) and Song and Park (2015). Park et al. (2011) construct the comparison group through propensity score matching and identify average treatment effects of SME policy loans by SBC, KODIT and KTFC by comparing differences in various performance indicators such as profit margin, return on assets and sales growth. The treatment group consists of beneficiaries of each loan program in 2006, and the change in performance measures between 2005 and 2008 for the two experiment groups is compared to give the final result reported in Table 10.6. It seems that the effectiveness of SME policy loans depends on who administers

Table 10.6   Average treatment effects of SME policy loans, 2011

	SBC	KODIT	KTFC
Profitability			
ROA	−0.079	0.150	0.702***
standard error	0.438	0.311	0.246
Profit margin	−0.091	0.139	0.284**
standard error	0.108	0.127	0.125
Growth			
Sales growth rate	−2.205***	−4.641**	0.916
standard error	0.810	1.932	1.405
Operating income growth rate	2.438	−3.836	6.977*
standard error	2.739	5.735	3.737

Note: *, ** and *** indicate statistical significance at 10 percent, 5 percent and 1 percent, respectively.

Source: Park et al. (2011).

the programs. In the case of loan guarantee programs by KTFC, the profitability of program participants has improved a lot more than that of non-participants. However, no significant difference is found between participants and non-participants for the loan programs administered by SBC and KODIT. Interestingly, participation in the programs of SBC and KODIT seems to have a negative impact on the growth of SMEs.

We cannot exclude the possibility that the result in Table 10.6 may have been derived from insufficient control for heterogeneity of program partic-ipants. In the case of KTFC's loan programs, the treatment group consists of relatively homogeneous SMEs, since most of the loan programs are targeting technology-intensive SMEs. On the other hand, both SBC and KODIT offer a variety of loan programs targeting SMEs with different characteristics. For instance, SBC offers separate loan program for each stage of the business life cycle: start-ups, growing SMEs, mature SMEs and temporarily distressed SMEs. Moreover, SBC and KODIT select beneficiaries of loan programs from diverse industries ranging from the traditional manufacturing sector to the information and communication technology sector. Without sufficient control for heterogeneity of program participants, the estimate for program effect could be seriously contami-nated. In order to cope with such criticism, Song and Park (2015) narrow down the scope of analysis and concentrate on individual loan programs. They select three loan programs of SBC: the loan for start-ups, the loan for fast-growing SMEs and the emergency loan for temporarily distressed

Table 10.7   Average treatment effects of SBC loan programs, 2015

	Loan for start-ups	Loan for fast-growing SMEs	Emergency loan for temporarily distressed SMEs
ROA	−3.85*	−2.51	−1.25
standard error	2.22	1.64	1.20
Sales grow rate	−225.05	−46.34	−509.81
standard error	298.67	42.44	544.40
Operating income growth rate	320.06	158.83	134.22
standard error	718.95	195.89	428.23

Note: * indicates statistical significance at 10 percent.

Source: Song and Park (2015).

SMEs. Adopting the propensity scoring estimator as in Park et al. (2011), they reach the conclusion that no loan program under investigation makes positive impacts on the performance of beneficiaries.

It is highly probable that the lack of accountability in SME financial policy has brought the results in Tables 10.6 and 10.7. A lot of loan programs without clear evidence for their effectiveness continue to operate mechanically without reorganization or restructuring. Both of the studies whose results are discussed above in Tables 10.6 and 10.7 were commissioned by MOSF to examine the effectiveness of SME policy loans. The negative assessments were not enough to change the upward trend in the scale of SME financial policy.

Inefficient Allocation of Funds

Another problematic aspect of lack of accountability in SME financial policy is the fact that financial support is provided to virtually all SMEs. As discussed in the previous section, SBC offers loan programs for three different groups of SMEs: the loan for start-ups, the loan for fast-growing SMEs and the emergency loan for temporarily distressed SMEs. Unlike its name, the first program (the loan for start-ups) is intended for firms whose age is less than seven years, and the second one is targeting SMEs that are seven years old or older. Therefore, all SMEs are qualified for the loans SBC provides, as long as they are small enough to be classified as SMEs by the Framework Act for Small and Medium Enterprises and possess the minimum financial soundness to pass SBC's screening process. This also true of loans programs offered by KODIT and KTFC. In addition, KDB

Table 10.8   Distribution of SME policy loans by firm age, 2014 (%)

Firm age	SBC (lending)	KODIT (guarantee)	KTFC (guarantee)	KDB (on-lending)
0–5 years	34.8	23.5	25.5	5.0
5–10 years	19.5	26.1	26.7	14.7
>10 years	45.7	50.5	47.8	80.3

Note: The figures are calculated based on outstanding volume at the end of 2014.

Sources: SBC, KODIT, KTFC and KDB data.

extends policy loans through an on-lending facility to SMEs belonging to the mature stage of the business life cycle, and to firms that are too large to qualify as SMEs but too small to be classified as large enterprises.[9] In other words, practically every SME in Korea can apply for policy loans in one form or another.

Table 10.8 illustrates the distribution of the outstanding volume of SME policy loans at the end of 2014 by firm age. Close to half of the SME policy loans were held by SMEs whose ages exceeded ten years. Firms with more than ten years of history since establishment are likely to belong to the mature stage in their business life cycle, so that the need for government support is not thought to be significant for reasons of information asymmetry or corporate restructuring, which implies that agencies for SME financial policy put much emphasis on financial soundness of SMEs in their allocation of funds. In other words, it seems that policy agencies behave like commercial banks rather than pursuing their mission of correction of market failure. It is likely that agencies administering loan programs on behalf of the government compete against commercial entities in SME financial market to attract SMEs with high ability to repay. On the other hand, mature SMEs apply for policy loans to take advantage of more favorable loan conditions, such as lower interest rates or longer maturities, even though they can acquire the necessary funds without government assistance.

We can also confirm the possibility that policy loans are provided even to SMEs that do not need government support, in Table 10.9, which shows that 27.2 percent of the beneficiaries of KODIT's guarantee programs had been using the facilities for more than ten years. The situation is similar for KTFC's guarantee programs. Two possible explanations can be offered for long-term dependency on policy loans. First, in spite of being able to raise necessary funds in the financial market without relying on policy assistance, some SMEs may participate in guarantee programs to take

Table 10.9   Length of guarantee utilization, 2014 (%)

Firm age	KODIT	KTFC
≤ 3 years	30.4	33.8
3−7 years	30.1	32.8
7−10 years	12.3	13.2
> 10 years	27.2	20.3

Sources: SBC, KODIT, KTFC and KDB data.

advantage of the favorable conditions that policy loans offer. Next, despite depending on government support for a long period of time, some SMEs may still encounter difficulties in acquiring funds and thus must depend on government programs. Given that the cost of policy loan programs is considerably high, further assistance to such SMEs cannot be justified, since there is little hope for self-reliance in the financial market.

We can find the reason for long-term dependence on government assistance from unclear delineation of policy objectives along with the misaligned incentive scheme. All agencies in charge of SME policy loan programs are subject to annual management evaluation conducted by MOSF, and evaluation results are incorporated into the decision-making process on important issues such as personnel change and budgetary adjustment. Therefore, evaluation results are crucial for welfare of all members of the agency, and influence their behavior. Various evaluation standards have been used, but the loan default rate is one of the most important performance indicators. Pursuing lower default rates in loan portfolios, program agencies have the tendency to favor larger and more financially sound firms over SMEs that do indeed need government assistance to acquire necessary funds.

Policy Directions

The most important task to enhance accountability and effectiveness of SME financial policy in Korea is to clearly delineate policy objectives and establish a strong performance management system. As discussed in the precious section, two important theoretical justifications for government intervention in the SME financial market are the correction of allocative inefficiency due to informational asymmetry, and the absorption of shocks to employment stemming from fast change in industrial structure. Consequently, we can set up two important target groups of SME financial policy. One is the group of SMEs that, despite plenty of potential to grow, have difficulties in obtaining funds because of lack of collateral or information on the ability to repay. The other is the group of SMEs that confront financial distress in the process of corporate restructuring.

Next, the crucial element of a strong performance management system is performance indicators well aligned with policy objectives. Therefore, it is very important to revamp performance indicators of the agencies of SME financial policy following newly established policy objectives. For instance, as for the policy objective of alleviation of financial difficulties from information asymmetry, candidates for performance indicators could be profitability, growth, productivity and financial soundness of a target SME. We can also suggest performance indicators that are more directly linked to the policy objective. Examples are the proportion of young firms (less than five years since establishment) among beneficiaries, the proportion of start-ups among beneficiaries, the proportion of ex-beneficiaries that stop relying on policy loans, and the average proportion of policy loans out of total external financing of beneficiaries. With these types of performance indicators, policy agencies have the incentive to reduce the length of policy loans and to make beneficiaries less reliant on policy assistance.

If the policy objective is facilitation of corporate restructuring, different performance indicators should be established. Possible candidates are the number of jobs saved or created by restructuring of beneficiaries, and the number of workers who found a new job.

Another important task to ensure accountability of SME financial policy is to explicitly designate an entity that controls the size of SME financial policy and coordinates allocation of roles and duties among policy agencies. More specifically, it is recommended that an SME Financial Support Holding Company be established and incorporate current policy agencies, KODIT, KTFC, SBC, KVIC and the on-lending function and venture capital business of KDB under the umbrella of the holding company. The government would assign the ceiling for the total amount of financial support to SMEs, and the holding company would allocate the total amount allowed among its subsidiaries. The government should establish the ceiling for government funding based on objective research on the state of funding gaps SMEs are facing,[10] and the ceiling should be updated on a regular basis.

CONCLUSION

SMEs have recently started to attract great attention as a new engine for growth and employment. Most governments provide various types of financial support to SMEs to facilitate their success and achieve policy goals of growth and employment. Korea is no exception.

SME financial policy in Korea has a long history. The first serious attempt by the government to provide financial resources to SMEs dates back to the early 1960s. Many commentators seem to agree that the policy has been playing a significant role in promoting the development of the SME sector. It is also true that serious criticism has been raised, pointing out problems such as repeated provision of scarce financial resource to a small group of SMEs, and provision of financial support to SMEs in better shape in terms of financial stability. In addition, some criticize that the magnitude of financial support to SMEs has increased without due regard to demand conditions, thus replacing the market allocation mechanism rather than complementing it.

This chapter examines the lack of effectiveness and efficiency in policies intended to provide financial support to SMEs, as well as the inadequacies of the current system in providing accountability, and attempts to identify solutions to these problems by enhancing accountability among policymakers. Staring with a political concept, accountability is discussed in various contexts, beginning with Bovens (2010), who perceives accountability from the perspective of the relations or mechanism between public opinion and policymakers. While policymakers have the obligation to provide information and justification for their actions and decision-making, public opinion asks questions and evaluates measures taken by the policymakers and imposes sanctions on them if necessary. Finally, measures to examine or evaluate accountability include the performance management system, the requirement to correct or make modifications, laws and rules, and criticism by the public or the press.

In terms of objective and transparent provision of information, accountability in financial support to SMEs remains far below a satisfactory level. Each agency provides fragmented information, and no agency has the responsibility to report information on any integrated and comprehensive topography of policy schemes to provide financial support to SMEs. It is particularly hard to obtain information on the policy effectiveness. There are institutional arrangements through which public opinion can raise issues and examine policymakers, but the incentive structure surrounding stakeholders in SME financial policy makes it almost impossible for the institutional arrangement to function well. It is obvious that SMEs would object to any attempts to reduce the magnitude of financial support or reorganize the current system based on an argument for improved effectiveness and efficiency. Government agencies would also oppose efforts to improve the system, out of concern for their reduced influence. The National Assembly does not have a strong incentive to raise issues on accountability of SME financial support policy, since the owners of SMEs form a strong political powerhouse in most communities. In addition, the public has a favorable attitude toward supporting SMEs, based on the presumption that SMEs should be protected from abuse by large conglomerates. It is hard to come to a favorable verdict on the final element of accountability: that is, performance evaluation and feedback of the result. Since the policy objectives are not clearly specified, it is difficult to reach any agreement on performance indicators between those who are evaluated, policymakers, the evaluators and public opinion. Consequently, it is very difficult to adopt any measures to adjust the budget size or to determine compensations or promotions based on performance.

The fundamental reason for lack of accountability in SME financial policy in Korea can be found in the absence of clear policy objectives. Mere support for SMEs themselves cannot be a policy objective. Theoretical or logical justification for supporting SMEs should be provided in terms of improved social welfare. Without clear policy objectives, the mechanism to secure accountability does not function well, and the magnitude of financial support to SMEs has been increased without rigorous examination of policy effectiveness. In addition, the system to provide financial resource to SMEs by the government is dominated by the supplier rather than by customers, such that criticism has been raised about financial support repeatedly provided to SMEs in better shape in terms of financial and operational stability.

Two policy suggestions are presented to enhance accountability in SME financial policy. First, it is essential to clearly specify policy objectives and construct a performance management system based on these policy objectives. Second, it is suggested that an SME Financial Support Holding Company should be established to manage and control the magnitude of financial support to SMEs.

NOTES

1. We may include the Industrial Bank of Korea (IBK) as an agency of SME financial policy. It was established in 1961 as a state-owned bank specializing in providing credit to SMEs. However, the bank was partly privatized by selling 49 percent of shares to the public after the foreign exchange crisis of 1997. It is now operated based on market principles, and a large share of its SME loans is covered by credit guarantee contracts issued by KODIT, KTFC and RCGFs. In order to avoid double counting, we exclude SME loans by the Industrial Bank of Korea from the list of policy financing for SMEs.
2. In 2015 seven ministries were providing funds to SMEs under 29 loan programs.
3. They are the Small Business Corporation; Ministry of Culture, Sports, and Tourism; Korea Intellectual Property Office; Korea Film Council; Korea Communication Commission; Ministry of Employment and Labor; Ministry of Health and Welfare; and Korea Sports Promotion Foundation.
4. The foundation is a non-profit organization established in 2012 based on contributions

from 18 members of the Korea Federation of Banks. The foundation provides financial and technical assistance to young entrepreneurs and makes investments to fortify the venture ecosystem.

5. The exchange rate was 1173.5 Korean won per US dollar on December 31, 2015.
6. For further information on the relative size of SME financing policy, see the discussion in the next section.
7. For analytical discussion of the topic, see Stiglitz and Weiss (1981) and Bester and Hellwig (1987).
8. They are the establishment of an efficient credit system, the facilitation of an efficient SME funding system, and smooth supply of funds to technology-intensive investment projects.
9. In Korea, they are called high-potential enterprises.
10. For discussion on the measurement of the funding gap in the SME financial market, see Canovi and Venturelli (2008) and Lopez de Silanes et al. (2015).

REFERENCES

Ashenfelter, Orley (1978), "Estimating the effect of training programs on earnings," *Review of Economics and Statistics*, **60**(1), 47–57.

Bester, Helmut and Martin Hellwig (1987), "Moral hazard and equilibrium credit rationing: an overview of the issues," in Günter Bamberg and Klaus Spremann (eds), *Agency Theory, Information, and Incentives*, Berlin and New York: Springer-Verlag, pp. 135–166.

Bovens, M. (2010), "Two concepts of accountability: accountability as a virtue and as a mechanism," *West European Politics*, **33**(5), 946–67.

Canovi, Luciana and Valeria Venturelli (2008), "An original equity requirement estimation model," in Elisabetta Gualandri and Valeria Venturelli (eds), *Bridging the Equity Gap for Innovative SMEs*, London: Palgrave Macmillan, pp. 43–60.

Harris, M. and A. Raviv (1991), "The theory of capital structure," *Journal of Finance*, **46**(1), 297–355.

Kim, H. (2005), "An evaluation of SME policy loan programs," *Journal of Economic Policy*, **22**(2), 45–88 (in Korean).

Kim, Junki, Young Bum Lee, Sukwon Lee, Kyungho Jang and Minho Lee (2008), "Effective analysis of the government small business loan program: comparing the types of loan program management," *Review of Administrative Studies*, **46**(1), 1–32 (in Korean).

Lopez de Silanes, Florencio, Joseph McCahery, Dirk Schoenmaker and Dragana Stanisic (2015), "The European capital markets study: the estimation of the financing gap of SMEs," Duisenberg School of Finance, available at https://studylib.net/doc/10867784/the-european-capital-markets-study-estimating-the-financi.

Park, C., K. Seo, S. Woo and K. Lee (2011), *Current State of SME Policy Loans and Evaluation*, Seoul: Ministry of Strategy and Finance (in Korean).

Song, H. and C. Park (2015), "Effectiveness of SBC loan programs", unpublished paper, Ministry of Strategy and Finance, Seoul (in Korean).

Stiglitz, J. and A. Weiss (1981), "Credit rationing in markets with imperfect information," *American Economic Review*, **71**(3), 393–410.

11. Enhancing economic growth and productivity through efficient public infrastructure management

Kang-soo Kim and Weh-Sol Moon

INTRODUCTION

Public infrastructure plays decisive roles in increasing the overall productivity and development of a country's economy, as well as the quality of life of its citizens. As a result, countries around the world are striving for sustainable public investment, and Korea likewise has used public investment as a cornerstone of economic development. However, the rapid growth of the aging society and the increase of social and welfare expenditure in Korea have led to the argument that the government should maintain a prudent attitude toward expanding public investment. In other words, institutional factors such as promotion of competition and deregulation policy are more important for economic growth, and the role of public investment as a policy tool to revive economy activity is gradually becoming weak due to the establishment of a private-led economic system (Koh 2004). Thus it is argued that public investment expansion may threaten long-term fiscal soundness, which could have a negative impact on economic growth.

On the other hand, there is another argument that in order to overcome the problems of weak domestic demand and a decline in the potential economic growth rate, it is necessary to establish a driving force for economic growth by expanding public investment. In particular, there is a claim that unlike some countries with high credit risk, Korea has sufficient fiscal space, and therefore it is necessary to reduce the future costs that the low-growth economic recession can bring about by expanding public investment.

Despite the debate between public investment and economic growth, there is no dispute over the importance of efficient public investment management (PIM).[1] This is because efficient PIM is believed to provide better-quality public services, to generate faster economic growth and to improve equity from the same amount of public investment. Furthermore, good PIM can enhance fiscal soundness by managing risks and uncertainties in public investment, because successful PIM involves identification, analysis, mitigation and management of budget deficits as a potential result in public investment. In particular, as fiscal soundness has become an important agenda in countries around the world, maximizing the efficiency through better selection and management of public investment spending has high attention.

The purpose of this chapter is to analyze the role of PIM to enhance economy growth through the efficiency of public investment, and to provide policy implications for strengthening the public investment management system in particular in Korea. Under the relationship between public investment and economic growth, this study investigates how efficient PIM can produce high-quality infrastructure and seeks to find ways for such efficient infrastructure to boost productivity and promote economic growth. The next section explains the data and provides literature reviews on the importance of PIM. The third section analyzes the relationship between efficient PIM and GDP per capita after controlling for variables that affect economic growth, such as the investment-to-GDP ratio, the educational level and trade openness. The fourth section analyzes the relationship between efficient PIM and gross domestic product (GDP) per capita after controlling for variables that affect economic growth, such as the investment-to-GDP ratio, the educational level and trade openness. The fifth section shows that an efficient PIM enables the establishment of high infrastructure quality, and this high-quality infrastructure can enhance the productivity that can bring economic growth. The concluding section presents the findings and implications for strengthening the public investment management system in Korea.

LITERATURE REVIEW AND DATA

Literature Review

The relationship between public investment and economic growth has been based on the relationship between public investment and productivity[2] (Sturm et al. 1998; Romp and de Haan 2007). Aschauer (1989, 1998) shows the role of public capital stock in improving productivity, and Munnell (1990) estimates the effect of public capital stock on economic growth. In the same context, Lynde and Richmond (1993) find that public services that were supplied from the public capital stock played an important role in the production process, and insist that the reduction of public capital stock per capita could reduce productivity by about 40 percent.

In relation to PIM studies, overall existing studies emphasize the importance of PIM in terms of increasing the return, transparency and managing risks in public investment to increase its effectiveness and efficiency. A study by the International Monetary Fund (IMF) (2011) has shown that public investment is distorted when the established infrastructure of the public investment management system is insufficient, and the remnants of poorly feasible projects can hinder the productivity of the public capital stock. The IMF (2011) also insists that the qualitative level of the PIM (such as the institutional basis, budget allocation, project management and *ex post* review) determines the success or failure of public investment. The IMF (2015) quantifies the effectiveness of PIM. In countries with high PIM efficiency, the output of the public investment increased by about 0.8 percent in the year of impact and 2.6 percent accumulative for four years. However, the output of public investment increased by only 0.2 percent and 0.7 percent accumulative for four years, respectively, in countries with low PIM efficiency. Continuing with the same argument, the IMF (2015) says that transparent budgeting and efficient project implementation and management need to be emphasized in countries with low levels of economic development. In addition, the IMF (2015) shows that the debt-to-gross domestic product (GDP) ratio tends to increase in countries with low PIM efficiency.

Data: The Efficiency Index of the Public Investment Management System

The efficiency index of the public investment management system (PIMI) is an index from 71 countries (40 low-income, 31 middle-income) as suggested by the World Bank and IMF (2011) and Dabla-Norris et al. (2012). The index is composed of 17 indicators grouped into the four stages of the public investment management cycle: (1) strategic guidance and project appraisal; (2) project selection; (3) project implementation; and (4) project evaluation and audit. To capture the efficiency of the public investment management process in each of the stages, countries are scored based on different indicators and subindexes, which are then combined to construct the overall index.

Most of the data used in the construction of the indexes is qualitative in nature, though available quantitative indexes compile available information regarding the characteristics and functioning of the budget process, practices and fiscal rules. For each question, a scale between 0 and 4 is used, with a higher score reflecting better public investment management performance. Further information on the index is provided in World Bank and IMF (2011) and Dabla-Norris et al. (2012).

Figure 11.1 plots GDP per capita against the PIMI for 2007–10

ln (GDP per capita)

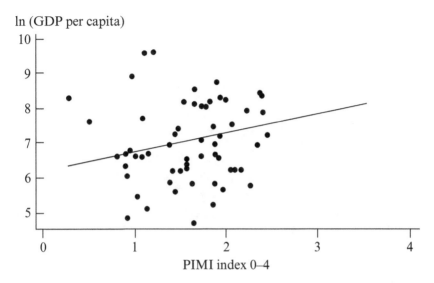

Note: 0.5472*PIMI+6.1809, R-squared = 0.0921.

Figure 11.1   GDP per capita versus the PIM$_1$ index, 2007–10

and demonstrates that GDP per capita and the PIMI are positively correlated. The correlation indicates that countries with an efficient public investment management system have a high level of income, and in the case of low-income countries there is almost no significant relationship between income and efficiency of public investment management.

The relationship of the PIMI with public capital stock coverage and infrastructure quality was further examined for the period 2007–10. The data on the public capital stock are mainly based on the World Development Indicators for 2016, and the coverage includes the rate of clean water supply, the number of teachers in secondary education, the number of hospital beds and the road length, which is based on data from the United States Central Intelligence Agency. The infrastructure quality data of each country utilizes the world competitiveness index for the 140 countries published annually since 2005 by the World Economic Forum.[3] The measure of infrastructure quality is a composite index, which consists of transport (high-quality roads, railroads, ports and air transport), electricity supplies and a telecommunications network.

As a result, the efficiency of the public investment management system shows a positive correlation with public capital stock coverage and infrastructure quality (Figure 11.2). In other words, countries with a highly

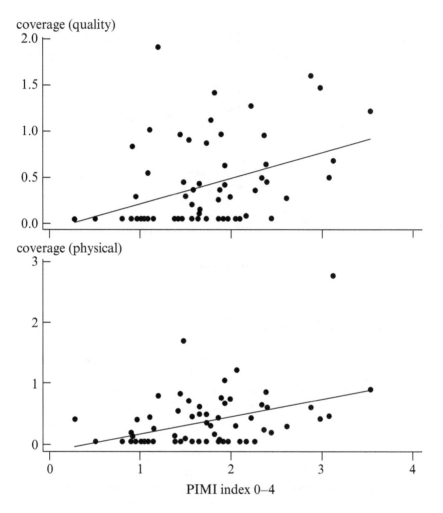

Note: In quantity coverage 0.270*PIMI–0.060, R-squared = 0.14. In physical coverage 0.284*PIMI–0.111, R-squared = 0.16.

Figure 11.2 *Public capital stock coverage and quality versus the PIMI index, 2007–10*

efficient public investment management system have high infrastructure quality and public capital stock coverage; or from the opposite view, countries with high public capital stock coverage and infrastructure quality have a more efficient public investment management system.

EFFICIENCY OF PIM AND INCOME

Model Specification

Empirical studies on income differences consider various control variables. Among others, Mankiw et al. (1992), based on the Solow growth model, include the investment-to-GDP ratio and the educational level as control variables, and later empirical works extend Mankiw et al. (1992) in various ways. On the other hand, Alesina et al. (2006) highlight the importance to economic growth of trade openness, measured by the ratio of imports plus exports to GDP.

We follow the previous studies of empirical growth to estimate the effects of efficiency of PIM. In doing so, we include a lagged variable of per capita GDP, PIM efficiency, infrastructure, education and trade in our regression equation:

$$ln\,y_{1,i} = \beta_0 + \beta_1 PIM_i + \beta_2 ln\,y_{0,i} + \beta_3 X_{1,i} + \eta_{1,i} \qquad (11.1)$$

where $ln\,y_{1,i}$ is country i's average current-period (log) GDP per capita level, and $ln\,y_{0,i}$, is country i's average past-period (log) GDP per capita level and $X_{1,i}$ includes country i's control variables – such as the public infrastructure to GDP ratio, the average level of education, the trade ratio, and others. PIM_i denotes the efficiency index of country i's public investment management, hereafter, PIMI.

We are concerned about a possible channel through which the past PIMI might affect the current PIMI. That is, there is a positive correlation between the PIMI (PIM_i) and the error term (η_1). In this case, β_1 will be biased. To handle this issue, we consider the following auxiliary equation:

$$PIM_i = \alpha_0 + \alpha_1 PIM_i^* + \alpha_2 ln\,y_{0,i} + \alpha_3 X_{1,i} + \eta_{2,i} \qquad (11.2)$$

where PIM_i^* is the past (average of the past period) PIMI. Unfortunately, we cannot observe the variable in the data. We assume that the past PIMI (PIM_i^*) depends on GDP, education, trade and a measure of government effectiveness.

To investigate which factors affect quality of institutions, it is common in the literature to employ variables measuring the rule of law, corruption, and governance. This study uses the variable of government effectiveness (GE) from the World Governance Indicator (https://info.worldbank.org/governance/wgi) of the World Bank.

Once employing the variable of government effectiveness, we can express equation (11.2) as:

$$PIM_i^* = \gamma_0 + \gamma_1 X_{0,i} + \gamma_2 lny_{0,i} + GE_i + \eta_{3,i}. \qquad (11.3)$$

After substituting equation (11.3) for PIM_i^* of equation (11.2), we have equation (11.4):

$$PIM_i = \delta_0 + \delta_1 X_{0,i} + \delta_2 lny_{0,i} + \delta_3 X_{1,i} + GE_i + \eta_{4,i} \qquad (11.4)$$

where $X_{0,i}$ denotes country i's past-period variables, including education ($edu_{0,i}$), the ratio of public investment to GDP ($inv_{0,i}$) and trade ($trade_{0,i}$).

Finally, we substitute equation (11.4) for PIM of equation (11.1) and have equation (11.5). Equation (11.5) exhibits the relationship between GDP per capita and PIM efficiency, given that differences in public investment, education and trade are controlled for:

$$lny_{1,i} = \beta_0 + \beta_1 PIM_i + \beta_2 lny_{0,i} + \beta_3 X_{1,i} + \eta_{5,i} \qquad (11.5)$$

where the current period indicates the period from 2010 to 2014, and the past period indicates the period from 2000 to 2005. All the variables are average figures over the corresponding periods. For example, $lny_{1,i}$ denotes country i's average (log) GDP per capita over the period 2010 to 2014, $lny_{0,i}$ denotes country i's average (log) GDP per capita over the period 2000 to 2005, PIM_i denotes the PIMI over the period 2007 to 2010 and GE (government effectiveness) denotes the average figure over the period 2000 to 2005.

Estimation and Results

First, we run equation (11.4) and compute the fitted value of the PIMI, denoted by PIM_i. Second, we run equation (11.5) in which we use the fitted values from the first-stage regression. Linear relationships exist between $X_{0,i}$ and $X_{1,i}$ in the first-stage regression; for example, between $edu_{1,i}$ and $edu_{0,i}$ as well as between $inv_{1,i}$ and $inv_{0,i}$. To resolve this problem, we use the residuals. We run a regression of $edu_{1,i}$ on $edu_{0,i}$ and compute the residuals, denoted by $edu_{1,i}^*$. Similarly, we run a regression of $inv_{1,i}$ on $inv_{0,i}$ and compute the residuals, denoted by $inv_{1,i}^*$. The same logic applies to the trade variable. In both stages, we use the residuals ($edu_{1,i}^*$, $inv_{1,i}^*$, $trade_{1,i}^*$) instead of the actual variables ($edu_{1,i}$, $inv_{1,i}$, $trade_{1,i}$). Table 11.1 summarizes the first- and second-stage estimation results.

Table 11.1 shows that the past income level and PIM efficiency have a positive impact on the level of income. Countries with more efficient public investment management are likely to have a higher level of income. We conclude that public investment coming through more efficient PIM has a positive impact on income.

Table 11.1   Efficient PIM and income

Dependent variable	First stage PIM_i	Second stage $lny_{1,i}$ (GDP per capita) 2010–2014
PIM_i	–	1.378***
	–	(0.453)
GE	0.511**	–
	(0.2170	–
$edu_{0,i}$	0.264	–
	(0.178)	–
$inv_{0,i}$	−0.955	–
	(1.917)	–
$trade_{0,i}$	−0.461	–
	(0.313)	–
$edu^*_{1,i}$	1.345	−2.607*
	(0.817)	(1.517)
$inv^*_{1,i}$	0.077	−0.461
	(1.671)	(2.546)
$trade^*_{1,i}$	0.011	−0.329
	(0.565)	(0.884)
$lny^*_{0,i}$	−0.092	0.836***
	(0.123)	(0.164)
Constants	1.986***	4.819***
	(0.488)	(0.830)
R^2	0.335	0.306

Notes:
Number of observations = 49.
*** = $p < 0.01$, ** = $p < 0.05$, * = $p < 0.1$.
Numbers in parentheses are standard errors.

To further analyze the relationship between PIM efficiency and income, we use the variable of government effectiveness as a proxy for the PIMI. One of the reasons why we employ the government effectiveness variable is that it allows us to perform panel analysis. We build up the first-stage regression equation as follows:

$$GE_{i,t} = \xi_{ge}GE_{i,t-1} + \xi^T X_{i,t} + \xi^{ge}_{i,t} \qquad (11.6)$$

where the lagged variable of $GE_{i,t}$ appears on the right-hand side because of the possibility of autocorrelation. $X_{i,t}$ includes $edu_{1,i}$, $inv_{1,i}$, $trade_{1,i}$ and other control variables that are used in the second-stage regression, and ξ^T denotes a vector of the corresponding parameters.

Table 11.2   Income and GE as a proxy for efficient PIM

Dependent variable	First stage GE	Second stage $\ln y$
GE	–	0.029***
	–	(0.009)
$\ln y_{i,t-1}$	0.085**	0.871***
	(0.035)	(0.010)
GE_{t-1}	0.631***	–
	(0.021)	–
inv_t	0.127*	0.199***
	(0.074)	(0.021)
edu_t	−0.151***	0.012
	(0.059)	(0.017)
$trade_t$	0.005	0.022***
	(0.021)	(0.006)
Dummy variable (year/country)	yes/yes	yes/yes
Within R^2	0.436	0.938
Number of observations	1524	1524
Number of groups	129	129

Note: Numbers in parentheses are standard errors.

We posit that GDP per capita has the following linear relationship with government effectiveness:

$$\ln y_{i,t} = \theta_y \ln y_{i,t-1} + \theta_{ge} GE_{i,t} + \eta_{i,t}^y \qquad (11.7)$$

where $\ln y_{i,t}$ denotes country i's (log) per capita GDP in time t. We put the lagged dependent variable on the right-hand side because the dependent variable presents autocorrelation. When we run regression equation (11.7), we use the fitted values of $GE_{i,t}$ which come from equation (11.6). Therefore, we employ a two-stage least squares regression analysis to estimate the effects of GE on income.

Table 11.2 reports the estimation results. It demonstrates that government effectiveness as a proxy for *PIM* has a significant effect on income.

EFFICIENCY OF PIM AND PRODUCTIVITY

In this section, we examine the channel through which efficient public investment management increases total factor productivity by improving the public capital stock in terms of quantity as well as quality. Before discussing the regression model, we briefly introduce data. A total factor productivity measure comes from the Penn World Table 9.1 (https://www.rug.nl/ggdc/productivity/pwt/?lang=en). A measure of infrastructure quality comes from the *Global Competitiveness Report 2015–2016* of the World Economic Forum. A measure of infrastructure quality is a composite index that consists of transport (high-quality roads, railroads, ports and air transport), electricity supplies and a telecommunications network. In what follows, we attempt to examine empirically the effects of PIM efficiency on total factor productivity by accumulating extensive and efficient infrastructure.

Model Specification

We begin by explaining how we choose variables and build up the regression equation. As mentioned above, the PIM indexes are available only for emerging economies, not for advanced economies. Even for emerging economies, each economy has only one observation. To avoid this sample bias, we employ a proxy variable for the PIMI. One good candidate is the measure of government effectiveness from the World Bank database. When the proxy variable is used, the number of countries in our sample increases to 92, and the sample period expands to eight years (from 2007 to 2014).

We posit that infrastructure quality of an economy depends on institutional factors, investment environments and tax policies. This assumption is consistent with the structural model discussed in the following section. In addition, we consider education and trade shares as other explanatory variables. All explanatory variables are included as lagged ones because of the possible endogeneity problem:

$$IQ_{i,t} = \phi_{iq}IQ_{i,t-1} + \phi^{T}X_{i,t-1} + \eta_{i,t}^{iq} \qquad (11.8)$$

where the lagged counterpart of the dependent variable appears on the right-hand side because the dependent variable may present autocorrelation. $X_{i,t-1}$ consists of $GE_{i,t-1}$ (government effectiveness as a proxy for the PIMI), $inv_{i,t-1}$ (the ratio of investment to GDP), $tax_{i,t-1}$ (the ratio of tax revenues to GDP), $edu_{i,t-1}$ (education), $trade_{i,t-1}$ (the ratio of imports plus exports to GDP) and other control variables. ϕ is a vector of the corresponding parameters.

We assume that total factor productivity (*TFP*) and infrastructure quality have the following relationship:

$$\ln TFP_{i,t} = \psi_{\alpha}\ln TFP_{i,t-1} + \psi_{iq}IQ_{i,t} + \eta_{i,t}^{tfp} \qquad (11.9)$$

where $\ln TFP_{i,t}$ denotes the country i's (log) *TFP* in period t. We also include the lagged (log) *TFP* in the set of explanatory variables because (log) *TFP* exhibits autocorrelation. When we run regression equation (11.9), we use the fitted values of $IQ_{i,t}$, denoted by $\widehat{IQ}_{i,t}$, instead of $IQ_{i,t}$. Therefore, we employ a two-stage least squares regression estimation by using instrumental variables. Finally, the error term $\eta_{i,t}^{tfp}$ includes country fixed effects and time fixed effects.

Estimation Results

Before we present our estimation results, we show the relationship between the PIM index and the measure of government effectiveness (*GE*). Figure 11.3 shows that there is a positive relationship between the PIM index and the average figure of *GE* over the period 2000–14 with a correlation coefficient of 0.49.

The results are given in Table 11.3. The estimated coefficient of *GE* in the first stage regression is 0.321, which is statistically different from zero at even the 1 percent significance level. In the second-stage regression, the estimated coefficient of *IQ* (infrastructure quality) is 0.014, which is also significant.

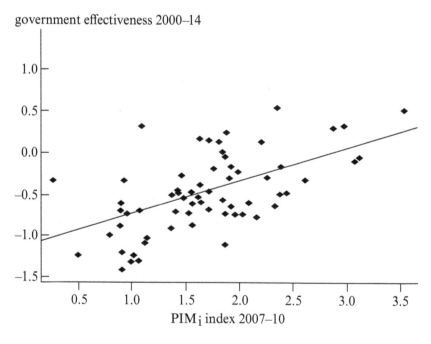

Figure 11.3   Government effectiveness versus the PIM$_i$ index, 2007–10

Table 11.3   GE (as a proxy for PIM), infrastructure quality and productivity

Dependent variable	First stage IQ	Second stage lnTFP
IQ	–	0.014***
	–	(0.005)
ln TFP$_{i,t-1}$	0.452**	0.746***
	(0.207)	(0.027)
IQ$_{t-1}$	0.658***	–
	(0.032)	–
GE$_{t-1}$	0.321***	–
	(0.083)	–
inv$_{t-1}$	−0.624**	–
	(0.252)	–
tax$_{t-1}$	0.479*	–
	(0.279)	–
edu$_{t-1}$	0.009	–
	(0.208)	–
trade$_{t-1}$	0.002	–
	(0.075)	–
Dummy variable (year/country)	yes/yes	yes/yes
Within R^2	0.683	0.658
Number of observations	659	659
Number of groups	92	92

Notes:
*** = $p < 0.01$, ** = $p < 0.05$, * = $p < 0.1$.
Numbers in parentheses are standard errors.

Table 11.3 demonstrates that countries with more effective government are likely to have a higher level of infrastructure quality and thus a higher level of total factor productivity. Given that the measure of government effectiveness is a proxy for PIM efficiency, efficient PIM improves the level of infrastructure quality and the improved level of infrastructure quality increases economy-wide productivity.

CONCLUSIONS AND POLICY IMPLICATIONS

Returns to public investment will depend on the effectiveness of management of public investment. This chapter investigates the relationship between the public investment management system and economic growth, and it finds that the strength of public investment management is a significant factor for economic growth. Furthermore, this chapter shows that efficient PIM (government effectiveness, *GE*, used as a proxy for PIM) is essential for the establishment of high-quality infrastructure, which has a positive effect on productivity. From the results of the study, one can also infer that good PIM can enhance fiscal soundness by managing risks and uncertainties in public investment, because successful PIM involves identification, analysis, mitigation and management of budget deficits as a result in public investment. Based on the results of the analysis, the policy implications are as follows for the current Korean PIM, though it is widely acknowledged that Korea has rigorous and transparent public–private partnership arrangements.

First, there is a need for further improvement of the appraisal (*ex ante* evaluation) of public investments. In the Preliminary Feasibility Study, which is a representative *ex ante* evaluation in Korea, the proportion of qualitative analysis consisting of policy analysis and regional balanced development analysis is gradually increasing in the evaluation of the comprehensive feasibility on the infrastructure. Considering the purposes of public investment for economic growth by raising productivity under the limited fiscal resources, it is desirable for this study to emphasize more economic efficiency rather than the policy aspects.

Second, there is also a need for reliable and subjective appraisal evaluation methods that can eliminate inefficient projects that are significantly less cost-effective. For example, although there is a general phenomenon of excess traffic demand forecasting in transport projects around the world, the forecasting errors for the road and railway projects in the Preliminary Feasibility Study still remain at about 15 and 17 percent, respectively (Korea Development Institute 2015). Therefore, it is necessary to have a reliable technique and process in such studies, to prevent overly optimistic forecasting in the appraisal of public investments.

Third, it is also necessary to seek a governance reform that can positively exclude political influence in the appraisal of public investment. In particular, the accountability of local government needs to be strengthened through the improvement of the subsidy system for the infrastructure, and it is necessary to improve the system to prevent "pork barrel" public spending where politicians intend to channel excessive public resources into their political districts for political purposes.

The limitations of this chapter are as follows. The efficiency index of its public investment management system (PIMI) is an index from only 71 countries, comprising 40 low-income and 31 middle-income countries. Returns of the public investment according to the PIM can vary according to the levels of development or income of a country, and it is necessary to build a model with different development or income levels. However, the data are too limited to analyze the segmentation, and further studies will be needed to analyze the issue.

NOTES

1. The efficiency of public investment is the relationship between the value of the public capital stock and the measured coverage and quality of infrastructure assets.
2. Productivity is the relationship between investment and economic growth, measured by the ratio of the average real rate of capital stock growth to the average real rate of economic growth.
3. Note that the data on infrastructure quality possibly have limitations, as the data are compiled under the subjective perception of the experts.

REFERENCES

Alesina, Alberto, Enrico Spolaore and Romain Wacziarg (2006), "Trade, growth and the size of countries," in Philippe Aghion and Steven N. Durlauf (eds), *Handbook of Economic Growth*, Volume 1B, Amsterdam: Elsevier, pp. 1499–1542.

Aschauer, D.A. (1989), "Is public expenditure productive?", *Journal of Monetary Economics*, **23**(2), 177–200.

Aschauer, D.A. (1998), "How big should the public capital stock be?," Public Policy Brief 43A, Annandale-on-Hudson, NY: Jerome Levy Economics Institute of Bard College.

Dabla-Norris, Era, Jim Brumby, Annette Kyobe, Zac Mills and Chris Papageorgiou (2012), "Investing in public investment: an index of public investment efficiency," *Journal of Economic Growth*, **17**(3), 235–66.

International Monetary Fund (IMF) (2011), "Efficiency-adjusted public capital and growth," IMF Working Paper, Washington, DC: International Monetary Fund.

International Monetary Fund (IMF) (2015), "Making public investment more efficient," *Staff Report (June 2015)*, Washington, DC: International Monetary Fund.

Koh, Young-Seon (ed.) (2004), *A Study on the Improvement of Productivity of Public Investment*, Seoul: Korea Development Institute (in Korean).

Korea Development Institute (2015), *Ex-post Evaluation of Preliminary Feasibility Studies*, Seoul: Korea Development Institute (in Korean).

Lynde, Catherine and J. Richmond (1993), "Public capital and long-run costs in UK manufacturing," *Economic Journal*, **103**, 880–93.

Mankiw, N. Gregory, David Romer and David N. Weil (1992), "A contribution to the empirics of economic growth," *Quarterly Journal of Economics*, **107**(2), 407–37.

Munnell, A.H. (1990), "Why has productivity growth declined? Productivity and public investment," *New England Economic Review*, (January–February), 2–22.

Romp, Ward and Jakob de Haan (2007), "Public capital and economic growth: a critical survey," *Perspektiven der Wirtschaftspolitik*, **8**, 1–140.

Sturm, Jan-Egbert, Jakob de Haan and Gerard H. Kuper (1998), "Modelling government investment and economic growth: a review and some new evidence," in Horofumi Shibata and Toshihiro Ihori (eds), *Welfare State, Public Investment and Growth*, Tokyo: Springer, pp. 61–83.

World Bank and International Monetary Fund (IMF) (2011), "Investing in Public Investment: An Index of Public Efficiency," Working Paper WP/11/37, Washington, DC: World Bank and International Monetary Fund (IMF).

World Economic Forum (2016), *The Global Competitiveness Report 2015–2016*, Geneva: World Economic Forum, database available at http://reports.weforum. org/global-competitiveness-report-2015-2016.

Index